Flexible Product Development

JB JOSSEY-BASS

Flexible Product Development

Building Agility for Changing Markets

Preston G. Smith

John Wiley & Sons, Inc.

Published by Jossey-Bass
A Wiley Imprint
989 Market Street, San Francisco, CA 94103-1741—www.josseybass.com

Wiley Bicentennial logo: Richard J. Pacifico

Readers should be aware that Internet Web sites offered as citations and/or sources for further
information may have changed or disappeared between the time this was written and when
it is read.

Limit of Liability/Disclaimer of Warranty: While the publisher and author have used their
best efforts in preparing this book, they make no representations or warranties with respect
to the accuracy or completeness of the contents of this book and specifically disclaim any
implied warranties of merchantability or fitness for a particular purpose. No warranty may
be created or extended by sales representatives or written sales materials. The advice and
strategies contained herein may not be suitable for your situation. You should consult with a
professional where appropriate. Neither the publisher nor author shall be liable for any loss
of profit or any other commercial damages, including but not limited to special, incidental,
consequential, or other damages.

Jossey-Bass books and products are available through most bookstores. To contact Jossey-Bass
directly call our Customer Care Department within the U.S. at 800-956-7739, outside the
U.S. at 317-572-3986, or fax 317-572-4002.

Jossey-Bass also publishes its books in a variety of electronic formats. Some content that
appears in print may not be available in electronic books.

Library of Congress Cataloging-in-Publication Data
Smith, Preston G., 1941-
  Flexible product development : building agility for changing markets/
Preston G. Smith. — 1st ed.
    p. cm. — (Jossey-Bass business and management series)
  Includes bibliographical references and index.
  ISBN 978-0-7879-9584-3 (cloth)
  1. Product management. 2. New products. I. Title.
  HF5415.15.S63 2007
  658.5'75—dc22
                                          2007013368

Printed in the United States of America
FIRST EDITION
HB Printing   10 9 8 7 6 5 4 3 2 1

Contents

Preface

You may have heard of *Developing Products in Half the Time*, a book I wrote with Donald Reinertsen, originally in 1991. It has become a classic in the time-to-market literature, but many managers report that they have absorbed its lessons. If this includes you, you will be pleased, because this book is the next generation in our quest for responsive new-product development.

We have learned that time to market has many meanings, and the common interpretation as time from the beginning of the project until you ship your first unit may not be an appropriate measure. Specifically, if the development environment is in flux, a better measure might be time from the last point where you can change the design until the first shipment, that is, the design freeze duration. In this case, the later you can make changes, the shorter will be your time to market. Making changes late in development without excessive disruption or cost is exactly the subject of this book.

Such flexibility is increasingly important today, for two reasons. One is that the world in which we live has become more chaotic. It is widely believed that Charles Duell, who was commissioner of the U.S. Patent Office in 1899, proclaimed, "Everything that can be invented has been invented." But today we find ourselves facing exploding technical change in our development projects. Thanks in part to the Internet, customers have become more sophisticated, more fussy about what they want, and consequently more likely to change their minds—another source of change during development. In addition, the global marketplace has become more turbulent. Yesterday your competitor was across town and did predictable things, but today your competition is likely to spring from a part of the world that you never thought of as competitive turf before.

The second reason that flexibility has become important is that the management approaches we use today—phased development systems, project office, and Six Sigma, for instance—are all oriented toward planning a project up front, then following this plan. We reward teams for following the plan, and we consider any deviation a weakness. In short, rigidity is encouraged and rewarded. When change happens, our brittle systems are unequipped for it, and managers certainly do not welcome it. This book is about accommodating and even embracing change in development plans.

This may suggest that this book applies to large, mature companies that may be carrying excess baggage. And so it does—but it also applies to small companies where flexibility means survival in their chosen environment. This book will help them focus their flexibility on areas most likely to provide business benefit, becoming truly nimble rather than simply chaotic.

Best wishes in your journey toward flexibility!

This is the first book in a new field—a first iteration, if you will. It is imperfect, and we will all learn more about flexible development as we apply these techniques to more projects. As with any new product, I would like to hear about successes and difficulties with this material. What enhancements have you added to it? Please let me know.

Preston G. Smith
New Product Dynamics
3493 NW Thurman Street
Portland, Oregon 97210 USA
+1 (503) 248-0900
preston@NewProductDynamics.com
FlexibleDevelopment.com

Introduction

This book's initial chapter, "Understanding Flexibility," opens the subject, introduces many key concepts, and sensitizes you to important points as you read the rest of the book. I therefore suggest that you read it first.

Chapters Two through Nine describe the tools, techniques, approaches, and strategies of flexible development. Think of them as a kit of tools. Just like the tools you might use to fix your car or repair the plumbing, you will not use all of the tools in your kit on every job, and certain ones are inappropriate under certain circumstances. I try to emphasize the limitations and inappropriate uses, but my advice here is limited, because I cannot envision all the applications that you may face.

These chapters are in largely arbitrary order. I have tried to keep them independent, and you could read them in any order and skip ones that do not seem to apply to your operations. Nonetheless, there is some order to the chapter arrangement. The chapter on customers comes first, because good product development always starts with the customer. Then I cover the core techniques of product architecture, experimentation, and set-based design to expose you to the meat of the book early.

Next I present a chapter that is also central to high-performance product development: development teams. You probably have already read plenty on teams, so I concentrate on what supports flexibility in teams. Because co-located teams are so critical to flexibility, these—and their opposites, globally dispersed teams—receive special attention. A chapter on decision making follows the one on teams, because most of the decisions involved are made within the team and depend on the strong communication channels that result from the tools in the teams chapter.

The next two chapters—on project management and development processes—appear at the end of the book for two reasons. First, flexibility deemphasizes structured processes and mainstream project management techniques, such as work breakdown structures, so these topics, in a certain sense, come last. Second, these are complex subjects that require an understanding of the nature of flexibility, which will come from the preceding chapters, so the earlier chapters will be helpful prerequisites.

Finally, I close with a chapter on implementation. This is a critical chapter with a sobering objective, for it asserts that none of the tools and techniques in the other chapters will be of any use in your business until you implement them. This often requires significant changes in values, so I provide an effective approach for making such transitions.

One important tool or approach does not have a chapter of its own at all, because it is so central to flexible development that it pervades all of the others: *iteration*.[1] In contrast with traditional methods, which generally plan activities in advance and execute them sequentially (with some overlap for speed), flexible approaches typically make many small loops through the process, obtaining interim feedback from tests, customers, or management before starting the next loop. Because flexible developers seldom know precisely where they are going—due to the uncertainty that is the hallmark of flexibility—it's essential to start with small steps in what seems to be the right direction and make adjustments from there. The tools of flexibility, covered in Chapters Two through Nine, will help you to iterate more effectively.

I wish the book had more examples of the techniques as they are applied in actual development projects. Readers always appreciate these and want more of them, I know. However, this presents a paradox for a new field with only limited experience to present in demonstrating how the techniques apply to development projects. If I waited until I had plenty of examples to present, the material would no longer be new. Thus, it would not offer the competitive advantage that it provides now. Consequently, in the spirit of incremental innovation (see Chapter Nine), I have chosen to launch this product with limited examples for now. I would be most pleased to include your examples in the next edition, so please send them.

Sources

This may be the first book on product development flexibility, but I did not invent the material. Rather, I have packaged techniques from diverse sources. Many of these tools have a rich history and extensive usage in other areas. Thus I provide comprehensive endnotes to indicate the roots or where you can find related material and a bibliography that supports the endnotes. I plan to provide links to future related literature online at FlexibleDevelopment.com.

Terminology

Why have I chosen to call this *flexibility? Agility* would do just as well, but that word is already in use for the same purpose by the software development community. Because this book must be a rebuilding of what the agilists have done and not merely a translation, I avoid *agile* except in reference to software development.

More important, what is the opposite of *flexibility? Rigidity* first comes to mind, but no one would admit to being rigid. Barry Boehm and Richard Turner, in an otherwise excellent book, use *discipline* in the title and *plan-driven* inside the book as opposites of *agile*. Agilists object to both terms on the basis that agilists have plenty of discipline, but it is of an unconventional variety. And they probably plan more than the plan-driven folks, but it is done where it is unapparent. *Structured* is another possibility, but it has some of the same problems. Consequently, I hope to avoid all these booby traps by using *traditional* as the opposite of *flexible*.

Flexible Product Development

1

UNDERSTANDING FLEXIBILITY

It is not the strongest of the species that survives, nor the most intelligent, but the one most responsive to change.

—*Charles Darwin*

Flexibility has existed in industry for years, but the emphasis has been different from what I address in this book. To sharpen perceptions of the many flavors of flexibility, I start, a bit negatively, by mentioning some types of flexibility that are *not* my focus here.

Manufacturing professionals have embraced flexibility for a couple of decades. A technique from Toyota called "single-minute exchange of die" (SMED) has allowed them to change manufacturing tooling, such as the dies used to stamp body panels, in minutes rather than days, thus changing from making one part to making another one far more easily. Similarly, flexible machining centers allow manufacturers to change from machining one part to machining another one instantly, which further enables them to move from making one product to making another with little changeover cost.

Going further, product development professionals have moved these lessons upstream by designing families of products (sometimes called platforms) that allow so-called *mass customization*, that is, the ability to adapt a product late in manufacturing—or even in distribution—to meet the needs of an individual consumer.

This is a popular view of product development flexibility, but it is not what I address here. Instead, I'm talking about the changes that occur during the process of *developing* the product. In particular, this book addresses a growing conflict between so-called best practice in product development—which says that one should plan the development project and then follow the plan—and the reality of today's industrial environment—where change from original plans is the norm, not the exception. I discuss this conflict more in the next section, but at this point it's useful to define the type of flexibility covered in this book:

> *Product development flexibility:* The ability to make changes in the product being developed or in how it is developed, even relatively late in development, without being too disruptive. The later one can make changes, the more flexible the process is. The less disruptive the changes are, the more flexible the process is.

You might be tempted to create such a mathematical formula: flexibility equals time-into-project times lack-of-disruption. Unfortunately, it is more complicated, because each change is different and leads to a different amount and kind of disruption. One change might affect marketability of the product, while the next might waste development labor. Furthermore, a change that is harmless in one phase of the project could be disastrous in the next.

Dealing with Change

Change is fundamental to product innovation, which, after all, is about bringing something into being that hasn't existed before. *The more innovative your product, the more likely you are to make changes during its development.*

Recent studies show that innovation connects strongly with long-term corporate success, and corporate executives regularly list innovation as a top critical success factor. For example, one global survey ranks innovation as the top strategic priority for 40 percent of senior executives and among the top three strategic priorities for 72 percent of these executives.[1] Nevertheless, research shows that corporate product portfolios are becoming less innovative. See Figure 1.1, which shows that over a fourteen-year period and

Figure 1.1   Decline in Innovation, as Shown by Portfolio Shift: 1990–2004

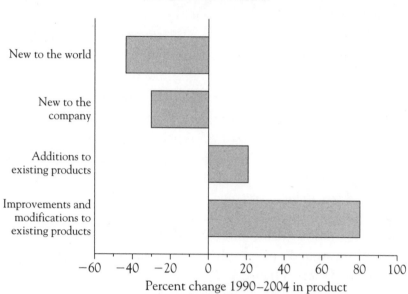

Percent change 1990–2004 in product portfolio category

Source: Cooper, 2005.

over a broad range of industries, the proportion of truly innovative products in corporate portfolios has decreased while the proportion of simple upgrades in portfolios has increased. In short, innovation is vital to business success, but contemporary businesses are losing the innovation battle.

Why is this? Many possible explanations come to mind, but I believe that it is due to competitive pressures and a short-term outlook forced upon executives by the financial markets. Today's executives simply cannot afford to be wrong. Seeing the great advances achieved in the factory by driving variation out of the manufacturing process, they also want to reduce product innovation to a predictable activity. This also explains the current great interest in Six Sigma, which is a methodology to drive variation out of all parts of the business.

Six Sigma, ISO 9000, and similar quality systems are not the only culprits. Stage-Gate®, PACE (Product and Cycle-Time Excellence), NPI (New Product Introduction), PDP (Product Development

Process), and similar phased product development systems encourage heavy up-front planning followed by sticking to the plan. And you can add to these the phenomenal recent growth of project management,[2] project office, and similar methodologies that promote a plan-your-work, work-your-plan approach.

None of these approaches is misguided or has net negative effects. When applied to high-risk, highly innovative programs, however, they have had an unnoticed side effect of putting innovation in a straitjacket, thus making it increasingly difficult to make changes in projects midstream in development. Those who must make such changes are often penalized and regret what they are doing—when, in fact, they are innovating. For stable projects, the current trends of greater planning and control are properly aligned, but for the more volatile ones aimed at correcting the portfolio problem illustrated in Figure 1.1, developers need more flexibility to make midstream changes.

What kinds of changes are these?[3] The first group is changes in customer requirements. Often, customers must see the actual product before they can relate to it, the IKIWISI (I'll know it when I see it) phenomenon. Sometimes they have unanticipated difficulties in using early versions of the product or they try to use it in unanticipated ways. Often they find completely new uses for or ways of using a product. Software developers call these *emergent requirements*, because they emerge in the course of development and no amount of market research is likely to uncover them in advance. Occasionally, features introduced by competitors drive changes. As customers or developers try prototypes, they discover better or cheaper ways of delivering the specified customer benefits.

Related are market changes. Competitors come into being or go out of business. They introduce unanticipated and disruptive products. Markets change in response to fads, shifts in customer preferences, government or regulatory action, or political events. Often, markets are new and thus poorly understood; for instance, it took 3M, manufacturer of Post-it brand sticky notes, nearly a decade to find a market for this item, which is indispensable today.[4]

Then there are technology changes. Sometimes a new technology does not work as advertised. Or it may work better than expected, and developers want to exploit this. It may have unexpected side effects or require additional work to render it acceptably reliable or user friendly. Sometimes patent infringement or licensing problems arise.

World events, such as terrorism or global warming, can lead to changes in a development project.

The next group might be called network changes. Seldom do companies today develop a product entirely by themselves. Sometimes they engage consultants who are expert in a particular area. Often a supplier provides components. Increasingly, partners develop subassemblies from general guidelines. Complicating this, these partners tend to be located in distant parts of the world. Such broad and dispersed networks are fertile ground for changes. For instance, a supplier receives a big, urgent order from another customer—maybe even your competitor—that compromises your order.

Finally, there are organizational changes. Managers are promoted or reassigned. Key employees leave. Managers move developers from project to project to resolve changing priorities. Project budgets are cut. Management lets some initiatives wither while starting new ones.

What can you do about these changes? You may have other options, but I see three. First, you can move faster to minimize exposure to change. This is an approach taken in agile software development, and one I have recommended in the past.[5] Agilists divide development into short iterations, typically of one to four weeks each. Then they can freeze the plans during an iteration while replanning between iterations. Broadly speaking, rapid development techniques rely on working quickly enough to avoid change during development.

Second, you can plan better in hopes of anticipating change. This is the approach followed by Six Sigma, phased development, and similar techniques mentioned earlier that emphasize more formal customer research, more structured risk management, and similar up-front work. This book also develops anticipation as a flexibility technique in certain cases. But the amount of anticipation possible is severely limited. An analogy here is the needle-in-a-haystack metaphor. Imagine building up a haystack by tossing more hay on top. Then, as the stack grows in all three dimensions at once, the difficulty of finding a needle in the midst of all that hay (that is, anticipating a certain change) is proportional to the third power of the haystack's height. See Figure 1.2.

This is an apt metaphor. Real-world projects change in several dimensions at once, so anticipating a certain change becomes increasingly difficult as one tries to extend the forecasting horizon. Eventually, the work put into planning to anticipate change reaches a point of diminishing returns.

Third, you can build a process and apply tools and approaches that are more tolerant of change—ones that accommodate and even embrace change as a natural consequence of working in the

Figure 1.2   Difficulty of Finding a Needle in a Haystack

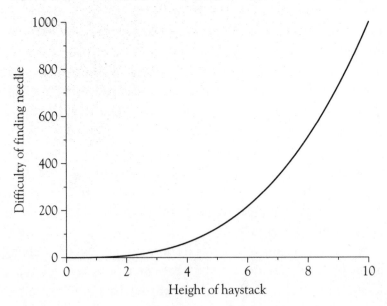

innovative domain where change is the norm. This is the direction I offer in this book. Change can have great opportunity associated with it, and it is better to exploit that opportunity than to suppress it.

How Much Flexibility?

From the definition of flexibility provided earlier, it would be easy to conclude that the more flexibility, the better. But flexibility can be expensive, so it must be used with discretion. This is an area where cost-benefit thinking pays off.

Benefits of Flexibility

The benefits of flexibility connect directly with the degree of innovation you seek. Figure 1.1 suggested that new products could benefit from more innovation, and this is generally true. But new-product experts also agree that a new-product portfolio needs balance between innovative products and line extensions.[6] In general, mature products provide reliable income for today; innovative ones ensure that you will be in business tomorrow.

Consequently, apply flexibility where you must be innovative. You can do this at several levels:

- Some markets for your products change faster than others.
- Some product lines within a company change more than others.
- Some products within a line are more subject to change than others.
- Some portions of a product are subject to greater change than others, due to immature technology, unstable customer needs, or market flux.
- Some departments or disciplines change faster than others, for example, the electronics in an airplane change much faster than its structure.

This is where competitive advantage resides—in distinguishing where the organization is going to pursue innovation and thus needs flexibility, and where it will encourage stability and its associated economies. No simple rules apply here, but these decisions should stem from your corporate strategy and from an understanding of the uncertain spots in your technologies and markets.

After this chapter, this book provides tools and approaches for enhancing flexibility. You should decide where and to what degree to apply them. Use discretion, but remember Figure 1.1: you probably could benefit from considerably more flexibility than you have today.

The Cost of Change

Managers resist change in a project—quite correctly—because it is expensive, and change usually leads to schedule slippage. Furthermore, change can open the door to product defects. So any attempt to encourage change must consider its cost. Although each change has different effects on the project, the cost of a change, in general, rises the later it occurs in the project. Barry Boehm has collected data for the cost of fixing an error in a large software program, averaged over many large projects from TRW, IBM, GTE, and Bell Labs. As shown in Figure 1.3, the cost rises exponentially by a factor of 100 from the requirements phase (cost: 1.6) to the operational phase (cost: 170). (Similar data for a few small, less formal software projects, however, indicate that these smaller projects only increase the cost of change by a factor of 5 from requirements to operation.)[7]

More recent data from Boehm confirm that the factor of 100 still holds for contemporary large projects, and he has also found that the Pareto principle applies: 80 percent of the cost of change comes from only 20 percent of the most disruptive changes, namely, those with systemwide impact.[8] Furthermore, this group of expensive changes is usually identifiable in advance, and by applying the tools covered in this book, you'll find you can often avoid

Figure 1.3   Cost of Changing Software

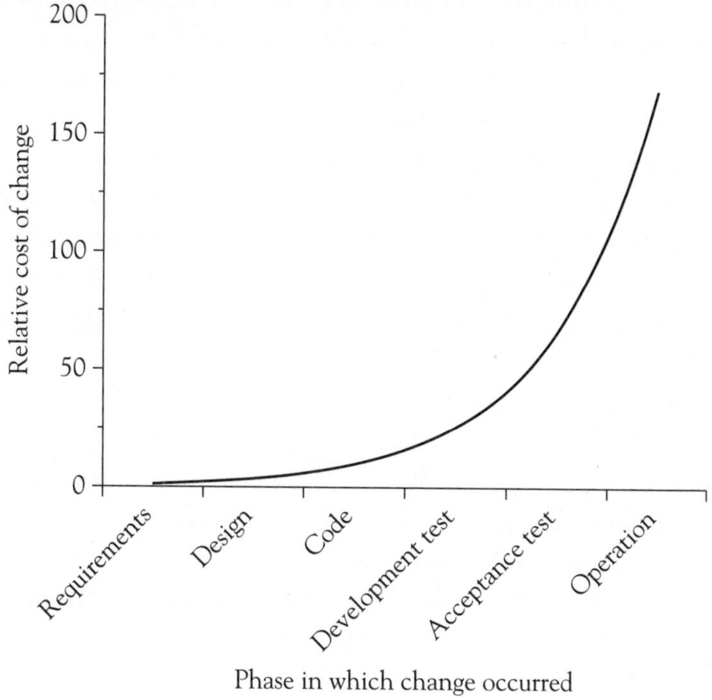

Phase in which change occurred

Source: Boehm, 1981, p. 40.

them. This, plus the fact that the cost of change is lower for small projects, is very good news. Product developers can take advantage of both these opportunities.

Earlier I suggested applying flexibility selectively and at a level where you believe change is most valuable or likely. Now another criterion appears for selecting the areas where you wish to be flexible: avoid the areas with systemwide impact—the ones most likely to have a high cost of change (if you cannot resolve them by using the tools in this book).

A word of warning. The cost of change is a hotly debated topic among developers, usually based on their own undocumented experience or perceptions. As far as I know, Boehm's data provide the only carefully collected and documented information available. Boehm himself is highly regarded and has collected his data from many sources over thirty years. You are likely to hear "rules of thumb" that the cost of change escalates by a factor of 10 for each phase of development, which would raise the Figure 1.3 factor to 100,000! Such factors seem to be pure conjecture. Please question your sources on the cost of change.

Also, notice that all of Boehm's data are for software projects, which unfortunately limits their application to other fields. I have thus far found only one limited source of cost-of-change data for mechanical, electrical, chemical, optical, or mixed systems, but I have little reason to doubt that Boehm's findings carry over in general.[9]

Usually, discussions about the cost of change revolve around a graphic like Figure 1.3, but as the discussion here suggests, we know little quantitatively about the cost of change. Nevertheless, this is a valuable concept, because midstream changes do have associated costs that should be kept in mind continually and tied to the related benefits of flexibility. Many of the tools in this book aim at reducing the cost of change.

Managing the Convergence of Flexibility

Figure 1.4 shows three levels of flexibility after the initial planning period. The restricted flexibility level is the most common, as it fits with popular good practice in phased product development. At the outset, the project has complete flexibility, since nothing is fixed yet. But at the end of the initial (planning) phase, the project budget, schedule, and product requirements are established and approved. From here on, this project has restricted flexibility, as shown in the figure.

Next, consider the completely flexible zone in the figure. In this idealized case, the ability to make changes is left wide open until the end of the project. This yields lots of flexibility but also leads to chaos at the end of the project when nothing is yet certain. The project schedule will most likely stretch, as will the budget. Consequently, complete flexibility is not a useful objective.

Figure 1.4   Three Levels of Managing Flexibility in a Development Project

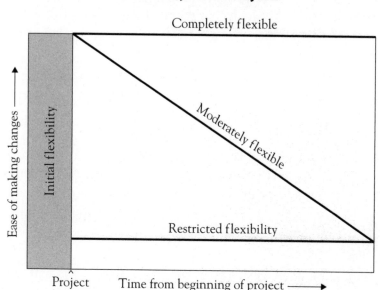

A project managed for flexibility will look like the moderately flexible zone in the figure. It starts with a great deal of ability to make changes. Decisions are not made until they must be made—what I describe in depth as the "last responsible moment" in Chapter Seven. But decisions are made when necessary, often by progressively tightening up tolerances on variables. Thus the ability to make changes narrows methodically as development proceeds. At Toyota, a major duty of engineering managers is to manage the rate of convergence of the design space: not so fast as to rule out change unnecessarily but not so slow as to leave too much uncertainty late in the project.

The Downsides of Flexibility

Flexibility has its place, which is in projects or portions of projects where change is likely to occur. However, this ability to accommodate change can be abused by managers who introduce unnecessary change simply because the system is now more tolerant of it. Think of a high-performance motorcycle: it can get you to your destination quickly, but it can also get you into the hospital quickly. To survive, you must ride your motorcycle with skill and wisdom.

Similarly, an advantage of a flexible approach is that it can follow customer reactions quickly, but if the customer vacillates or is flighty, the project can become chaotic.

Flexibility can be a crutch for indecisiveness, for not committing to decisions, or for reversing prior decisions. Sometimes, flexibility is abused by those who do sloppy research or planning, thinking that a flexible system will allow their work to be fixed later. More broadly, it can be an excuse for skipping the planning and thus emphasizing firefighting and tactical views over a strategic view.

If you use flexibility as an excuse to be sloppy, you will derive no benefit from it.

The Roots: Agile Software Development

To my knowledge, no other books on flexible product development have been written, and only a few articles. However, non-software developers can draw on a rich body of material in a parallel field: agile software development. Although its roots go back further, agile development has arisen since about 2001. Its starting point is the Agile Manifesto (see Exhibit 1.1), which appeared in February 2001. The annual agile conference has grown in attendance from 238 in 2001 to 1111 in 2006, a compound annual growth rate of 36 percent. More than fifty books and countless articles now exist on agile software development; Craig Larman provides a good overview.[10] The remainder of this chapter provides some highlights of agile development to provide background for the non-software flexibility material covered in later chapters. Toward

---

Exhibit 1.1   Manifesto for Agile Software Development

We are uncovering better ways of developing software by doing it and helping others do it. Through this work we have come to value:

> **Individuals and interactions** over processes and tools
> **Working software** over comprehensive documentation
> **Customer collaboration** over contract negotiation
> **Responding to change** over following a plan

That is, while there is value in the items on the right, we value the items on the left more.

Kent Beck, Mike Beedle, Arie van Bennekum, Alistair Cockburn, Ward Cunningham, Martin Fowler, James Grenning, Jim Highsmith, Andrew Hunt, Ron Jeffries, Jon Kern, Brian Marick, Robert C. Martin, Steve Mellor, Ken Schwaber, Jeff Sutherland, and Dave Thomas.

The Agile Manifesto. © 2001, the above authors. This declaration may be freely copied in any form, but only in its entirety through this notice. Source: agilemanifesto.org (Accessed April 23, 2007).

the end of this chapter, I discuss the differences between software and non-software development that prevent us from adopting the agile development approaches directly.

I refer to the Agile Manifesto more later, but for now, notice that it is four statements that contrast values. Although the second value of each pair is acknowledged as being valuable, the agilists emphasize the first value more. Also notice that the second values align closely with generally considered "best practice" in the traditional development of new products (*product development* can be substituted freely for *software development* in the manifesto). The themes of the Agile Manifesto pervade the agile approach to software development. Accompanying the manifesto is a set of thirteen principles that underlie it.[11]

In practice, agile software development is a collection of about seven identifiable methodologies:

- Extreme Programming (XP)
- Scrum
- Adaptive Software Development
- Crystal (a collection of methods for various types of projects)
- Lean Development
- Dynamic Systems Development Method (DSDM)
- Feature-Driven Development (FDD)

On a given project, developers often use a mix of these methods, a combination of XP and Scrum perhaps being most common.

More important than the differences between these methods is the commonality among them. They all follow the Agile Manifesto. They all develop software in short iterations—from one to four weeks, occasionally to six weeks. They all produce working software at the end of each iteration. They all deliver releases to customers frequently. They all involve the customer either directly or through a surrogate (such as a product manager), usually at the end of each iteration and sometimes on a daily basis. They all invite change at the end of each iteration (but essentially prohibit it during an iteration). They all tend to do planning and risk management as they proceed with the iterations. They all emphasize small, co-located teams. They all use emergent processes (those that emerge during the project, not determined at the beginning of the project). Observe that most of these characteristics can be adapted to non-software projects.

Extreme Programming

Extreme Programming (XP) is perhaps the most widely discussed and illuminating of the agile methodologies, so it's worth considering in detail.[12] It is based on a dozen or so practices that fall into the context of about four values. Although the values actually come first, I will start right off with the practices. Once you absorb them, the values that create an environment in which the practices have a chance of working will make more sense.

XP Practices

I use the terminology of those who practice XP here so that you can become used to it, then switch to more conventional product development terminology later. I urge you simply to observe these practices now without concern about how they might ever apply to non-software products. This is the task of later chapters. However, do observe as you read these that many of them improve flexibility by lowering the cost of change.

The Planning Game. Some people accuse agilists of not planning. True, initial project planning may be light—because so much is likely to change before it is used—but this is more than compensated for by detailed planning within an iteration. This iteration planning is always a balance of business and customer needs against the team's capability and capacity. The business and customers lead in deciding on the features to be developed, their priorities, and the timing for a release (a release usually comprises several iterations). The developers lead in estimating how much effort a feature will require (and thus how many features can be completed in an iteration), the work processes the team will use, and detailed scheduling and prioritization within an iteration. The important factors are that developers plan iteratively and that there is strong interplay between the business or customer people and the technical people—and clear roles for them all.

Small Releases. The emphasis is on small and thus frequent releases to customers to enhance opportunities for feedback and flexibility. For instance, a company using these techniques for educational software used in public schools (not an industry subject to frequent change) plans releases every eight weeks. Clearly, this requires that the fixed cost of a release, such as costs of documentation, training, and flushing the distribution channel of old products, be reduced.

Product Metaphor. This is a vision of the product, held in common by the team, that indicates what it will do or how it will differ from what exists now. It provides the team with a compass to know whether it is going in the right direction in the stormy seas of change. I cover product visions in detail in Chapter Two. Of all the practices of XP, this one has been the most difficult to implement. This may be because a metaphor cannot capture all products crisply, or it may be that it has not received enough attention, whether by the methodologists in describing how to create a metaphor or by the teams in allocating adequate time for creating a captivating metaphor.

Simple Design. This one runs counter to the way designers normally operate. It says that one should design and implement *only* what is necessary to satisfy today's requirement or what the customer needs today. The idea is that if the landscape is changing constantly, speculating on tomorrow's needs will most likely be wrong. Not only does this waste resources, it complicates the design and thus raises the cost of change for tomorrow's work. The agile term for this is "barely sufficient." Following the fourth item of the Agile Manifesto, it means that one places more value on adapting than on anticipating. Note that while this premise is appropriate for projects subject to a great deal of change, it is not wise for projects that are predictable. Also, it runs counter to the principle of providing reserve performance, which I cover in Chapter Three.

Test-Driven Design. Much like non-software development, software traditionally is developed in large batches of features. When development is complete, programmers turn their code over to a tester, who then designs tests to ensure that the features work properly and do not cause damage elsewhere. XP turns this around by having the programmer, working a feature at a time, write the test first and then code the feature to pass the test, rather like being offered the final exam when you start a class. Among other things, this encourages simple design, because developers can code a feature in a barely sufficient way to pass the known test. In addition, they write all tests to be automated with a clear pass/fail outcome for each one, so that tests accumulate and can be run repeatedly to confirm that existing features still work as others are added.

Refactoring. This is a process of cleaning up code without changing its behavior. The cleanup could be to render it more understandable, to improve its internal consistency, to streamline its design or remove duplication, or to make it easier to work with in the future. Explicitly, refactoring does not add capability to the code. There is nothing basically new here: programmers have often cleaned up code as a first step in preparing to modify it. But in XP and other agile methodologies, refactoring is a routine activity done apart from adding new features and, indeed, whenever an opportunity to refactor appears. Agilists are meticulous about the cleanliness of their code, as this keeps the cost of change low. Notice that the automated tests just mentioned are a prerequisite for refactoring, because the developer must run the refactored code through the test suite to confirm that its behavior hasn't changed.

Pairing (Pair Programming[13]). XP requires that all production code be written by two programmers sitting at one computer with one keyboard and one mouse. One of them, called the driver, enters code while the other, the navigator, plays various roles as needed: strategist, checker, planner of next steps, or contrarian. They operate as equals, and they trade roles a few times every hour and change partners once or twice a day. Although you might assume that this would double labor costs, several studies have shown that it adds 10 to 15 percent to costs while reducing defects by about 60 percent and shrinking schedules by about 45 percent.[14] A major benefit is that it gives everyone a shared understanding of all of the code, which sets us up for the next practice, collective ownership.

Collective Code Ownership. This means that the entire team owns all the code, and anyone on the team has the right to change any of it at any time—in fact, the obligation to refactor it if an opportunity to do so appears. Clearly, this could lead to errors, but pairing and continuous automated testing protect against undesirable results. A major advantage of collective ownership is that the code is not hostage to the specialist who created any particular part of it, again lowering the cost of change.

Continuous Integration. Pairs may be working with their version of the code, but they frequently integrate it with the common version on the server and run all the automated tests immediately. Then they discover quickly if they have broken the code (that's *fast feedback*, an important theme of this book). Clearly, the beauty of this is that problems surface quickly and clearly compared to the normal situation, where integration happens infrequently, obscuring the fault. Notice that continuous integration takes advantage of modern technology (fast computers and easy-to-use integration software) for process advantage, which is another theme of this book.

Sustainable Pace. All agile methods are people-oriented. The authors of the Agile Manifesto were no strangers to the burnout—or death march, as one popular book on software development is titled—that accompanies too many software development projects. Although this concept does not appear in the manifesto itself, it is explicit in the published principles behind the manifesto. The rule in XP is clear: if you work overtime one week, you can't work overtime the next week. The thinking is that if a problem requires two consecutive weeks of overtime, more overtime will not fix it.

Customer on the Team. We all recognize the value of having access to a customer when detailed questions of usage surface or priorities must be set under limited resources. Again, XP goes to the extreme. The rule is that a real customer must sit with the team. As you might guess, teams sometimes sidestep this, but it stands as the XP rule nevertheless. Observe that many software projects are IT (information technology) ones done for a customer who is within the organization, for example, order-taking software for the company. Thus, for many XP projects, it is easier to identify and assign a customer than it would be for many non-software projects.

Coding Standards. The practice of maintaining coding standards supports other practices, such as collective ownership, pairing, and refactoring. With so much built-in fluidity (to provide flexibility), the team simply cannot allow a laissez-faire approach to formatting, style, and similar matters. It should be impossible to tell who wrote which part of the code. The team can establish its own standards or it can assume them from company standards or those supplied by the software language in use. Common standards are one strength that Toyota uses to remain flexible much deeper into the development process than its competitors. Viewed another way, by standardizing things that normally remain constant, you gain latitude to let variability run longer in the design itself.

It is important to recognize that the practices do not stand alone. They fit together and support one another mutually. There is a worn story about two programmers meeting and one says, "We are doing XP."

The other asks, "Are you doing pairing?"

"No."

"What about test-driven design? Are you doing that?"

"Nope."

After a couple more rounds, in frustration, the first programmer asks, "What *are* you doing?"

"We've stopped doing the documentation."

Clearly, effective use of XP goes beyond eliminating obnoxious activities; it must extend to recognizing that these practices are designed to fit together like a puzzle to provide a safety net for one another. For example, see Figure 1.5, which shows the support structure for one practice. Similar support is possible for all the other practices as well.[15]

How Did XP Arise?

The story about how XP started is instructive.[16] Kent Beck, one of the originators of the technique, was consulting at Chrysler in 1996 when he was asked to lead a programming team. He observed what seemed to be best practices and asked the team to do them, things such as testing early in the project and co-location. The next time, there was more at stake and he was under pressure, so (as he told an interviewer later), "I thought, 'Damn the torpedoes' ... [and] asked the team to crank up all the knobs to 10 on the things I thought were essential and leave out everything else." So, for example, test-ing early seemed to be a good idea, so why not write the test *before* writing the code? Co-location seemed to be beneficial, so why not put two programmers side by side? Thus, XP was born. What are you doing today that is working and might be cranked up to 10?

XP Values

Extreme Programming may not be completely transferable outside the software development world, but its underlying values are. What are they? Beck lists four: communication, simplicity, feed-back, and courage.[17]

Communication. Communication is at the very core of much of human activity, and nowhere more so than in product devel-opment. Good communication is difficult. We forget to tell people things that are critical to their work, or we are unaware that this information is critical to their work. Sometimes we hide information purposely, because it is embarrassing. On occasion, people ignore what we are saying or they miss it because they are distracted by something else.

Figure 1.5 "Safety Net" for Collective Code Ownership

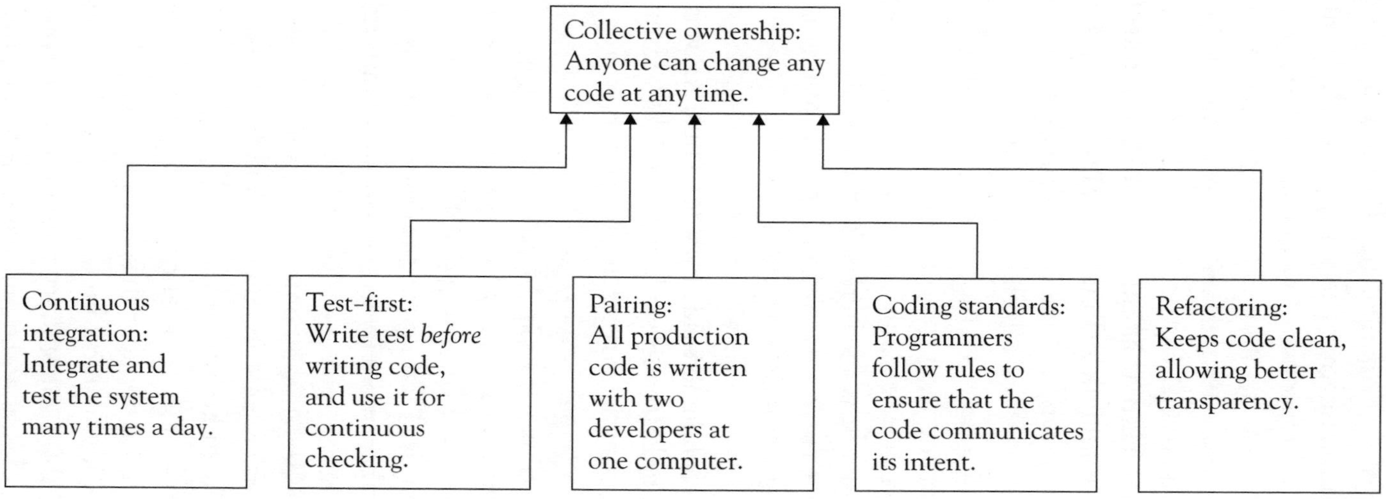

When we are working in the flexible mode, another dimension enters: communicating the certainty or flexibility in your basic statement, for example: "I would like to have ten units by Friday so that I can test them over the weekend, but next Tuesday is my absolute deadline. And if you can't get new ones at a decent price, functional used ones will do."

Another factor that enters these days is the effect of cultural factors on communication. For example, I do some training for a Chinese training company, and I recently went with them to conduct a workshop in India. The Chinese trainers were amazed at the contrast between the two countries. In China, the students are reticent, and we spend our time drawing them out and seeding a discussion. In the Confucian manner, subordinates defer to the boss. In India, it is the opposite: the discussion expands and we must strive to manage it and bring it to closure. Each student has an opinion that must be expressed.

Simplicity. In XP, simple design and refactoring aim directly at simplicity. The idea is that something simple is easier than something complex to understand and thus to change. Complexity hides problems and extends the time needed to understand how something works and would work if you were to change it. In other words, simplicity lowers the cost of change. As Albert Einstein put it, "Everything should be made as simple as possible, but not simpler." The principles provided with the Agile Manifesto describe simplicity as the art of maximizing the amount of work not done.

Simple design is a knobs-at-ten approach to simplicity that, as noted earlier, does not always apply. However, the value of simplicity is much broader than this. Most of us overload ourselves when we travel with clothing that we never wear, we cover our desks with piles of paper that have outlived their utility, and we carry older, low-volume products in inventory just in case someone wants them. Simplicity is about clearing out these things in order to be clearer and more adaptable where it matters today.

Feedback. Feedback drives flexible systems better than plans do. The fourth value of the Agile Manifesto is "responding to change over following a plan." Note that half of the XP practices exploit feedback:

- The Planning Game, to plan the current iteration based on what you learned from the preceding one
- Small Releases, so that you can learn early what the market-place thinks
- Test-Driven Design, so that you discover quickly whether your work is right
- Pairing, to correct incorrect thinking even earlier
- Continuous Integration, to learn sooner whether you have problems
- Customer on the Team, to know what the customer thinks as early as possible

Courage. When Kent Beck said "Damn the torpedoes" and cranked the knobs up, he didn't know if it would work. That took courage. Several of the XP practices require courage. One is simple design—purposely not putting in the design what you might need tomorrow. It takes courage to refactor code that someone else wrote, possibly causing it to break. Pairing takes courage; it is a good way to get your ego bruised.

Observe that courage is supported by the other values of communication, simplicity, and feedback. Good communication gives you the best information for taking action, so you have the best chance of success. Simplicity allows you to see through the haze, further raising your chances of success. And feedback allows you to revise and redirect quickly if you are wrong.

Does XP Work?

Extreme Programming is certainly a radical departure from traditional "best practice" in software development. What is its record of accomplishment? You certainly can find naysayers who trot out failures, and you can find plenty of advocates with wonderful success stories. Perhaps the most even-handed assessment is reported by Boehm and Turner, who advocate a balance between agile and traditional methods.[18] They found that for thirty-one agile (mostly XP) projects in several industries (aerospace, computer, and telecom, among others), compared to traditionally run projects of similar complexity:

- All were average or above average in budget performance.
- All were average or above average in schedule compliance.
- All were about the same as traditional projects in product quality.

They also observed that these projects followed most XP practices strongly, but that a full-time co-located customer and a forty-hour week were admirable aspirations but difficult to achieve in practice.

The big advantage of these methods for us is in flexibility. During each iteration (one to four weeks), the set of features being implemented is replanned, so

- Customers or marketing people can add a new feature in under a month with no penalty.
- They can drop a feature that hasn't been processed yet with no penalty.
- Management can terminate the project at any time with the most valuable features completely coded and tested.

However, XP has been used mostly on smaller projects where it was possible to have a co-located team in one room (I have much more to say about co-located teams in Chapter Six). Also many of these projects were internal IT ones where it was relatively easy to involve the customer. As experience with XP and other agile methodologies is growing, however, these restrictions are loosening.[19]

Moving from Software to Other Products

Software is a special medium that lends itself to agile approaches. Here are some of software's characteristics that agilists have exploited:

- Object technologies, which allow modularization to isolate change and enable substitution of modules
- The low cost of an automated build, which facilitates frequent and early testing
- The logic basis of software, which allows relatively fast automated checking for many types of errors
- Relatively easy divisibility of product features, which enables developing a product feature by feature and subdividing features to split tasks
- (For IT projects) customers who are relatively easy to find and involve in development
- In general, the malleability of the software medium, which makes change relatively easy

Nevertheless, agilists have worked hard to exploit the special characteristics of software to their advantage. Many of the principles agilists exploit apply equally to non-software products, principles such as iterative development with customer feedback, self-organizing teams, and emergent processes. We can exploit the special characteristics of non-software media to our advantage. For example, an advantage mechanical systems possess is that they are quite visible, lending themselves to physical prototyping, and electrical systems have the advantage that programmable components, such as field-programmable gate arrays, allow quick changes in a system that may be difficult to redesign and rebuild quickly.

Consider how Johnson & Johnson Worldwide Emerging Markets Innovation Center (Shanghai) has translated many of the XP practices to their business of developing personal care products, such as lotions, creams, shower gels, and soaps:

- Small releases: Conduct fast prototypes and test immediately. They separate the development of fragrances, preservative options, and base formulas, and then merge them eventually.
- Simple design: Remove unnecessary materials in the formulation.
- Test-driven design: For example, when concerned about skin moisturization, look at how the test is done and design the product accordingly.
- Pairing: Adopt a buddy system. Have two formulators working on the same project, which helps both in finding better solutions and in broadening skills.
- Collective code ownership: For difficult issues, conduct group prototyping wherein a pair of buddies shares their issue with others, whereupon other pairs create solutions in the lab and forward them to the requesting buddies for further development.
- Continuous integration: As soon as formulators create an innovative product, forward it to others who optimize the formulation.
- Customer on the team: Expose fast prototypes to consumers and get their assessment, then revise, evaluate again, and so forth.

A Note of Caution

I have mentioned that these tools and techniques must be applied selectively to some projects and not to others, and they should be applied only to certain portions of a project. The next section provides more on this. Some of the tools and approaches, such as simple design, are exactly the right thing to do in some cases and absolutely the wrong thing to do in others (see "Providing for Growth" in Chapter Three, for instance). I point out many of the potential pitfalls as I go along. I wish I could resolve the essential ambiguity for you, but this is impossible given the broad variety of potential applications.

This is new material. Tomorrow it will be applied in ways undreamt of today, and this will lead to clearer rules for when and how to apply it. You could wait for the material to be pack-aged neatly for you by your competitor, but that is probably an unattractive option.

Consequently, these tools and techniques should be applied by a seasoned manager who understands the unique objectives and capabilities of the target organization, as well as its culture and the demands of its marketplace.

The Project Analyzer

Flexibility is inappropriate for some projects, nor is it necessarily appropriate for all parts of a product. The Project Analyzer suggests where to allow flexibility and where it is necessary to stay closer to more traditional approaches (See Figure 1.6). It measures a project in four dimensions: quality management, project planning, docu-mentation, and requirements management. Each of these dimen-sions is independent and is influenced by various project attributes, as shown in Figure 1.6b.

As indicated in Figure 1.6a, a project can rate high on one axis, necessitating a greater amount of structure and control there. On the other hand, other dimensions might be relatively light, allow-ing more flexibility on them. For instance, in Figure 1.6a, Project 2 can be managed using a more flexible approach than Project 1— except in requirements management, where it should be even more structured than Project 1. Also note that the total "thumbprint" area of a project indicates the amount of project overhead required, and the area left over outside the thumbprint represents the resid-ual effort, after overhead, for actual product development.

Figure 1.6   a. The Thumbprints of Two Projects.
b. Attributes of a Project That Push Its Thumbprint
Along the Indicated Axis

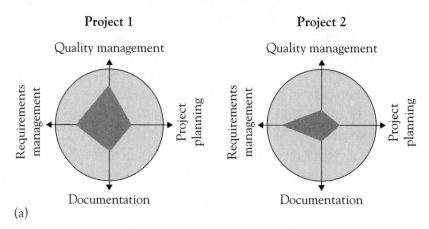

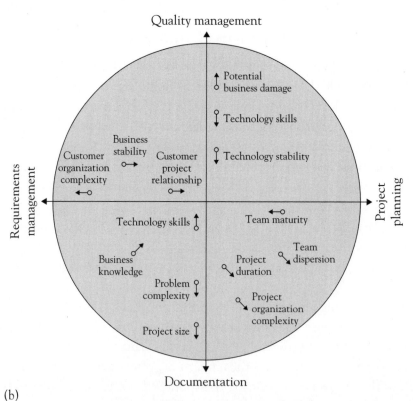

© 2002 Anne Bjerre Jorgensen and Ole Jepsen. Used with permission.

The point of Figure 1.6 (and my motivation for placing the Project Analyzer so early in the book) is only to alert you that each project should be viewed separately for areas where flexibility will be beneficial and where it might be harmful. Each project will have its own characteristic flexibility thumbprint. In Chapter Nine I explore this topic further and provide a means for actually balancing the needs for flexibility with the needs for structure.

Should you decide to use the Project Analyzer as portrayed in Figure 1.6 for your project, note that it was created for IT software projects. Although it seems relatively general, please modify it to the attributes of your project.

Summary

This chapter provides a foundation for flexible development. Some key points:

- I aim to provide customizable tools, techniques, and approaches that will help you accommodate—even embrace—change rather than suppressing or denying it.
- Change is essential to innovation, and industry's record over a recent fourteen-year period is one of decreasing product innovation.
- Not all projects or parts of a project need be flexible, and it can be inadvisable to make them all flexible. Use flexibility with discretion when its benefits outweigh its costs.
- Agile software development, Extreme Programming in particular, is a motivating model of the possibilities for increasing flexibility, but most agile practices do not translate directly to non-software products. This book develops similar practices for use outside the software industry.

In contrast with this introductory chapter, the ones to follow present the tools and approaches of flexibility. Think of them as a tool kit. Each chapter presents a category of tools. For a given project, you will need an assortment of tools but not necessarily all of them.

I present the categories of tools by chapter only because it is easier to assimilate them separately. Like the practices of XP though, they fit together and mutually support each other. They tend to be synergetic $(1 + 1 = 3)$. Some may not seem to fit your business, but this may only be because you are not thinking creatively enough about them. For instance, at first, modular product architectures (Chapter Three) may not seem to apply to homogeneous chemical products like paint, but they may apply to the manufacturing or distribution processes of such products to make them more flexible.

2

CUSTOMERS AND PRODUCT REQUIREMENTS

Your most unhappy customers are your greatest source of learning.

—*Bill Gates*

The customer is the starting point—and the ending point—for all effective product development, so it is appropriate to start by exploring ways businesses can improve flexibility through their relations with customers.

The changes developers encounter during development frequently can be traced to the customer. Customers change their minds; they do not know what they want until they see it; they do not use the product as they are supposed to (that is, the way developers assume they will); they do not read the instruction manual; they abuse the product; they undervalue the product's marvelous features while complaining about minor problems; and they return it for warranty service when it is working perfectly. Even for high-tech products, where one might think that technology changes would dominate a project, many technology changes actually stem from customers' difficulties in relating to the new technology. Oh, if we could just live without customers—but of course, we can't.

The Fallacy of Frozen Requirements

So-called best practice in product development advises that the development team should do a thorough job of understanding the customer, write down exactly what the customer needs in a specification or requirements document, and then design to that.[1]

Although many of us know that it seldom works this way, we continue to believe that this is the way it should be. Moreover, the development processes we use reinforce this myth. Phased development systems generally require a requirements document as a deliverable at the end of an early phase with the expectation that it is final. For medical device development in the United States, the U.S. Food and Drug Administration (FDA) recently tightened up procedures for specifying the product in advance and then sticking to that specification during development.

Does this fit with reality, or is a frozen specification simply fiction? Donald Reinertsen has been collecting data on this discrepancy for thirteen years, from the thousand-plus product development managers who have attended his class at the California Institute of Technology. Here is what he found:[2]

Question	Answer
Out of hundreds of projects, how often did the requirements remain stable throughout design?	Never
How many developers had complete specifications before starting design work?	5 percent
On average, what proportion of requirements were specified before design commenced?	54 percent
For each developer who waits for at least 80 percent of the requirements, how many have already started designing?	Five

So it is not that specifications seldom remain constant during development; it is that they *never* do. The concept of frozen requirements is complete fiction in the real world. Reinertsen went beyond this with his last three questions. He found that it is foolhardy even to try to specify the product completely before you start design, because if you try, you will be late to market.

Requirements Evolution Versus Scope Creep

Changing requirements have a bad reputation with designers and engineers. They usually mean *added* requirements, and these additions are imposed from outside—often by management or marketing. Thus the project grows in difficulty while the schedule and resources remain the same. Commonly, this phenomenon is called *scope creep*.

In effective flexible development, the situation is much different. First, a requirement is just as likely to be removed as added, and a new one could be easier or more difficult to develop than an old one it replaces. The objective is to provide customer value, not to make your product bulletproof against anything a competitor might add. Ideally, the change occurs before much is invested in the changed requirement.

Such changes are standard fare in agile software development, and agile processes accommodate them naturally by making a place for requirements changes in each iteration cycle. During an iteration (typically, two weeks), requirements remain fixed so that developers can concentrate on assigned tasks. But at the end of an iteration, the complete team, often including the customer, reconsiders all the remaining features—called the backlog—and allocates to the next iteration the features that currently seem most valuable, as shown in Figure 2.1. Thus, changes in unstarted

Figure 2.1 Feature Replacement in Agile Software Development

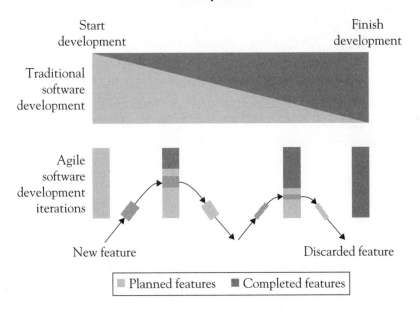

Start development   Finish development

Traditional software development

Agile software development iterations

New feature   Discarded feature

■ Planned features   ■ Completed features

features are routine, and the priority of a given feature can change from iteration to iteration. A feature that seemed important at the beginning of the project might be bumped repeatedly and never make it into the final product.

Consequently, the first reason that this is not scope creep is that the requirements list does not continually grow more demanding. The second reason is the cross-functional deliberation regarding the pros and cons of making each change. Changes are not thrust upon the project from the outside but rather balanced internally to provide maximum customer value from the available resources.

The Value of Customer Feedback

The Reinertsen data clearly show that frozen requirements are a myth. Two other studies take the next step, showing us that frozen specifications would not be effective even if they were possible. Both of these studies come from the software world.

The MacCormack and Boehm Studies

Professor Alan MacCormack, of the Harvard Business School, investigated Internet software development, a fast-changing field. He contrasted development projects that were commercially successful—made a lot of money—with those that were not commercially successful, and he made some amazing discoveries.[3] Most startling, he found that the managers of the commercially successful projects did *not* believe they were successful. To understand this, it's necessary to look first at his other conclusions. He found that commercial success depends on

- Placing a working product in users' hands as early in development as possible
- Rapid feedback on product definition changes
- Team members with broad experience in delivering new products
- Strong attention to product architecture

I consider team member experience in Chapter Six, and I cover architecture in Chapter Three, but the first two bullets are the key to understanding why the managers of successful projects did not believe they were successful.

Consider what is happening in the successful project. The team is developing working prototypes and placing them in users' hands early. (MacCormack found that what matters is the earliness, not the number of early prototypes.) Of course, these prototypes are not fully baked. Users are not bashful in telling the developers about the flaws. So the developers fix these flaws and build another working prototype, only to have users tell them that it now has other flaws. And so on.

Internally, this project looks like an unplanned mess—in constant flux and with many customer problems. Consequently, managers are not proud of their work on this project, and they rate it as unsuccessful. However, in terms of responding to customer feedback, thus producing a product with exceptional customer value (commercial success), the project is first rate.

Barry Boehm and his associates conducted a similar study. Boehm is a professor of software engineering at the University of Southern California now, but he previously spent many years managing large software projects and investigating software methodologies in the aerospace industry. In one interesting experiment he had seven teams develop the same small (2000–4000 source instructions) software application.[4] The dominant part of this application was a user interface, which makes it a likely high-change situation. Four teams used a traditional plan-driven approach where they documented their requirements, then documented their design, and finally coded the program from the design. The other three teams used a prototyping approach, where they concentrated on building a prototype in lieu of formally documented requirements and design. They then obtained user suggestions on the prototype before completing the code.

The prototyping approach required substantially less effort and created substantially less code (see Figure 2.2). There were other differences between the two groups. The prototyped products were

Figure 2.2   Prototyping with User Feedback Is More Effective Than Specification-Driven Development

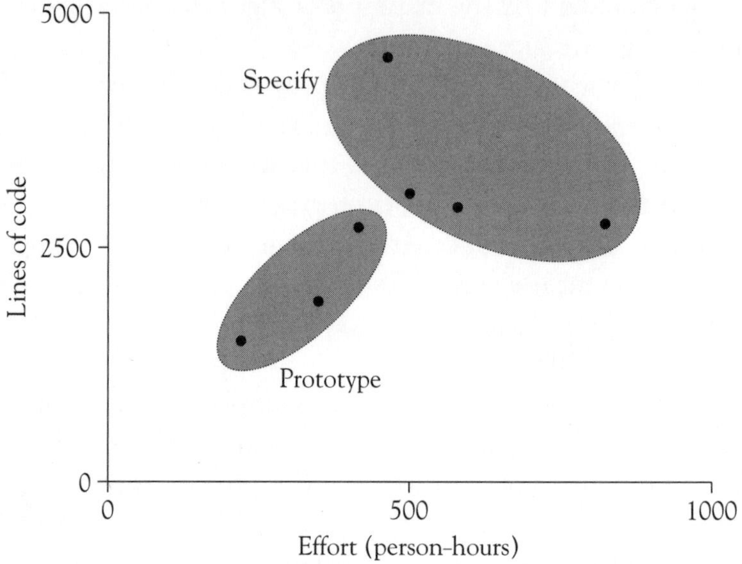

Figure used with permission from IEEE.

judged easier to use and easier to learn, presumably due to the changes made midproject from user feedback. On the other hand, the traditionally developed products had more features (because these teams completed all the features in the original require-ments) but, interestingly, no greater usability (the omitted features were of marginal utility, the prototypers apparently discovered). Also, the traditionally developed products were easier to integrate, because they had better interface specifications.

Both the MacCormack and the Boehm studies demonstrate that an iterative approach that obtains early feedback from customers and users has a great deal of power.

The Overspecification Trap

As the Boehm study suggests, obtaining early feedback from customers and using it to adjust the design is effective, in part, because it allows the team to develop the most valuable features and skip some of the others. Everyone knows that some features in a product are more valuable than others, but traditional development methods have no effective way to separate them, especially when such distinctions become clearer as development evolves.

Think about some of the products you use—DVD players, digital cameras, automotive air-conditioning systems, word processors, and food processors. What portion of their features do you actually use? How about the high, medium, and low power settings on a vacuum cleaner: how many people set it to low power? Maybe those who love vacuuming and wish to stretch the chore out as long as possible.

The Standish Group studied software product features and found that people do not use 45 percent of the features in software products, rarely use another 19 percent, and sometimes use 16 percent, which leaves only 20 percent that they use often or always.[5] So overspecification is not only a problem for a few of the products that you use. It is widespread across a broad array of new products.

Why does this happen? In large part, it is due to rigid development processes that attempt to forecast all possible features that users might need or competitors might offer. Such processes seem attractive because of an assumption that there will be no opportunity to add features later or that the cost of change associated with adding them later might be prohibitive. In short, it seems easy and cheap to add one more feature today, just in case it might become important later. Developers are rewarded for providing all the features that customers might want, and they are penalized for missing one. Consequently, traditional development processes encourage overspecification.

The Principles of Iteration and Customer Feedback

This concept of iteration incorporating customer or user feedback is fundamental to flexible development. It is relatively straightforward in software development projects, and all agile methodologies exploit it. In fact, the agilists use very short iterations—one to four weeks—precisely to amplify feedback and learning. Feedback is one of the four basic values of XP, as explained in Chapter One. It is also fundamental to all the non-software tools and approaches considered in this book. The idea is to build the very basics of what the customer seems to want, let the customer assess what you have done, and go on from there, repeating until it is good enough. The real customer requirements emerge from the interaction, and they are likely to be less demanding than originally envisioned. Another advantage is that iteration and feedback, especially if it occurs early in the project, forces the change to occur early in the project—when the cost of change is relatively low.

Although this seems simple enough, it is not easy. First, some people are quite uncomfortable without a clear destination. They want to know when they will be finished. Management, in particular, tends to have concerns about any project without a clear end point. Even if the project plan is fiction, having it is more comfortable than believing that the customer will tell us when the results are acceptable.

In practical terms, management does need a schedule at the beginning of the project to plan resources and coordinate with other projects. Thus, a flexible project does have an initial schedule, but everyone recognizes that it is likely to change as the project proceeds.

Second, some people are uncomfortable revealing their ignorance or asking others for help, and this is exactly what happens when you show an early prototype to customers. The notion that customers might know more about a product than professionally trained developers seems a bit strange. After all, developers would not be developers if they were not best at it.

Third, there is clearly some waste here. The team will repeat some activities, and some of their work will go unused. This is true, and this is why these flexibility techniques work best for developing novel products. For routine upgrades, you know where you are going, and you do not need customer feedback. But for innovative products, the apparent waste associated with some dead ends and rework is the price of a winning product. Keeping the cost of change low will help minimize this waste.

Lowering the Cost of Iteration

There is one more difficulty with iteration. Even if you know exactly where you are going and thus avoid rework or unused work, you still have to endure the cost of repeating some activities that could be done only once if you were not iterating. These are the cycle costs. Each time you complete a cycle of iteration—from the time that you show a customer one prototype until the time that you show the next prototype—you incur the costs outlined in Figure 2.3. Such cycle costs are generally proportional to the number of iterations.

Consequently, your ability to do extensive iteration and customer sampling will depend on your ability to reduce these costs, and for radical iteration, you may need radical cost reductions. This depends greatly on the nature of the prototyping cycle involved. Here are some cost-reduction possibilities to consider:

Figure 2.3   Costs That Accumulate in Each Customer Iteration Cycle

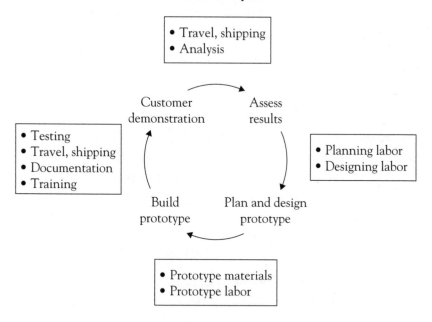

- Automate tasks. This is what agilists have done with their software testing so that they can repeat it almost continuously.
- Hold off on some tasks, such as documentation, until you are finished.
- Find less expensive ways to make and change prototypes. I discuss this more in Chapter Four, but here are some useful avenues:

  Many teams find ways to replace prototypes with computer simulation.

  Automotive developers use "mules": existing cars with only the system in question—say, the power steering—changed.

  Electronics developers use field-programmable gate arrays (FPGAs) that they can reprogram easily.

  Software developers use "scaffolding" that allows them to build and test only a small part of the system.

- Find more efficient ways to assess prototypes, especially when you conduct the same type of assessment repetitively.
- Combine cycles, for instance, by modifying the prototype at the customer site overnight.
- Think at a higher level: what is the fundamental learning you need from a loop, and what are you doing that is extraneous to this?

Another approach is to gather your team and give them a challenge goal that is almost outlandish. Ask them to cut cycle costs by 90 percent. At first, the proposals might be outlandish too, but in them, you are likely to find the seeds of some much cheaper ways to complete a cycle.

Specify at a Higher Level

I've found two general ways to handle customers and requirements that increase flexibility. One, covered here, is to specify the product at a higher level that is less likely to change. The other, covered in the next major section, is to anticipate changes in requirements.

Product Vision

Rather than specifying the product at a detailed feature-by-feature level, which will most likely change, provide guidance to developers with a vision of what the product will do, who it will serve, how it will differ from what your company or your competitors are providing now, or how it will make life more enjoyable. This vision is comparable to the product metaphor (described in "XP Practices" in Chapter One). The vision is like a compass used on a trail. Although the trail wanders, you can check your compass to verify that you are proceeding in the desired general direction and not heading the wrong way entirely.[6]

A product vision is typically less than a hundred words, and you can state it in many ways. For instance, the vision for the original Lexus automobile, which appeared in 1989, was a compound of apparently conflicting goals:[7]

- Great high-speed handling/stability yet a pleasant ride
- Fast and smooth ride yet low fuel consumption
- Super quiet yet light weight
- Elegant styling yet great aerodynamics
- Warm yet functional interior
- Great stability at high speed yet great C_D value (low friction)

This statement was demanding, but it gave developers a great deal of freedom to maneuver in the uncertain waters Toyota was entering to upset Mercedes Benz, BMW, Jaguar, and other luxury makes.

The original Hewlett-Packard DeskJet printer, which appeared in 1988, resulted from an even simpler vision statement:

- Laser-quality print

- Plain paper printing
- Price under US$1,000

Given the great advances in inkjet printing since then, the challenge in this vision is difficult to comprehend today. The competition at the time was dot matrix printers, which did not offer true letter-quality printing, and laser printers, which did but cost thousands of dollars at the time. In addition, the only inkjets available required special coated paper. Consequently, this simple vision provided plenty of room to explore with a clear objective in a fluid market.

Moving forward to today, DeskJet printers are selling for under US$50, and in this competitive market, manufacturers make their profit from the associated ink cartridges, not from the printers themselves. Consequently, HP management found that their printers were not competitive, because they were overdesigned for the current market. So an HP development manager, to create a dramatic vision of the product needed, placed a current production printer on the floor in front of the developers and stood on it, proclaiming that they make printers, not footstools; their printers do not need to be as strong as footstools. The developers walked away with a very clear vision that their design must be good enough but no better, and the way in which the manager presented the challenge (not-a-footstool) left plenty of design latitude.

It might appear that a vision statement is created by the resident visionary or by the development team huddling together. This is far from the case for effective vision statements. They are not so much a creative statement as the carefully composed essence of broad-based customer research. You listen to many customers, walk in their shoes, and survey the market for directions and gaps. Then you create a statement that circumscribes a discovered gap in the market. For instance, Ichiro Suzuki, the chief engineer for the original Lexus, conducted considerable research of the market, customers, and competitors. From this, he compiled a list, in descending order, of what Mercedes Benz customers said they wanted:[8]

1. Brand prestige
2. Quality
3. Resale value
4. Performance (ride, handling, acceleration, for example)
5. Safety

Suzuki knew that he had to go beyond what current customers said they wanted, and he knew that items like quality and resale value arose from more basic characteristics. This is what led him to the list of six Lexus contrasts presented earlier.

An automobile is a complex product created by a complex team. Even so, Toyota is able to boil its requirements document (called a "chief engineer's concept paper") down to fifteen to twenty-five pages that are completely cross-functional and based on the customer. Contrast this with a typical automobile company, whose requirements documentation runs for hundreds of pages in disjoint departmental documents with only the one from Marketing having any orientation toward the customer.[9] For example, a Chrysler minivan had 1,700 functional requirements for the body alone![10]

Once you have a product vision statement, the project leader maintains and communicates it and monitors the project relative to it. The vision statement provides a wonderful filtering mechanism for the project leader. Outside demands, proposed new features, shifts in emphasis, changes in resources, and project progress all can be checked against the product vision to ensure that the project is remaining on track. This filtering mechanism is valuable when the project is subject to ongoing change: you admit items that fit with the vision, and you reject those that do not.

Using a vision statement rather than the sort of specific requirements list found in a traditional project will lead to more team discussion as open items are sorted out. Thus a flexible project will benefit greatly from a close-knit, cross-functional team that provides such intense communication flow (see Chapter Six).

Personas

Another way to describe a product without anchoring yourself prematurely in details likely to change is to describe instead the people who will use the product.[11] Developers call these characters *personas*. A typical project will have three to five personas, a primary one and some who fill secondary but essential roles. For instance, if you are developing an automotive audio system, you might create four personas:

- The owner and primary driver of the car (primary persona)
- Spouse (a professional violinist)
- Teenage son
- Repair and service technician

Each persona receives a name, say, Juan, Amelia, Carlos, and Filipe, respectively, in this case.

Then you provide a portrait and create a personality for each one, consistent with your market research. For instance, Juan's portrait might be of a distinguished middle-aged gentleman. His description portrays a busy businessman with no time for trivia or the unexpected. Everything has its place. In his spare time, he likes to entertain others on his yacht. For music, he prefers traditional jazz.

As with vision statements, these personas are not works of fiction; they are constructed carefully from thorough market research. The primary persona should represent your dominant user group, and each secondary one should represent an important but distinct user group that to some extent conflicts with the primary user group. Together, they should provide the balance that you desire for your product. Although you want them to be accurate from a market research perspective, you create personas to come alive so that members of the development team will relate to them.

Use personas by asking whether a persona would be pleased with a design direction being taken. Would Juan be frustrated with these knobs to reduce static on weak stations? Would Amelia be able to relate these level controls to her sense of musical balance? Will these speakers produce enough bass for Carlos? Will Filipe be able to replace the unit before Juan becomes impatient waiting for him?

Unlike a requirements list, which aims to answer questions for the team—often prematurely, according to what is presented in Chapter Seven—personas aim to ask the right questions as the team proceeds. Consequently, again you need a strong team communication network to use personas.

Use Cases

The use case technique applies to products dominated by a procedural element. It arose from object-oriented software development, and it has been applied to business process engineering as well.[12] As a non-software development example, consider a rice cooker. Not all important portions of a rice cooker relate to its operating procedure, but key portions concerning customer value do. Thus, important portions of the rice cooker could be specified through use cases. As with product visions and personas, the advantage of doing this is that, in a fluid environment, use cases are more likely to remain stable than are traditional specifications.

A bit like personas, use cases employ a variety of *actors* acting on a *system*. Unlike personas, each actor has a different role. For example, you create one actor for preparing rice, another for serving rice, and a third for doing the cleanup. You create a *primary scenario* for each separate procedure (cooking, serving, and cleaning), which describes exactly how the actor interacts with the system step-by-step when all goes well. Then you create *secondary scenarios* that describe nonstandard events, such as the cord not reaching the electrical outlet, or too little rice for the water already in the cooker. Use cases can be written using a number of diagramming techniques or—probably best—in simple prose. An advantage of use cases is that they are nontechnical, facilitating understanding by customers and marketing.

User Stories

Use cases arose in the pre-agile era, and agilists mostly have moved to user stories, which fit the agile software development style better.[13] A user story has three parts, the most apparent of which is a story card (or sticky note) that states one user feature as a simple sentence. For instance, the rice cooker might have these two story cards:

- A user can cook brown or white, long-grain or short-grain rice interchangeably without making adjustments.
- A user can clean the rice-cooking portion separately from the electrical portion.

You usually post story cards in the team room, and you use them for planning iterations (see "The Planning Game" in Chapter One). However, the story card's main role is a reminder of the more significant second part of the user story: a conversation with a customer to elaborate the details of this functionality. The third part is a set of tests (see "Test-Driven Design" in Chapter One) that, in addition to allowing developers to check their work after coding, essentially provide documentation of the feature. That is, because developers write the tests before writing the code, they can then use them as a guide for implementing the feature successfully.

Unlike the techniques discussed earlier in this section, user stories aid flexibility not by rising above change but by keeping the cost of change low.[14] You invest very little in the story card, and it acts as a placeholder to complete the feature's definition and documentation later when you are certain that you will use it and have fresher information about it. Thus the technique is akin to "Rolling-Wave Planning," covered in Chapter Eight.

Anticipate Customer Needs

The preceding section showed how to keep a product's definition flexible by remaining at a relatively high level of definition, where change was less likely. The companion approach involves anticipating where change might happen so that you can prepare for it. Of course, better anticipation can be valuable in traditional development as well. It is a matter of degree. If you are facing a great deal of potential change and thus need the flexibility, you should make a heavier investment in these anticipatory techniques than you would make traditionally.

Anticipation is dangerous in that it can be confused with forecasting, a practice I caution against in Chapter One (see Figure 1.2). However, there is a difference. Forecasting is an attempt to *know* what will happen in the future, and this effort has serious limitations. To *anticipate* is to give advance thought, preparation, or attention to something. So it is a matter of becoming sensitive to areas that might change, so that if they do change, even though you do not know exactly how they will change, you are in position to deal with them effectively. For example, you can attempt to forecast whether it will rain next Wednesday, when you will have to walk to the train station, or you can anticipate the possibility and buy an umbrella to deal with the rain if it occurs.

Recall that the Extreme Programming practice of simple design described in Chapter One advised against any anticipation. This is appropriate when change is likely and unpredictable, but you are likely to find that some parts of a project are relatively stable and the trend is clear. In this case, anticipation pays. Use your judgment in such cases.

You can improve anticipation by adding a section to your requirements document discussing areas of the product most likely to change, so that you can focus anticipatory efforts on them. If you can gather a representative group of customers together, you can discover what might change in your product by playing carefully constructed games with them. Luke Hohmann provides a selection of games of this type: Remember the Future, Spider Web, Buy a Feature, and Speed Boat.[15]

You can also improve your anticipatory capabilities by appreciating the customer experience, or by staying in touch with "lead users"—the people who are likely to be the first to encounter changed needs.

Get into the Customer Experience

You can understand and anticipate changes in your marketplace better by immersing yourself in your customer (or user) environment.[16] The customer often operates in a world far different from yours, as this example shows. The customer service department of a computer printer company had received a number of warranty returns from the same customer. Finally, they found some bits of dough in one of the returned printers. Upon investigation, they discovered that the customer was a *tortillería*, and its operators were attempting to make their tortillas distinctive by imprinting the firm's logo on them as a watermark! Once the customer service staff understood what was happening, they disallowed these returns as, in industry jargon, "unsupported media." In this case, although customer service personnel were exposed to this unusual application, the designers—who really needed to experience it— were shielded from it.

I find that the companies that are best at appreciating their customer environment find ways of getting designers in contact with customers that are unique to their products and markets.[17] The examples I provide here are offered in the hope that they will inspire you to find one that works well for you.

Surgical implements present challenges in that few design-ers are in a position to see how their products are used. However, many designers arrange to observe surgeries in the operating room. Others, including a colleague of mine, go further and try surgery themselves on dead animals for firsthand experience. Another col-league, associated with a start-up company without much money, got permission to hang out in the staging room in a major hospital, where surgeons wait to enter the operating room, and obtained free feedback from these surgeons on his prototypes. This is the type of creativity needed to find effective ways of learning about your customers' product experience.

Credit Suisse formed a team to investigate handicapped acces-sibility to their facilities, then required each member of the team to spend an entire day working completely from a wheelchair. The biggest problems they encountered were things they had never imagined. According to David McQuillen, head of the cus-tomer experience team, "Sitting in the wheelchair was an emo-tional experience for everyone on the team, and we could see that we didn't need to focus so much on fixing buildings or Web sites, but on teaching our employees how to interact with people with disabilities."

Many companies have designers staff their help desks regu-larly—say, one day a quarter—to understand their products' short-comings firsthand. A client making consumer electronics had its executives (not its designers, unfortunately) spend one day a year in a department store selling their own and competing products in order to appreciate the buying experience.

A contemporary equivalent of this is employee blogs. Some companies encourage—or at least allow—their employees to inter-act with the public regarding their products by making their work the subject of their personal blog. If this is done well, employees can learn a great deal about what concerns customers. Clearly, they can also divulge proprietary information, so companies' poli-cies and tolerance for employee blogs vary greatly. Microsoft is quite open (even without a corporate policy on employee blogs) while Apple Computer is very closed; Yahoo! is open, but Google is closed.[18]

Pushing this further, have your designers actually get their hands dirty using your product in its normal environment (best for industrial products). See the Apprentice Game for an example of this type of activity.[19]

A manufacturer of power tools requires designers to spend a day each quarter riding with a service technician who visits construction sites where the company's products are used (and abused) and superstores where they are sold. A maker of building alarm systems had the whole team visit technicians who were installing its equipment, and this team learned some important lessons about how difficult it is to work with subminiature wires and terminals atop a swaying four-meter (12') stepladder.

This kind of practical insight becomes more difficult—and more critical—when your products are used overseas in an environment where you have little experience. Japanese automobile manufacturers routinely send teams to the United States to experience motoring conditions there. For instance, the chief engineer of the 2003 Toyota Sienna drove his team fifty thousand miles through Mexico, the United States, and Canada in the then-current Toyota minivan to understand the North American market. Two design features that resulted from this were more cup holders and the capacity to hold standard 1.2×2.4-meter ($4' \times 8'$) sheets of plywood. Another Toyota chief engineer moved into a Southern California household to understand the Generation X lifestyle.[20]

I provide two examples of how not to do it. First, consider certain U.S. automobile manufacturers that provide new cars to their senior employees, ostensibly as a product evaluation program (it is really more of an executive benefit program and a tax write-off, but the objectives become confused). However, because these cars rotate for new ones every three months, these key decision makers never have to deal with a car out of warranty, a dead battery, or insurance or maintenance problems. They thus lead a sheltered life and have a distorted view of their products.

The second example comes from the highly technical world of ultrasound medical imaging devices. These devices have three subsystems: the hand-held transducer, the computer that processes sophisticated digital signal processing algorithms, and the display that incorporates the latest electronic hardware and user interface software. The engineers are most comfortable with the more technical part of the system (the computer, the display, and their associated software), as they can exhibit their technical prowess better here, and marketing professionals gravitate to these subsystems also, because they are easier to specify. Consequently, they both leave behind the transducer, which is the part most apparent to the user and ripest for improvement. When designers experience the user environment firsthand, such distortions of priorities are less likely.

This field of observing customers is called ethnography, and many sources are available on it.[21]

Lead Users

Efforts to understand where your customers are today are worthwhile, but it would be even better to anticipate where they might be tomorrow. The lead user approach will give you a perspective on your customers' life tomorrow. Thus, lead users are a leading indicator of change.

Lead user research operates on the principle that a few of the people using your product are leading the way for how the product might be used in the future by others. Even beyond them, there may be others in a related application who face a similar need in an extreme form. These lead users have certain earmarks:

- They are generally professionals in the field.
- They are willing to modify (and have modified) your product to suit their needs—that is, they have already invented your next product.
- They are willing to pay premium prices for an effective solution.

- They will tolerate some inconveniences with the product.
- They are likely to profit greatly from certain advances in your product.

Lead user research is a matter of identifying these categories of users, finding the users themselves, and investigating how their usage of the product might be a forerunner of the field.

Consider an example from the 3M unit that makes surgical drapes—thin plastic films with adhesive backs that stick to the skin. Drapes are used at the site of surgery to prevent infection. However, they are expensive, and they do not control infection very well. 3M wanted a better solution and a blockbuster product, so its developers sought lead users who could move them toward the next generation of their product. They found several. One was surgeons in developing countries who worked under less hygienic conditions and could not afford surgical drapes. Another, surprisingly, was makeup artists in Hollywood, who must apply many materials to the skin and remove them without irritating it. Finally, they found veterinarians; as one veterinary surgeon commented, "Our patients are covered with hair, they don't bathe, and they don't have medical insurance, so the infection controls we use can't cost much." From these lead users, 3M found several new directions in surgical infection control.[22]

I am not suggesting that you invest in a formal program leading to a new product, as 3M did, but you can seek lead users of your current products who are extending their applications into new areas and pay careful attention to them as an indicator of future change. However, on your journey to understand your customers, also notice what others who are not your customers are doing to solve their problem, like the surgeons in developing countries who could not afford 3M's product.

Pitfalls of Customer Feedback

You can learn much from your customers, and it is clearly good policy to keep in touch with them. But these same customers can lead you in inappropriate directions and down blind alleys. Thus a few cautions are in order.

Expert Customers

Expert customers can teach you many things about your products and their deficiencies, but you must always remember that they are not typical. Lead users (who are expert customers by another name), for example, are willing to put up with shortcomings and cope with workarounds that would bring many complaints from mainstream customers.

Furthermore, expert customers can obscure deficiencies in your products. For instance, in the orthopedic joint implant market, manufacturers typically hire a leading orthopedic surgeon as a consultant to advise them in developing, say, a knee joint implant. This surgeon then tests the joint in experimental surgeries, and in some cases, if the surgeon is famous enough, the surgeon's name goes on the product: the *Chen Knee Joint*, for instance. The problem is that a surgeon at this level can make almost any joint work by deftly adjusting the ligaments and tendons, an important skill in such surgeries.

Consequently, be careful that your expert customers do not cover up problems with their expertise.

Customer Desires and Customer Needs

Seldom do customers actually suggest your next product. The best customer research methods search below the surface of what customers say they want in order to understand the underlying customer problem to be solved. In essence, this means not asking customers *what* they want but *why* they need it. Such research is called voice of the customer (VOC).

Contract design houses, which conduct engineering and industrial design to develop new products for manufacturers, often face a situation where the client has done what it regards as sufficient market research and comes in with a fully formed notion for a new product. The design house faces a dilemma here: does the client really know what its customers need, or is this just a hunch? Consequently, the design house uses a two-stage approach. Its people first listen carefully to what the client wants, and then they conduct their own investigation. As one of them put it, "We start with what customers say they want as a warm-up exercise."

In the same vein, customers sometimes are so wedded to the existing solution that they cannot envision a disruptive technology.[23] Make sure that you listen not only to your customers of today but also to the ones you will need to serve tomorrow. Lead users and similar means of breaking out of the present can help here.

Internal Customers

Internal customers—downstream players in your own organization—can also confuse you. *Internal customer* was a popular term a decade or two ago in the total quality movement. It was important to please internal as well as external customers—say, by designing a product that is easy to manufacture or for which your purchasing department can obtain parts easily.

Although this has merit, confusing internal and external customers can also lead you astray. As Jim Highsmith (an author of the Agile Manifesto) puts it, "Customers define value. Other stakeholders define constraints." (Here Highsmith is referring to the agile tenet that delivering customer value is the developer's highest priority.)[24]

Some companies have changed their terminology from *internal customers* to *partners* to enforce this distinction.

Summary

Here are some of the important points made in this chapter:

- Frozen requirements are a myth; it is healthier to acknowledge that requirements will change and then prepare for such change.

- Frozen requirements are undesirable from the standpoint of commercial success.

- Iteration with customer feedback is fundamental to flexible development.

- To reduce change in requirements, specify at a higher level.

- Seek to anticipate change in the customer environment by finding ways to stay close to your customers and thus appreciate their trends in using your products.

- However, be aware that customers can also lead you astray if you ask the wrong customers or ask them the wrong questions.

3

MODULAR PRODUCT ARCHITECTURES

> Minimizing connections between modules also
> minimizes the paths along which changes and
> errors can propagate into other parts of the system,
> thus eliminating disastrous "ripple" effects, where
> changes in one part cause errors in another,
> necessitating additional changes elsewhere, giving
> rise to new errors.
>
> —*Larry Constantine*[1]

Product developers are fond of talking about *product architecture*, but seldom are they very specific. Moreover, each developer tends to have a personal notion of what architecture actually is. Consequently, I start here by describing what I mean by product architecture and why it is important to flexibility:

> *Architecture* is the way in which one assigns the functional elements
> of a product to its physical chunks and how these physical chunks
> interact to achieve the product's overall function.[2]

Because this definition is rather abstract, and the concepts of *chunk* and *functional element* may be unclear, take a look at the corded telephones shown in Figure 3.1 as an example. The schematic on the left shows the functional elements of any corded telephone. On the right, the top photo shows one way of assigning these functions to chunks, specifically, the electronics and keypad to one chunk and the microphone and earpiece to another chunk. In the lower photo, the keypad has moved to the other chunk.

Figure 3.1   Two Corded Telephone Architectures

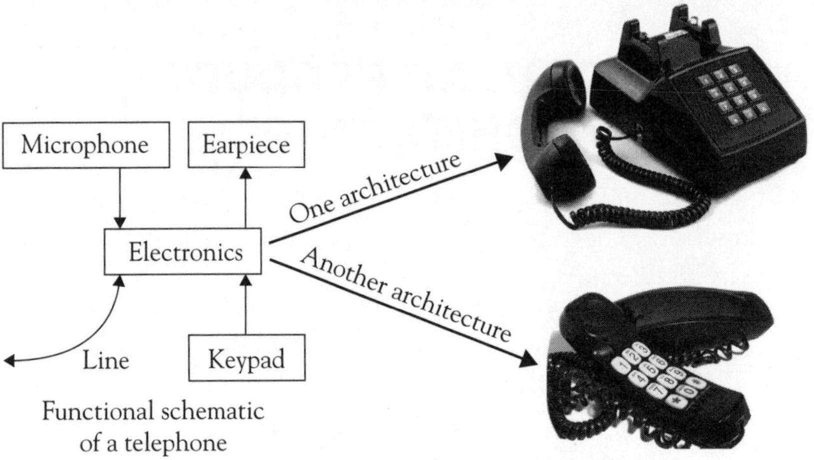

Functional schematic
of a telephone

Photographs © iStockphoto.com, members dpriebel and LizV, respectively.

Now think about today's mobile phones. Some of them place all functional elements in one chunk, while others—flip phones—split them into two chunks. In the early flip phones, only the microphone was in the lower chunk, while today it is more common to place the keypad and controls in the lower chunk and the display in the upper chunk. The bulk of the electronics can be in either chunk. Instead of the hinge of a flip phone, some designs employ a slide-out keypad with the controls in the upper chunk with the display. These are all different architectures, and if you were to look inside some mobile phones, you would probably see even more architectural variations in how the circuit boards are divided and laid out, how the display connects to the circuit boards, how tightly the batteries integrate, and so forth.

Modular versus Integral Architectures

Architectures come in two main types, plus a third one that is related more to manufacturing and distribution than to development. The type most important to flexibility is a modular architecture. In it, chunks of the product connect strongly within themselves and weakly to the other chunks. Some chunks may be cleanly isolated, but usually they have degrees of modularity and resulting degrees of isolation. Engineering standards and standard interfaces are often employed to enforce isolation through, for example, electrical plugs or mechanical threads.

The opposite is an integral architecture. Its chunks interconnect heavily, and one chunk of the product often implements several functions. For example, the bodies of many cars and airplanes serve as a stylistic element, provide aerodynamic and weather shielding, and also carry structural loads. When thinking of an integral architecture, visualize a bowl of noodles or spaghetti.

The third type is platform architecture. This defines a product comprising many parts planned and scaled to work together and to be fairly interchangeable within the platform. For instance, a compact car is one platform and a large car is another platform. You can interchange parts from one compact car to another within the platform, swapping a six-cylinder engine for a four-cylinder one or switching between steel and aluminum wheels, for example. You have the same freedom of choice in the large car platform, but you generally cannot use parts from the compact car on the large one or vice versa. Platforms are a popular topic today for achieving *strategic* flexibility, that is, the ability to make changes in product configuration during manufacturing or distribution to satisfy changes in market demand quickly and with minimal inventory, what is often called postponement or mass customization.[3] However, this is quite different from *development* flexibility—making changes during development of the product—pursued in this book, so I do not discuss platform architecture further.

Advantages and Disadvantages of Modularity

Modular architectures have great power to facilitate flexibility, but they also have their shortcomings. Like all the means of achieving flexibility, this one has its price, so I discuss both costs and benefits so that you can made wise choices in employing this approach.

Table 3.1   Contrasting Modular and Integral Architectures

Type of Architecture	Modular	Integral
Characteristic	Chunks are decoupled, operate independently	All portions are interdependent
Example	Desktop personal computer	Sony Walkman
Advantages	Ease of changing design, independent testing, reusable portions	Cheaper to make, lighter, more compact
Limitations	Planning time, performance weaknesses, integration burden	Harder to change, late testing

Refer to Table 3.1, which contrasts a modular architecture exemplified by a desktop personal computer with an integral architecture illustrated by a Sony Walkman. The chunks (modules) of a modular architecture connect strongly within themselves but weakly to other chunks. This makes it easy to swap one module for another, to test one module by itself, or to modify one module without affecting the others—hence the power of modules for enhancing flexibility.

On the other hand, integral architectures usually are cheaper, lighter, and more compact, simply because the interfaces and potential redundancy inherent in modular architectures cost money, add weight, and consume space. Usually, such advantages lead to product performance improvements and often to greater product value for the money.

Each type of architecture has its limitations also. Modular architectures carry a burden of greater upfront planning and—if not planned well—the risk of fundamental (expensive) changes later. Although modules can usually be tested independently, thus relatively early in development (beneficial), they carry the corresponding burden of final integration late in development (integral architectures have this burden too, but its impact is usually more gradual). Finally, modular architectures often suffer performance and reliability problems—usually in the interfaces that modularization introduces. Bolts connecting mechanical modules slip and loosen. Separate electrical modules can have problems with crosstalk, phase shift, and electromagnetic interference. In software, interfaces contribute delays, thus slowing the system. More fundamentally, the interfaces that separate modules introduce constraints on the design, which limit designers' ability to optimize the design, thus reducing its performance.

In contrast, however, integral architectures are difficult to change, because a change in one part tends to ripple through the whole design, necessitating changes elsewhere. Imagine pulling on one noodle in your bowl of noodles; as you pull, it disturbs many other noodles. Also, because nothing is ready to test early, all testing tends to occur late in development, where each failure creates the greatest disturbance and costs the most to correct.

Wise designers take advantage of this distinction. Consider the Walkman. Today, this is a mature product, and Sony has considerable experience in manufacturing and marketing it. Unexpected changes are unlikely at this point in its life cycle, so the advantage of easy design change has little value. Conversely, these products today are under great price pressure, and customers make their selections based on size and weight, all of which suggest an integral architecture. Consequently, this is what Sony uses.

This was not always the case. In the early days of the Walkman (the 1970s), the market was fickle; the technology was in flux; and what customers wanted, how they would use the device, and what they were willing to pay for it were all to be discovered. The early units cost hundreds of U.S. dollars. Consequently, Sony used a modular design then. As the product matured, Sony shifted to an integral design.[4]

Figure 3.2 vividly illustrates the contrast between a modular and an integral architecture. At the top is the highly modular jeepney—a popular means of public transportation in the Philippines. These interesting vehicles stem from U.S. Army Jeep vehicles left behind after World War II. Entrepreneurs extended them and added roofs. Over the years, as genuine Jeep parts

Figure 3.2   Contrast of Modular (Flexible) and Integral (Performance) Architectures

Top photo by Tarmo Soodla, www.ourworldtravels.com (Accessed April 23, 2007); bottom photo provided with permission from Ferrari North America, Inc.

disappeared, nearly total design change occurred, encouraging modularity. Today, the Jeep front styling is still apparent, but these vehicles have no Jeep parts. The chassis and power train are from used Japanese diesel trucks. Many of the body parts are made in China. Owners decorate their jeepneys to their own taste, usually following a too-much-is-not-enough theme (this photo is far more intriguing in color). You can change almost any part without affecting the remainder.

The lower photo is an integral architecture, a Ferrari F430 sports car. Every detail has been executed to exploit Ferrari's racing experience. "The side mirrors, for example, now have specially profiled twin mounting arms that channel airflows to the engine intakes."[5] Consequently, changing a mirror could asphyxiate the 360-kW (490-horsepower) engine, thus compromising the car's astounding performance: a top speed of over 315 km/h (196 mph)!

Actual architectures, such as these cars, are never purely modular or purely integral. The jeepney could be even more modular, and the Ferrari could be even more integral. Choosing an architecture is always a balancing act. Some parts of a product might be quite modular, while other portions clearly should be integral. Clever designers exploit this freedom to their advantage.

Modularity Objectives

Modular architectures are popular because of the variety of objectives they allow designers to achieve:

- Isolate portions of the design subject to growth or high uncertainty.
- Enable changing one part of the design without affecting other parts.
- Simplify organizational structures, for example, allow smaller design teams.
- Support design reuse and incremental innovation.

- Protect portions of the design where change would require heavy engineering, testing, or regulatory approval.
- Simplify or accelerate product testing.
- Manage product complexity.
- Enable user configuration and mass customization.
- Allow different parts of the design to be worked on concurrently.
- Render the product easier to service.
- Facilitate incorporating suppliers into design process.

Not only is product architecture an abstract and rather intangible subject, its variety of possible objectives further clouds the picture. Most designers pursue objectives other than flexibility or—worse—lack a clear objective. To benefit from architectural choices, tie them to a clear business objective.

To enhance flexibility, it is especially useful to follow the first two objectives in this list. The idea is to place fences around parts of the design that are most subject to uncertainty and to anticipate and allow for growth. These fences allow you to change the design within a module without having to change other modules. That is, changes do not ripple through the design causing massive redesign but are contained in a small area. This lowers the cost of change.

Examples of Architectural Choices

A desktop computer provides good examples of using modular architectures to enhance flexibility. (Laptop computers are less useful as examples, because here weight and compactness play a bigger role, which encourages integral architectures.) Computer designers know that computers will become faster and need more memory, so they provide standard, robust interfaces for the processor modules and memory modules. When these modules change, new modules can plug right into standard sockets without disturbing the rest of the hardware, even if these modules have characteristics somewhat different from those originally planned. In addition, designers plan to accommodate any other changes that may be needed for a different processor or memory module through software changes, where the cost of change is lower than for hardware changes.

Another area of anticipated change is in peripherals. Thus current computers provide USB ports, which constitute a versatile interface accommodating many types of design change in peripherals—even in types of peripherals not yet envisioned—without having to change the computer itself.

Automobile Design

Toyota applies the isolation principle in reverse to great advantage. Rather than focusing on areas subject to change, its designers concentrate on areas that are difficult, time-consuming, or expensive to change. For instance, Toyota engineers have found that noise and vibration emanate from a small area involving the engine mounts and sheet metal cradle supporting the engine. Noise and vibration are critical customer value criteria, and minimizing them involves considerable experimentation, testing, and prototyping with uncertain results. Consequently, Toyota structures its architecture to fence off this area from change. Whereas the rest of the car is subject to model changes every few years, Toyota keeps the engine-mounting system stable for up to fifteen years. It does the same for other areas that require heavy design-testing iteration and do not affect vehicle style, such as the structures that determine crashworthiness. This includes the inner construction of the front end, the underside of the hood, the door beams, and the inside of the roof.

Toyota's radiator supplier, Denso, applies modularity with a different twist. An automotive radiator has three natural chunks, the core: the highly engineered portion providing the heat transfer function, and the top and bottom tanks, which are the fluid and mechanical interface with the car. Denso divided the radiator into these three modules. Then it invested heavily in engineering and tooling for the core, exploiting sophisticated cooling concepts to improve performance and lower cost. By designing a family of cores to suit most car models and makes, it benefited from economies of scale on this complex but relatively stable module. The two tanks, which were more subject to change, were relatively simple and thus had a low cost of change.

Cordless Screwdriver

Black & Decker applied the principle differently on an early model of a cordless screwdriver. The first model, patterned after the company's popular drills, had a pistol grip and enough power to both drive screws and do light drilling. When introduced in June 1985, it was a market failure. A competitor's product took the sales, it turned out, because its straight shape looked more like a screwdriver than the pistol-shaped B&D model.

B&D initiated a crash program to develop a straight cordless screwdriver for Christmas 1987. Now its designers knew that handle size and shape were important to customers. They also knew that the engineering—thus, most of the development effort—was concentrated in the front end of the tool: the motor, gearbox, and chuck. Consequently, they introduced an interface between the front end and the handle to isolate the front end from likely changes in the handle as they researched handle configurations. See Figure 3.3.

Figure 3.3   Black & Decker Model 9018 Cordless Screwdriver (Slim Handle)

Photo and text used with permission of The Black & Decker Corporation.

The first round of market research on handle shape was incon-clusive. Some customers, mainly women with smaller fingers, preferred a slim handle that would accommodate only two cells. Others appreciated the power available with a fatter handle that would hold three cells. Given the long lead time to make the molds for the handle, they wanted to make a decision, but instead decided to proceed with both handle molds while they conducted additional market research. (This is an example of delaying a deci-sion to accommodate change, as covered in Chapter Seven.) In August, when they had to start production to fill the distribution channel for Christmas, the preferred handle shape still was uncer-tain. They decided to start production with the fatter handle. In October, the market research finally showed a clear preference for the slimmer handle, so they switched to it. Observe that because B&D introduced an interface to fence off the engineering-intensive front end from likely changes in the handle, it was able to make changes very late without an excessive cost of change.

CD-ROM Drive

The CD-ROM drive industry provides an interesting case study. These products appear on the front of your desktop computer; to read or write on a CD, you place it on a tray that slides out of the drive.

As with many computer products, the industry measures these drives in terms of a single parameter, in this case, speed, which is a multiple of a basic speed. Thus, the early drives were 4X units—operating at four times the basic speed (there may have been 1X or 2X drives before they became popular). Then came 8X, 12X, and so on. The current standard is 52X, which seems to be the limit.

Today, these are mature products, but in the 1995–2002 era, change occurred rapidly—and predictably. It's useful to look at two CD-ROM drives to see how the manufacturer arranged their archi-tecture to accommodate predictable changes in speed. Figures 3.4 and 3.5 show two models, respectively a 32X unit made in 1998 and a 40X unit made in 2002. Another change that occurred in

Figure 3.4   TEAC Model CD-532E CD-ROM Drive (Read-Only), Speed 32X, Manufactured 1998. No Audio

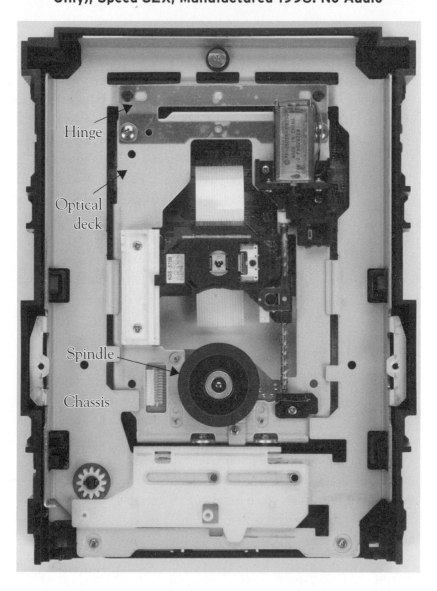

this period is the shift from read-only units to read-write ones, so Figure 3.4 shows a read-only drive and Figure 3.5 has a read-write one. Observe a few similarities. The entire chassis, the largest part of the drive, is identical, as is the plastic tray (not shown) that

Figure 3.5   TEAC Model CD-W540E CD-ROM Drive (Read-Write), Speed 40X, Manufactured 2002. Includes Audio

holds the CD. The manufacturer does not anticipate change in these areas.

The optical deck, which attaches to the chassis with the hinge, provides a spindle that spins the disk and sled rails that guide a sled, on which is mounted the pickup that slides in and out to access the desired track on the disk. Change is limited to the optical deck, specifically to the sled, the sled rails, the spindle, and the pickup. Notice in Figure 3.4 that a motor twists a worm shaft that drives the sled, and this shaft also acts as the right sled rail. In contrast, in Figure 3.5 a rack and pinion on the left side of the sled drives it. Inspection of other CD drives of this era suggests that this change has nothing to do with speed and is simply an improvement to reduce cost or improve accuracy. Consequently, putting aside this change in how the sled is driven, the only areas that change are the sled, the pickup, and the spindle, which encompass a quite small part of the drive, especially in recognition of the simultaneous change from read-only to read-write.

The flexibility technique that I've discussed most thus far involves isolating areas of change, but another technique also aids flexibility: providing for anticipated growth. The lower left corner of Figure 3.5 shows an example of this. You can see a round volume-control knob that does not appear on the 32X unit. Although it is not apparent in these top shots, the 40X unit also has an earphone jack that the 32X unit lacks. However, the 32X unit has places on its circuit boards for these two audio components. Designers anticipated audio capability in the 32X unit and included wiring on the circuit board to add it later if desired, but they saved most of the cost of audio on the 32X unit by eliminating the volume control and earphone jack. This is a technique for reducing the cost of change.

On the bottom of these units (not shown) are the circuit boards, which offer more lessons in arranging architecture for flexibility. The same architectural principles apply in the electrical domain as in the mechanical or software domains. For instance, the circuit board in the W540E unit is labeled "W532E." Apparently it was designed in the 32X era but in anticipation of higher speeds. This is another example of arranging the architecture in anticipation of growth or change.

Figure 3.6 is an electrical schematic of the unit. The dashed line encloses the portions that are speed sensitive: the RF

Figure 3.6   Electrical Schematic for a CD-ROM Drive

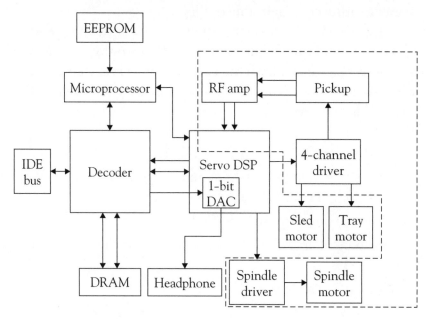

Used with permission and adapted from the Master's thesis of Chih-yu Chao at National Taiwan University, 2002.

amplifier, the pickup, a portion of the servo DSP (digital signal processor), the 4-channel driver, the spindle driver, and the spindle motor. The essential element here is the clock crystal in the DSP; the clock speed must increase to raise the speed of the drive. Other changes in the DSP and other elements inside the dashed line are possible, depending on how much anticipated growth the designers provided for in these elements, such as bandwidth in the RF amplifier. Consequently, by providing for anticipated growth here, developers would have to change only the clock speed, a very small part of the schematic. This involves an economic trade-off, because greater performance in the RF amplifier, spindle motor, and other speed-related elements costs more—sometimes much more and sometimes trivially more. Balance this cost increase against the cost of change. Thus, the apparently technical decisions involved in planning the electrical design are actually business decisions that balance manufacturing cost against flexibility.

Drive speed, the transition to writing capability, and the addition of audio on this CD drive are useful illustrations of the way managing change can keep the cost of change low, thus improving flexibility. The architects could have considered several other types of change as well:

- Modes of operation (CD, CD-R, DVD)
- Disk size or form factor (the common 120-mm disk diameter versus 80-mm minidisks)
- Electrical interface (IDE, SCSI, USB)
- Component upgrade or obsolescence (especially integrated circuits)
- Outsourcing alternatives

Each of these types of change would have resulted in a different architecture, and orienting the architecture toward multiple objectives becomes increasingly difficult.

Architectural Approaches

All these examples can be boiled down into guidelines that help in designing products for flexibility. First, many modern products involve multiple types of technology: mechanical, electrical, software, and sometimes chemical and optical as well. Each of these portions of the product can have its own architecture, as in the CD drive, and it is possible sometimes to shift functions from one technology to another, most often from electrical to software, to improve flexibility.

Generalizing is a bit dangerous, but often you can modularize to meet only one architectural goal well. Thus, by emphasizing flexibility, you might forgo architectural choices that would improve serviceability, offer sourcing opportunities, or reduce production cost.

It is difficult and expensive to make a whole product modular. As Black & Decker did, you must usually choose the portions of the product to make modular. Consequently, to improve flexibility, you must understand your technologies, markets, and customers well enough to know where change is most likely so that you can place modules and interfaces effectively. Recall how Toyota made these decisions from two directions, looking both at likely changes and at places where change was undesirable. You will not always guess correctly about change. For example, the Microsoft Windows XP operating system had a different name during development; "Windows XP" was a relatively late marketing change for which this product's architecture was not prepared. Rather than making the change in one place in a configuration file, as the designers could have provided, they had to search millions of lines of code and make hundreds of changes at the last minute.

Architectural decisions tend to persist. Often, they follow on to subsequent products and perhaps to generations of future products.

It follows that architecture is too important to leave to a few technical specialists. Especially in the computer and software fields, the highest grade of developers are often called architects, and management assumes that architecture can only be done by these technical wizards. However, architecture is a business decision, and it should follow from your business strategy. Rather than leaving it to a coterie of arcane specialists, you're better off assembling a cross-functional team of experts to look at the possibilities from several angles. Executing an architecture may be a technical matter, but planning one goes well beyond technology.

Reduce Coupling

The main use of architecture to improve flexibility is to design modules so that coupling between them is minimized.[6] Then when one module changes, the change does not propagate to other modules. Another way to look at this is to design a module with the complexity hidden inside it (high cohesion within a module). Thus, the design of interfaces between modules becomes critical. These interfaces are the fences mentioned earlier.

Isolate Volatility

A similar objective is to identify areas of the design subject to change and isolate them. If an area is likely to change, try to build a fence around it as closely as possible to minimize the portion of the design subject to change. This is what designers of personal computers do with the central processing unit (CPU), a volatile part of the computer as technology advances and allows higher and higher clock speeds. Designers offload as many functions as possible from the CPU to chipsets to minimize the portion of the computer subject to change as clock speeds rise.

Provide for Growth

As with the CD drive, often you can identify certain portions of the design that are likely to expand or progress in a predictable way. The fact that the CD drive would progress from 32X to 40X or that some users would want audio is no surprise. Thus it makes sense to provide capability for this change.

Align with Organizational Boundaries

Because a characteristic of architectures is high cohesion within modules, which implies a heavy communication burden within a module, and low coupling between modules, with correspondingly minimal communication needed between modules, you can align your development organization with the product architecture to simplify communication during development. You can observe this in most development organizations. For instance, automotive development organizations are normally divided by module: body, power train, suspension, interior, and so on.

The question here is whether the organization is aligned to the product architecture or vice versa. Usually, the organizational structure exists first, and the product architecture is aligned to it, rather than taking advantage of architectural opportunities by, for example, organizing a separate team specifically for a volatile module. Try designing your ideal product architecture first, then exploring how you can modify your organizational structure to realize this product architecture as well as possible.

Four Steps in Designing an Architecture

Given the characteristics of a flexible architecture, how do you go about creating such an architecture? The process outlined in this section follows one in a popular mechanical design textbook.[7] As an example, I use a desktop computer that also houses an out-of-the-way printer for those who have essential but infrequent printing needs.

Step 1 is to draw a schematic of the elements of the product, as shown in Figure 3.7. (Only the solid lines shown in the figure are drawn in the first step.) These elements may be a mix of functional units (such as a power supply), physical concepts (cooling), and actual components (a 19-inch flat-panel display with a DVI interface). That is, some components may be portrayed at a finer level of detail than others, depending on your current state of knowledge, existing constraints on the design, or your desire to emphasize a certain area. Furthermore, some elements actually essential to the function of the product, such as the keyboard and mouse here, can even be omitted if the designers consider them incidental to the flexibility focus.

This is a creative exercise. Many variations on a schematic are possible, each with its strengths and weaknesses. Consequently, re-approach the problem from several angles that emphasize and deemphasize various portions, represent elements at different levels of abstraction, and perhaps arrange elements differently. Ignore

Figure 3.7 Schematic for Creating a Desktop Computer Architecture

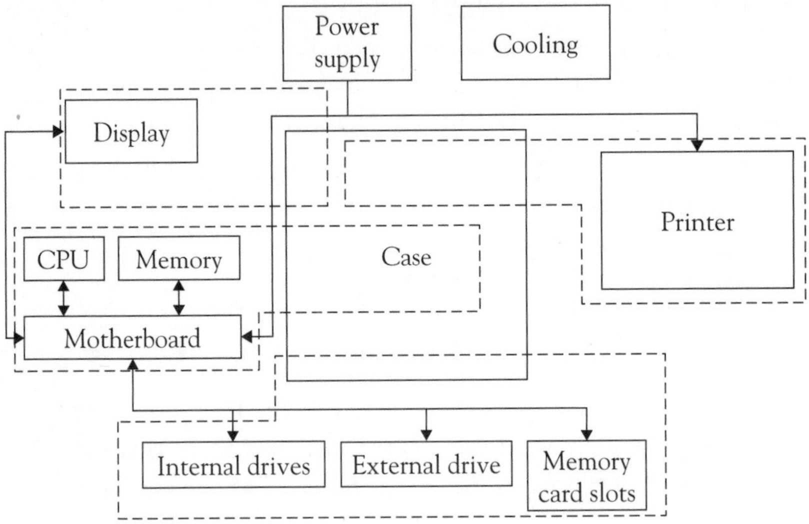

Note: Solid lines are drawn in step 1; dashed lines in step 2.

incidental elements so that you can focus on the critical ones. After creating several schematics through brainstorming, select the one that offers the greatest potential for flexibility, that is, for isolating probable areas of change or for providing for growth in certain areas.

Step 2 involves clustering the elements into clumps. The dashed lines in Figure 3.7 show one way of doing this, but here again, this is a system design step where you should consider many options before settling on a final clumping. Depending on your architectural objectives, many strategies are available for discovering clumping options. For flexibility, look for elements likely to change so that they can be isolated from the rest of the design. Or you could do the opposite, as Toyota did, by clumping the areas where you either do not expect change or will actively prohibit it. Another approach is to identify the areas where you anticipate growth so that you can accommodate it easily.

In step 3, you sketch a layout of your design. This could be a set of orthogonal views, as shown in Figure 3.8, or it could be an isometric (three-dimensional) sketch or even a physical model made of foam, cardboard, or other materials—whatever portrays the geometrical relationships and constraints well. Such sketches or models are reality checks. Is there actually space for everything? Is there growth space where you need it? Do two chunks occupy the same space or straddle each other? Can important parts be changed or serviced easily? These would be the reality checks for a mechanical product; for an electrical or software one, translate this into other pertinent reality checks on your work in step 2. This step also involves many possibilities, so sketch up some alternatives and select the one that satisfies your objectives best. To find the best solution, you may have to iterate back to step 2 to reassign elements to chunks so that the layout works well.

Figure 3.8 Layout of the Physical Arrangement of Modules: A Feasibility Check

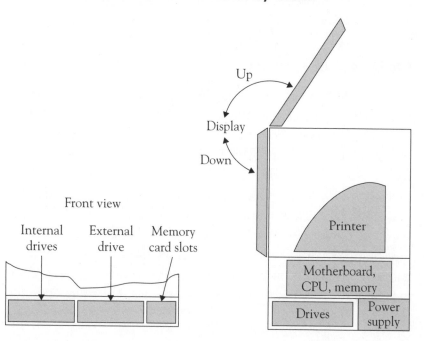

In step 4 you specify the interfaces and other interactions between the chunks. For flexibility, you want clean, well-defined interfaces to isolate changes, as discussed in the next section. Some interfaces you might specify for the desktop computer include

- ATX motherboard form factor
- Socket A CPU interface
- IDE, SCSI, and USB external drive interfaces
- VGA and DVI display interfaces
- 400-Watt minimum power supply with ATX connectors

Architectural Decisions

Designing an architecture necessitates making decisions on several levels. Many of these are a natural part of the four-step process just described, but they bear repeating explicitly. The first is how much modularity you actually need. Although modules have advantages, they also have costs, so you will want to limit them to where they are most beneficial.

Placement of Functions

The next decision is where you place the functionality. If possible, a function should not be split across modules—but such splitting sometimes happens. For instance, in an inkjet printer, the motion of the print cartridge relative to the paper (one function) is normally split so that rails going across the printer provide sideways motion and the paper feed mechanism provides vertical motion. This complicates communication, control, and accuracy of alignment. It consequently makes design change difficult, because any change in one module links to changes in the other module through the basic printing process. In the case of the inkjet printer, it is difficult to separate these two modules, but independence should be the goal.

Interfaces

The next—and probably most important—decision is the design of interfaces. Interfaces are the fences that isolate change or the insulators that hide operations in one module from its neighbors. Good interfaces are stable, robust, and standardized.

Stability is advantageous because if an interface changes, all modules connecting to that interface must be redesigned, raising the cost of change greatly. Thus you will find that the interfaces are probably the oldest part of any long-lived design, and you will seldom need to redesign a good interface. In personal computers, the IDE and VGA interfaces have been used for over a decade while everything around them has changed many times. The USB interface is newer, but will probably be with us for many years to come. In automobiles, the 14-mm spark-plug-to-engine interface dates to the early twentieth century and the Schrader tire valve to 1898, with neither showing any signs of retirement.

Toyota uses this concept to advantage. For example, the (floor-mounted) shift lever in an automobile has two quite different portions. The upper one, which you see, is a style item, and it changes with every interior redesign, perhaps every two or three years. The lower part (hidden below the boot) is the interface to the transmission. Toyota hasn't changed this interface for twelve years.

Robustness means providing growth potential in the interface so that capability can be added later without changing the interface. In an electrical interface, this might mean extra bandwidth or unused pins. In a mechanical interface, it might mean extra strength or some physical space for growth. The ATX motherboard interface that has been used in personal computers for more than a decade allows boards to grow (within limits) without relocating the fasteners that mount it to the computer's case.

Observe two things about robustness. First, it contradicts the agile concepts of *simple design* and *barely sufficient* discussed in Chapter One. There are solid arguments either way for going barely sufficient or for providing for growth. It depends on your confidence that factors related to the interface will remain stable. It also depends on the relative costs and benefits of the currently unused growth potential. This is comparable to buying insurance against change. The other observation is that robustness helps provide the stability just discussed.

Standard interfaces provide great benefit. Although such interfaces as the Schrader tire valve are not very exciting, and any decent engineer could improve upon their design, familiarity is precisely the advantage of a standard interface: everyone designing modules employing it knows exactly to how to relate to the interface. For the tire valve, wheel designers can work without consulting with the designers of inflation equipment, because each knows how to accommodate the interface. In short, standard interfaces minimize communication needs between modules. They also focus designers' creativity on the guts of the modules, where it will provide the greatest commercial benefit.

One last important characteristic of interfaces is that they tend to decay over time. An interface is a set of rules about how modules will interact.[8] When module designers are under pressure to improve performance or reliability, cut cost, or save time, they sometimes take shortcuts with interfaces by violating these rules. As this happens, the interface's ability to isolate one module from another decays. Consequently, if you use interfaces to fence in change, you will need to monitor the interfaces to ensure that they are not violated for expediency. The refactoring discussed in Chapter One is a means of repairing this damage.

Providing for Growth

In addition to providing for growth in the interfaces, as discussed in the last section, you can provide flexibility by anticipating growth in a module. The CD-ROM drive discussed earlier illustrates this: the manufacturer used a 32X circuit board in a 40X unit, apparently by anticipating the need for 40X when designing the 32X unit and providing extra performance before it was needed.

Such growth decisions are driven by economics. Clearly, the flexibility gained has economic value. So do the cost savings made possible by economies of scale (in the CD drive, the 32X board can be used in both the 32X and the 40X units, so production runs for it are larger) and in inventory reduction (no 40X boards need be stocked). Offsetting all these economic advantages is the extra cost of a module that has more capability than it needs today. Sometimes the extra cost of the growth potential is minor and worth having, and sometimes you pay dearly for it.

Architecture at the Design Level

Although architectural decisions should be made at a high, cross-functional level, as discussed, designers also make many architectural decisions at lower levels every day. An organization that fails to appreciate this impairs flexibility through daily design decisions that unknowingly raise the cost of change. Here is an example that shows how such decisions occur when using contemporary mechanical computer-aided design (CAD) software. The same principles apply to systems other than mechanical ones.

Suppose that you are designing a product that includes a keypad. Such items involve close interplay between the form design (look, feel, intuitiveness, and ergonomics) and function design (the underlying switch mechanism and its mounting on a circuit board or chassis). Typically, an industrial designer addresses the form issues while a mechanical engineer handles the function issues. The mechanical engineer invests time assuring that the mechanical pieces line up and function with other components under the keypad. Meanwhile, the industrial designer is likely to go through many prototyping iterations in arriving at a style that is attractive and easy to use. Consequently, unless their work is coordinated carefully or is forced into a time-consuming sequential mode (complete the form design before starting the function design), the mechanical design is likely to be redone many times before the industrial designer is satisfied.

However, modern CAD technology has so-called parametric and associative features that allow certain types of design changes to be automated. For instance, you might anticipate that change in the keypad design is likely to involve the amount of taper from top to bottom. (See Figure 3.9.)

Given that insight about probable change, the mechanical engineer can set up the CAD model to adjust the keys and their underlying parts automatically for any amount of taper. If this anticipated change is not communicated to the mechanical engineer, the cost of redesigning the keypad repeatedly or rebuilding the model to accommodate it could be high. Alternatively, the anticipated change might be in the shape of the individual keys or in the curvature of the rows of keys. In principle, the mechanical engineer can build the CAD model to accommodate any of these changes, but each requires extra work. None of these specific types of flexibility is likely to be accommodated unless the mechanical engineer is in close contact with other decision makers who are doing their best to anticipate the areas of most likely change.

Figure 3.9   Evolution of a Keypad. a. Original Design with No Taper. b. Revised Form Design Imposed on Original Mechanical Design. c. Tapered Keypad Adjusted in the CAD Model

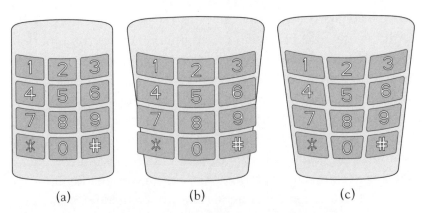

(a)   (b)   (c)

Source: Figure courtesy of Sherpa Design, Inc., www.sherpa-design.com.

In short, architectural issues propagate down to the lowest level, so designers must understand what is most likely to change in the design so that they can arrange the architecture appropriately at their level.

Shifting the Hardware-Software Boundary

As discussed, architecture can be applied to your advantage in whatever domains the product may have—mechanical, electrical, and software, for example. Although you usually consider these three domains of architecture separately, sometimes you can exploit opportunities to gain flexibility by shifting functions from one domain to another. Most common is to shift electrical functionality to software by using relatively recent electronic technologies called programmable electronic devices. The most popular of these are digital logic devices called field-programmable gate arrays (FPGAs). Such devices can be changed (reprogrammed) quickly, whereas the application-specific integrated circuits (ASICs) they replace have long and expensive change cycles.[9] More recently, small, inexpensive microprocessors, which also incorporate configurable analog sections, provide even more power to shift electrical changes to software, where the cost of change is lower.

In products where mechanical and hydraulic systems are controlled by electronics, you might shift areas of change from relatively difficult-to-change mechanical and hydraulic parts to electrical circuits with a lower cost of change—and even on to software if you have planned with change in mind.

Summary

These are the key points of this chapter:

- Modular architectures offer great potential for limiting change and accommodating growth.

- Modular architectures also have weaknesses and costs when compared to integral architectures.
- Modularity tends to reduce product performance.
- Because modules tend to add cost and degrade performance, assign modules selectively only where change is anticipated.
- It is difficult to accommodate multiple architectural objectives, so designing for flexibility may preclude other objectives.
- Product architecture influences many business outcomes and has long-term consequences, so architectural decisions should extend far beyond the Engineering department.
- Modularity tends to decay over time if architectural rules are not enforced.

4

EXPERIMENTATION

The real measure of success is the number of
experiments that can be crowded into twenty-four
hours.

—*Thomas Edison*

What is an experiment? This term is so broad that it is a bit difficult to define, but an exact definition really isn't necessary. The beauty of experimentation is that each experimenter can extend the concept in unique ways to fit special circumstances. Nevertheless, here are three definitions that suggest a direction:[1]

- Learning by trying things out
- Something one does deliberately to see what happens
- The process of an action followed by an observation

Notice that, in all cases, experimentation is more than simply observing what is happening. You provoke a situation and see how it responds.

The next question is, How does experimentation enhance flexibility? This is easiest to see in the negative. Suppose that a project has no uncertainty. You could plan, schedule, and budget it initially, knowing just what customers wanted and that they would not change their minds. Furthermore, the product technology is stable. In this case, you could proceed methodically through your project, planning and conducting only one test (experiment) at the end to ensure that the product possessed the planned properties. Experimentation would not be needed.

To the extent that your project includes uncertainties requiring flexibility, experimentation is essential to "try things out," "see what happens," or "observe," as the definitions I just listed indicate. The more uncertainty, the more flexibility will be needed, thus the more experimentation will be needed to check on progress. Sometimes, you might even need to conduct an array of experiments to map out uncertain territory to find your way.

Experimentation ties into the subject of the next chapter, set-based design. Set-based design emphasizes exploring and keeping the design space open so as not to lock into an option prematurely. Experimentation is a tool for conducting this exploration of the design space.

Experimentation allows product designers to investigate a new technology, testing its limits without committing to how they will use it, or indeed, whether they will use it. Likewise, they can probe what customers need and what satisfies them. In short, experimentation allows the project's maneuvering room to be enlarged while decreasing the cost of change by developing options in advance.

There is another reason for considering experimentation today. Contemporary computer technology provides huge improvements over previous methods in many kinds of experimentation, improving efficiency or throughput by ten to a hundred times or even more in many cases. These improvements open experimentation to completely new approaches that alter development processes dramatically to exploit technological advances.

Kinds of Experiments

Experimentation, as used here, is a broad term. It includes

- Testing a candidate technology
- Sketching a concept
- Carving a shape
- Showing this shape to customers or customer surrogates

- Analyzing a mechanism to see how it responds
- Simulating a circuit
- Testing a module to see how it functions
- Making a prototype
- Having someone use the prototype
- Building mock-ups
- Exploring with customers which mock-up they prefer
- Trying a procedure or process
- Overloading a machine to see what breaks (a smoke test)
- Trying a product in an application for which it was not designed

The common element here is that these are all activities that help us learn and move to the next step of development. Often, the most effective experiments are ones that go beyond this list or that combine these basic experiments in creative ways, for instance by exploring with customers the failure mode revealed by a smoke test. Another example is to combine experimentation with product architecture (see Chapter Three) by experimenting on paper with various architectural approaches.

A factor to keep in mind as you consider which experimental medium to use is to pick one that is comfortable to those whom you want to assess the experiment. For instance, if you plan to show an experiment to customers, avoid an abstract representation that only an engineer would grasp.

The Value of Failure

The essence of an experiment is learning. Interestingly, learning also includes a failed experiment. As Thomas Edison put it, "I have not failed. I've just found ten thousand ways that won't work." Conversely, if you do not learn, the experiment is valueless: "Before ordering a test decide what you will do if it is

(a) positive or (b) negative, and if both answers are the same don't do the test."[2]

Stefan Thomke draws an important distinction between failures and mistakes.[3] A failure is an experiment whose outcome is unexpected, which teaches you something. On the other hand, a mistake is a badly planned or conducted experiment whose outcome you cannot interpret, which thus teaches you nothing. Mistakes can result from not considering possible outcomes beforehand, not controlling extraneous variables well, not recording important conditions, being sloppy in your observations, or being unable to reproduce the experiment consistently.

This is a fine distinction and an exaggeration of the difference between the customary definitions of *failure* and *mistake*. However, for successful experimentation, it is vital. Although learning from failures is valuable, it is not easy to achieve. To the extent that an organization encourages failures by conducting many early experiments, it will necessarily encounter some experimental mistakes. Hence, the goal is not to eliminate mistakes but to obtain the highest ratio of failures to mistakes. This chapter will help you improve this ratio.

Although organizations pay lip service to the value of failure, they usually tacitly discourage it. Management is unlikely to be thrilled upon seeing a failed experiment, and seldom is the experimenter encouraged or rewarded—even though organizations that manage to do so may prosper amazingly. Consider this oft-told story from the early days of IBM: A young executive managed to lose US$10,000,000 in a risky venture. He was called into the office of Thomas Watson Sr., IBM's founder, fully expecting that Watson was about to fire him. Instead, Watson explained that the company needed him because it had just invested millions of dollars in educating him! This story is nearly a century old, and it's still told—not just because it's a good story but because we lack newer ones to replace it, an indication of the rarity of the phenomenon.

Another example of how ingrained success is in most corporate cultures is the maxim managers are fond of: *Do it right the first time*. Such guidance does not encourage learning.

So why is failure so valuable? It is valuable because product innovation is a process of learning, and the greater the uncertainty in the project, the greater the need for learning. An interesting characteristic of experimentation is that if an experiment turns out exactly as you expected, you have not learned much. You just shrug your shoulders. It is when the results are other than expected that you learn. See Figure 4.1 for an illustration.

This figure compares the expected outcome of an experiment with its actual outcome. Developers conduct most product-development experiments late in a project to verify that their product is performing as intended, and they learn little from such experiments—naturally enough, since the experiments are not intended for learning but simply for verification. For making progress and dealing with uncertainty, the objective should be learning, and the rate of learning is highest when the experiment turns out unexpectedly.

Figure 4.1   Learning from an Experiment

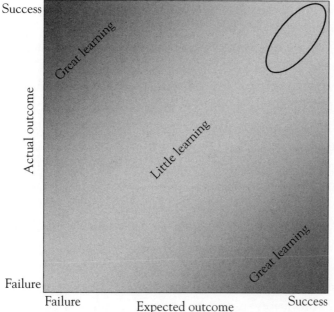

Most developers know this, and it is natural in many human activities. Consider how you look up a name in a telephone book. You probably turn to the most likely place in the book, splitting your uncertainty as to whether you are too far forward or too far back. You check where you are and try again to split your uncertainty as to being too early or too late. And so forth. Notice that at each step you magnify your uncertainty about whether you would be ahead of or behind the desired name.

Although we know this truth intellectually, most corporate cultures connect failure with waste and thus discourage it. Realigning the objective of experimentation—including dealing with the negative connotations of failure—is one of the major challenges most organizations face as they move toward more flexible product development.

Exploration as Experimentation

Experiments come in many styles. For instance, physical scientists—and to some extent, academic management researchers—conduct formal hypothesis-based experiments. This is an exacting process usually intended to prove a theory. It is slow, and it requires extreme and sometimes unnatural control of conditions. Such experimentation is not very useful to product developers.

Most experiments associated with flexibility aim more at exploration.[4] They help developers understand the design space and comprehend what will and will not work, to verify that they are on a productive path, and to assess the merits of alternatives. Exploration is suited perfectly to situations with a great deal of uncertainty.

Exploration is a relatively lightweight version of experimentation, intended to provide lots of useful information quickly and cheaply—to fit with the needs of flexible development. Nevertheless, it is not the kind of sloppy experimentation that results in mistakes. Mistakes mislead developers and waste resources. Consequently, exploration should balance experimental creativity

Figure 4.2   A Four-Step Iterative Exploration Process

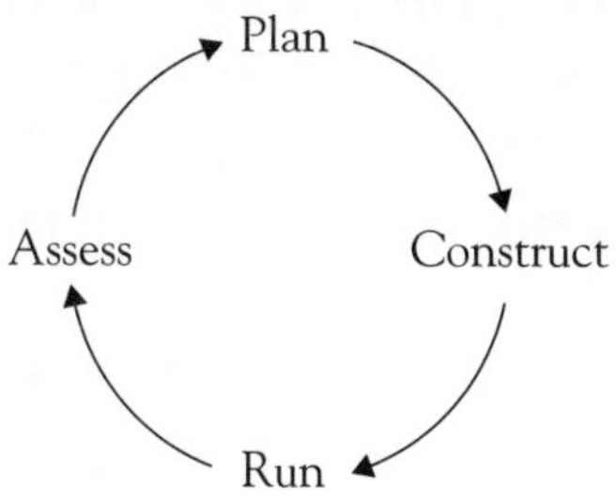

with rigor. The process and guidelines I outline here—sketched in Figure 4.2—provide a basis for effective exploration. Note the similarity with Figure 2.3, which illustrates another aspect of the same process.

Seldom does one experiment answer a question completely, especially when you are exploring, so it's best to think in terms of a program of several experiments conducted iteratively. You should have an objective for the program: what do you expect to learn from it? What are your associated gaps in knowledge? Is there a connection with a past experimental program? Is a basic trade-off involved, like the one between weight and fuel economy of a motor vehicle? Is one parameter likely to characterize the results, such as the boxiness of a motor vehicle (a more angular shape like that of a truck is likely to have poorer economy than a sleek one of the same weight). That is, characterize what you seek in this program, how it connects with what you have already done, and what major factors are involved.

Although I explain this process here as an experimental one, in reality it is embedded in an iterative product development process. Each cycle of experimentation also includes product design activity that takes advantage of the learning arising from the experiment. Marco Iansiti and Alan MacCormack provide many examples of such interaction of design and experimentation.[5]

Clearly, for this exploration cycle to be helpful to designing, you must be able to complete it quickly. A counterexample is automotive crashworthiness testing. Designing, building, and testing a vehicle to see if it survives a crash takes months. Meanwhile, the designers have moved on with their design. Thus, the test results arrive too late to be useful to them in designing. This forces them into a mode of verification rather than learning.

Planning Step

In this step you plan the next iteration. First, you establish an objective for this iteration, which should fit with but be more specific than the program objective. What do you expect to learn from this iteration? What outcome do you expect, and how sure are you about this outcome? This is the time to leave calculated room for failure. Maybe you should push this iteration a little further and move back next time should you overshoot.

How will you assess the outcome? Are useful measurements available to you? Can you handle the subjective factors involved? Are any variables outside your control, and if so, how will you handle them? Here is where you ensure that after you have run the experiment, you will have results that you can assess.

What extraneous variables must be controlled? How well? How complete does your experiment need to be? If you are building a prototype, do you need a model that functions, or one with refined cosmetics and finish, or both? An experimental model must be accurate in certain ways that affect the outcome, but it can skip details in other areas for expediency. For instance, a motor vehicle being tested for fuel economy needn't have a finished interior, but it may need ballast to compensate for the weight of the interior. The best prototype is the simplest one that meets the current objective.

Construction Step

Here you design and build any models, prototypes, or apparatus needed for the experiment. You may decide to run several experiments simultaneously in this iteration (more on this later). Based on the iteration objectives and the nature of the variables being controlled (information available from the last step), you design the simplest, cheapest test articles that will provide a valid experiment.

Experimenters in various fields have found effective shortcuts to construction. In automotive development, they use what they call "mules"—convenient production vehicles modified to test a specific subsystem, for instance, a car with a prototype cooling system replacing its production one. Software developers do the same with scaffolding and stubs. *Scaffolding* provides a temporary environment for a piece of code being tested when its surrounding system does not exist yet. A *stub* does the same on a smaller scale. It replicates a module not yet developed that interacts with (is called by) the code under test. Electrical engineers sometimes simulate (on a computer) currently undeveloped pieces of a circuit. Observe that using any of these tricks allows you to test a module earlier than otherwise possible, which is the idea of the front-loaded prototyping practice discussed later. Front loading keeps the cost of change low by resolving problems early in development.

The Run Step

This is where you actually conduct the experiment. Few decisions are left at this point. However, an important one is who should observe the experiment. Could any skeptics, managers, or customers be convinced by seeing the test? Can you think of anyone likely to see something that others might not notice?

Assessment Step

Here you draw conclusions. What did you learn? How should you document it—*barely adequate* being the guideline? (A digital camera can be a wonderful shortcut to documentation.)

This step naturally leads to planning the next iteration. So ask yourself what remaining gaps of knowledge should be filled. You may not need to know everything, but you need to know enough to assess whether you are making progress on the project. Maybe you can stop for now and continue later if necessary.

Thus, this step accomplishes three things:

- Establishes and documents your learnings
- Clarifies remaining gaps in knowledge
- Helps you reach a decision as to whether the exploration program can be terminated—at least for now

Front-Loaded Prototyping

Prototyping is a popular means of experimentation, and it is an effective vehicle to illustrate some general principles of effective experimentation. That is, many of the learnings from prototyping apply equally to other types of experimentation. The next section addresses testing, which involves some special considerations.

A prototype is an object that shares certain characteristics with or represents in a certain way a final object. Thus, a prototype can be a physical model, either made manually or by modern computer-driven technologies; it can be a software simulation of an analog or a digital circuit; it can be quick-and-dirty code used to demonstrate a software concept, or it can simply be a set of sketches or renderings. This discussion centers on prototypes as physical models of mechanical systems, but the principles carry over to other media as well. A prototype can represent only the form of the product, only its function, or both form and function. It can represent the whole product or only a small part of it. Seasoned prototypers make creative use of these options to suit the objectives at hand.

One strength of prototypes is that they often expose invalid assumptions or holes in your logic. As a result, they allow you to make changes while the cost of change is low, provided that you prototype early!

Although prototypes have traditionally been the domain of engineers, today marketers demonstrate them to customers, purchasing professionals use them in negotiating with suppliers, and customer service personnel might use them for training.

Traditional Versus Front-Loaded Strategies

Prototyping (like experimentation in general) is a means of gaining information about the options available in a development project without making commitments to a particular option, thus preserving flexibility. This information is most valuable early in the project while the cost of change is low. However, traditionally, most prototyping has occurred later in development, for several reasons:

- Prototyping has been expensive and time-consuming, making it best to wait for the design to stabilize before expending resources on prototypes.

- Building a prototype has required a detailed design, which—prior to the advent of computer-aided design (CAD) tools—appeared relatively late in the project.

- Product development management has moved toward more complete front-end planning, which has given management a false sense of confidence in the plan and thus a lack of interest in prototypes for checking it.

- Prototyping tends to expose developers' ignorance, so they feel more comfortable leaving it until the design is certain.

However, these factors are changing. The cost of many types of prototypes has fallen dramatically. As suggested, CAD now makes it easier to design a prototype. Some managers are recognizing that project plans may not be good indicators of market success. Finally, these first three factors are pushing developers toward revealing their work earlier.

Table 4.1   Contrast Between Traditional and Front-Loaded Prototyping

Characteristic	Traditional Prototyping	Front-Loaded Prototyping
Prototype cost	High	Low
Prototype build time	Slow	Quick
Number of prototypes	Few	Many
When used in development	Late	Throughout
Prototype's objective	Verify	Learn
Prototype's scope	Broad, vague	Narrow, specific
Prototype attractiveness	Refined	Perhaps crude
Departmental affiliation	Primarily engineering	Any

The driving factor behind these changes is the plummeting cost of making prototypes and the corresponding drop in build time, both due to computer-driven technologies that change the prototyping process dramatically, just as word processing has changed the process of creating a document. Consider Table 4.1. The cost and build time factors now allow developers to make many more prototypes than before, employ them much earlier in development (hence the *front-loaded* term), use them to learn for the future rather than just verify past decisions, and focus on narrower design issues.

Unfortunately, the inertia of organizational change is retarding this transformation, so it is not as easy as simply buying the new technology. Many of the technologists involved in rapid prototyping have concentrated on improving the technology—raising part strength, refining surface finish, adding color, and introducing new materials such as metals. At the same time, management has tended to look at these new tools in terms of cost savings rather than opportunities for changing their development process.

However, a few product development leaders have recognized the potential of these prototyping technologies to change the product development process radically, just as the transformation from typewriters to word processors has changed document creation.

Enabling Technologies

Consider a physical prototype, for instance, a nonfunctional full-scale model of a mobile telephone (something that looks like a mobile phone but is unable to make calls or do anything else).

Twenty years ago, this model would have been made by hand or perhaps by using the latest technology of the time, computer numerical control driving a conventional milling machine to make the model from blue foam, plastic, or aluminum. In 1988 a technology called stereolithography (SL) appeared (now more generally called additive fabrication), and other competing technologies appeared soon thereafter. SL remains popular for high-end prototypes, and it has cut the cost and time for making that mobile phone prototype by a factor of about ten. Then a decade later a second-generation technology appeared, often called a 3-D printer, so called because the devices could be connected to an office computer to produce—or "print"—a three-dimensional part, just as a conventional printer prints in two dimensions on paper. The new 3-D printers avoid the often toxic chemicals of the SL systems, so they can be used in an office. More important, they are substantially faster and less costly than SL-type systems, as shown in Table 4.2.

Consequently, these two generations of technology improvement have brought nearly a hundredfold improvement in investment

Table 4.2   Comparison of a 3-D Printer and Stereolithography

Basis of Comparison	Z Corp 3-D Printer	Viper Stereolithography
Purchase price of machine	US$20,000	US$220,000
Cost of making a part	US$100	US$250
Cycle time	2.5 hours	6 hours

Notes:

- The cost and time estimates are courtesy of Wohlers Associates, Inc., May 10, 2007.
- The part fits inside a 75-mm (3") cube.
- Cycle time is the actual part build time.

expense, R&D expense, and cycle time. As mentioned, most managers have simply pocketed the savings, perhaps building a few more prototypes than before, but not viewing this as an opportunity for fundamental change in the way they develop new products. I suggest that this improvement be used instead to front-load prototyping in the development cycle, that is, to change the development process radically by building many more prototypes much earlier and using these prototypes as vehicles for exploration.

Such front-loaded prototyping is probably the major contribution of this chapter. Table 4.2 suggests the potential by using physical prototypes of mechanical systems, but similar opportunities occur in electronics, software, chemicals, pharmaceuticals, and other types of development.

The Front-Loaded Style

Here's an example of front-loaded prototyping from Orion, a sensor technology company located in Boston, Massachusetts.[6] Orion staff developed the hand-held portion of a cosmetic surgical laser using a front-loaded strategy and compared it with their prior approach. The results appear in Figure 4.3 with the project broken into three phases: concept ideation, concept development and refinement, and detailed development. In the conventional approach that Orion had been using, its staff would have made a total of eleven prototypes over the three phases, which would have taken eighteen weeks in total. Using a 3-D printer, they produced seventy-five prototypes in total over the same three phases, but front loading allowed them to explore faster and thus make progress faster. Specifically, they finished the project in just seven weeks, a 60 percent reduction. However, because they made seven times as many prototypes (seventy-five versus eleven), was the prototyping bill huge? No, because the 3-D printer prototypes were so much cheaper than conventional ones. Orion estimates the cost of the seventy-five prototypes to be only US$4700 versus US$7500 for the eleven conventional ones.

Figure 4.3   Conventional Prototyping versus Use of a 3-D Printer

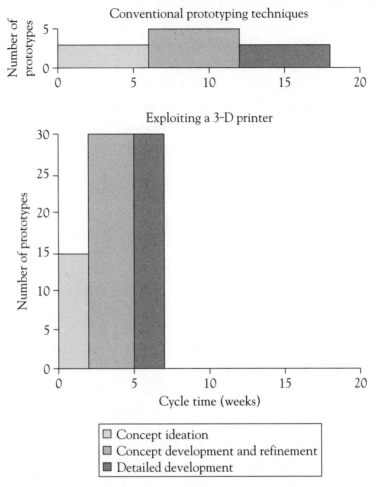

Used with permission of *Time-Compression Technologies* magazine, 6(3): 22 (April 2001).

Observe the difference. In the conventional approach, prototypes were relatively expensive and slow to make. Thus, the developers used only a few of them, mainly to check their work after they had moved on to other tasks. In the 3-D printer approach, they made prototypes much faster, and these prototypes appeared soon enough and often enough to actually guide them in improving the design.

This is not an isolated case. Thomke found that Japanese automobile manufacturers produce their first functional prototypes almost four times earlier (after first drawing release) than car companies in the United States do.[7] This gives the Japanese companies a huge advantage.

In Orion's case, front-loaded prototyping shortened development time dramatically. Although this is clearly a benefit, flexibility is the objective of this book. From the perspective of flexibility, front-loaded prototyping enables Orion's developers to explore the design space early and thoroughly so that they know what will and will not work. It enables them to use a set-based design approach to enhance flexibility, as explained in Chapter Five.

Front-Loading Considerations

Several factors influence a front-loaded strategy. The guidelines in this section will lead you toward making more prototypes than before, as Orion's developers did. This raises other problems: to take advantage of front-loading, you must ensure that you have the capacity to make many more prototypes, If not, you will choke on front-loading before you experience its benefits. The key is to make it easy for developers to obtain prototypes whenever they want them. (See Chapter Nine for more on capacity and bottlenecks.)

When to Start? When using front-loaded prototyping, the first consideration is when to start making prototypes. The answer: as early as you possibly can. In fact, you cannot start too early in the project. Turn back to the description of Alan MacCormack's research in Chapter Two. The most successful product developers, especially when facing uncertainty, are those who place prototypes in customers' hands early. Share early prototypes with those within your organization too.

How Refined? Your first prototypes should be simple. They should be low-level models of the product—a single feature, a component, or a critical interface. The idea is to start early with simple, inexpensive, quick-to-make models. As your ideas mature, you move to more complete and complex models. Of Orion's seventy-five models, the first seventy-four were 3-D prints. Only the last one was a model of the final product made on a high-end rapid prototyping system.

Keep each prototype as focused on its objective as possible. Eliminate extraneous portions not needed for the objective at hand. This keeps your models simple, allows for making more of them, and pushes them earlier in the process. To build and maintain options, consider building variations in parallel so that you can assess several alternatives at once.

How Many? The next question is how many prototypes to make. This is solely a matter of economics. Prototypes cost money, and you expend labor planning them, having them built, and assessing them, which translates into additional cost according to the burdened labor rate of those involved. Offsetting these expenses are benefits with financial value:

- The information gained
- The development effort that would have been spent on unfruitful approaches
- Calendar time saved because of the learning gained from each prototype

All these can be quantified. For instance, calendar time saved translates into money through the cost of delay, which you can calculate for your project.[8] This is often a quite large number that will swing any decision on making a prototype in favor of doing it, assuming that the prototype shortens development time (is on the critical path).

If you plan to run many experiments in a series, say to explore the design space (see Chapter Five), especially if the experiments are corrupted by random errors, the Design of Experiments methodology can greatly reduce the number of experiments needed.[9]

How Many in Parallel? At a certain point in development, you can build one prototype for the next step, or you can build several in parallel to expand your options or help you select the best option sooner. This too is a matter of economics, but there is more to it. The first thing to consider is the economic trade-off between the cost of building multiple prototypes and the benefit derived from the time savings this yields.

To understand this, consider the analogy of a lock.[10] You wish to open a lock that someone has given you, but unfortunately, they did not give you the key. This is analogous to a development problem for which you wish to find the best answer. Say that you know the lock has ten thousand possible tumbler patterns, of which only one will open it. You can have a locksmith make any number of keys for you (not repeating a key made previously), and you can test them all in parallel. It takes you one hour to have a batch of keys made and test them all. However, they cost €1 each. Figure 4.4 portrays the situation. If you make keys individually, you

Figure 4.4   Optimal Batch Size of Keys (Prototypes)

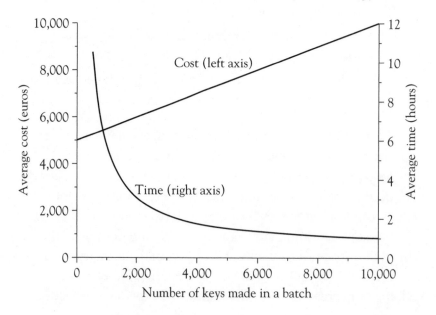

will have made five thousand, on average, before getting the one that will open your lock. This costs €5,000 but takes five thousand hours. At the other extreme, you can have your locksmith make all ten thousand keys in one batch, and you will have the correct key in one hour but at a cost of €10,000. The best solution is somewhere in between where the total cost of making keys and the monetary value of your time are balanced.

In addition, you also need to consider the learning that you can expect either within a cycle of prototyping (by making multiple prototypes within that cycle) or from cycle to cycle. Each situation is different. Observe that for the lock analogy, essentially no learning occurs either within a cycle or between cycles. (After all, locks are designed this way on purpose!) All you could learn from trying a key was that the future now held one less possibility. You can visualize this as a terrain with one isolated spike on an otherwise completely flat plain.

In contrast, consider Figure 4.5a, which resembles a single well-formed mountain. In a few tries here—either in parallel or in sequential cycles—you will know which direction to go to reach the peak. There is much learning available here, and you should plan your

Figure 4.5   Learning Terrain. a. A Cleanly Structured Design Space. b. A More Typical Design Space

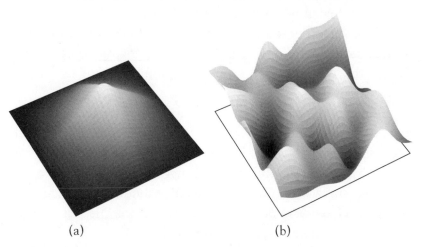

(a)   (b)

experimental strategy to take advantage of it. Figure 4.5b is a more typical mountain range. A sequential approach here is likely to head you to the top of a lesser peak rather than the highest one. To ensure that you have access to the highest one, you should use a parallel approach with dispersed prototypes in each iteration—essentially sending several mountain climbers up from different starting points. In this case, there is partial learning, but you can be fooled.

Testing

The preceding section used mechanical prototypes to illustrate the principles of applying experimentation to enhance flexibility, simply because mechanical prototypes are easier to visualize than other equally pertinent types of experimentation, such as a software simulation of an electrical circuit or an optical breadboard. However, testing offers some special and important lessons, so I consider it separately.[11]

Front loading applies especially to testing. Recall the discussion in Chapter One on Extreme Programming, in which agilists identified techniques that work well in development and cranked them up. For testing, they found that the earlier it occurred, the better, so they invented test-driven design, where the test code is written before the production code, and when the production code is finished, it is run through the test suite.

For media other than software, this probably will not work as well, because tests in other media involve more than code. Nevertheless, this is an excellent example of pushing testing far forward in development.

Test-driven design automates testing. Once the tests are available, in a collection that grows as additional modules are developed, the team has available a comprehensive test suite they can use easily to retest anything that changes. This retesting happens regularly—in fact, continually—in XP as modules are added and changed. These tests catch any flaws that break the system right away while they are easy to localize and fix.

It will not be as easy to automate non-software testing, but you might still be able to automate certain routine parts of it. For instance, mechanical CAD software provides an automated capability to highlight interferences—points in the design where two components occupy the same physical space—allowing the designer to correct the problem immediately. A similar example is the spelling checker on your word processor. It is imperfect, but it does catch many mistakes and thus helps you produce clean writing.

The challenge for non-software products is to find ways to push testing into the early stages of the project. Observe that modular design helps here, because you can test modules easily as they are finished—before other parts of the system are ready—by using the equivalent of scaffolding and stubs.

Tom Peters made this point dramatically by publicizing the "chicken test" for aircraft jet engines.[12] For years, the ultimate test of an engine has been to run it up to full power and pass a live chicken through it to see if the engine survives. This may seem cruel, but it replicates, as no other test can, the serious hazard of an aircraft encountering a flock of birds on takeoff. This is a high-risk test, and typically it occurs very late in development. Peters's point was that the developers, at Rolls-Royce in this case, should be conducting their chicken test much earlier in development.

This is a memorable instance of an all-too-common situation. Traditionally, testing has been regarded as a tail-end activity aimed at verifying and perhaps certifying the final design. This timing leaves no room for failure (learning). Such verification testing may be essential for life-critical products such as aircraft engines, but early, learning-oriented tests are crucial to the flexible organization.

One way to push your testing up front is to make a habit of asking yourself, every time you find a problem in a full system test, how you could have discovered this flaw earlier in component or subsystem testing. Then act on what you observe so that the learning occurs earlier next time.

A final caution: the opportunity to enhance flexibility through customer-driven front-loaded testing, great as it is, does not replace thorough final testing, especially if you are developing life-critical systems. In addition to a methodical approach that checks the product against its requirements list, you may want to have your testers think diabolically about the worst things that customers at their stupidest could do, and look for ways to ensure that your system fails gracefully.

Summary

Here are the high points of this chapter:

- Experimentation fits perfectly with the needs of flexible development to deal with uncertainty effectively.
- Experiments come in many types, including prototyping, testing, and simulation.
- Think of experimentation as exploration—discovering what will work and what will not.
- The emphasis must be on front-loading experimentation: learning as early in the project as possible to keep options open and the cost of change low.
- Failure is a valuable learning outcome from an experiment, but most organizations have a quite unhealthy attitude toward failure that undermines learning.

5

SET-BASED DESIGN

When you come to a fork in the road, take it.

—*Yogi Berra*

Yogi Berra really didn't say all the things he said, but he is right on with this one.[1] Most of us, when faced with a fork, feel compelled to reach a decision about it, thereby closing off the option not taken. The lesson of this chapter is to keep these options open longer, which retains flexibility in the design, reducing the cost of change.

This chapter draws heavily on techniques used in motor vehicle design, primarily at Toyota, that enhance flexibility. Interestingly, these techniques are simply considered good engineering practice at Toyota, not techniques to enhance flexibility, and they are not even called "set-based" there (this term was coined by American investigators studying Toyota's unique design process). Toyota designers use these techniques to ensure holistic designs and to reduce the possibility of designing themselves into a corner, thus having to redesign later. Consequently, set-based design is partially responsible for the fact that Toyota experiences fewer late-stage engineering changes than other automakers.[2]

Although many companies admire and seek to emulate Toyota's practices, this one has not been used significantly (to my knowledge) outside Toyota and perhaps a few other Japanese automakers, so industry's experience with using it specifically to enhance flexibility is quite limited. Nevertheless, I see great power in it to improve flexibility, and it integrates well with other techniques discussed in this book, such as product architecture and experimentation.

What Is Set-Based Design?

Designers usually practice *point-based design*—that is, they select what they perceive as the best course of action and concentrate on that, in contrast to *set-based design*, which would involve maintaining sets of options or a range of possibilities. Clearly, a designer who can keep a range of options open is creating and preserving flexibility. Another way of looking at this is that the set-based designer is deferring decisions. As noted earlier, a deferred decision has not incurred the cost of change, so this keeps the cost of change low.

For instance, consider the effect of deferring decisions on something apparently far from design: a hike in the mountains. Suppose some hikers drive to a trailhead, as indicated by the dot at 750 meters (2460 feet) in the lower left corner of Figure 5.1. They survey the terrain and notice a peak that would be a nice challenge, which appears in the center of the figure at about 1050 meters (3450 feet). Using a point-based approach, they head for this peak.

Figure 5.1   Topographical Map: Trailhead and Peak

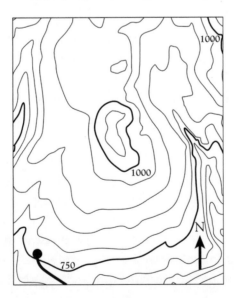

Set-based hikers would take more time to understand the terrain instead of immediately heading straight for the nearest peak. First, they might survey more of the area and notice a somewhat higher and more interesting peak (1150 meters, or 3770 feet) to the northwest of the trailhead. Furthermore, they would notice an area of mud on the southern slope of the 1050-meter peak—just where the point-based hikers intended to go. They also see some other obstacles: a couple of ice patches on the northern faces, and a steep cliff between the trailhead and the 1150-meter peak.

All these terrain features show up in Figure 5.2. What that figure does relative to Figure 5.1 is locate the constraints on the hikers' routing. This emphasis on constraints is what sets the set-based approach apart from point-based thinking. With an understanding of the constraints they face, the hikers have more flexibility in choosing a viable route. In this case, they decide to head north from the trailhead, skirting the mud to the right. When—and only when (for flexibility)—they reach the north end of the mud, they will take stock of their energy and the current weather conditions. Then they might go to the right, around the mud, to the easier 1050-meter peak. Or, for more exercise, they might go to the left, north of the cliffs but staying south of the ice, to reach the higher peak.

A Focus on Constraints

The essential characteristic of set-based design is its emphasis on constraints. In the hiking example, the mud, the cliffs, and the ice fields are constraints. Even after they were ruled out of bounds, the group still had considerable routing freedom. In fact, the hikers had not lost any useful routes by imposing these constraints.

In contrast, point-based development concentrates on choices—deciding which branch to take at a fork in the road. This narrows flexibility unnecessarily quickly. Making choices is a natural part of modern life. We make choices repeatedly during the day. Life is simpler and more efficient, as is product development, if we make these choices quickly and move on to the next one.

Figure 5.2   Topographical Map Expanded to the West of Figure 5.1, Revealing a Higher Peak and Some Obstacles

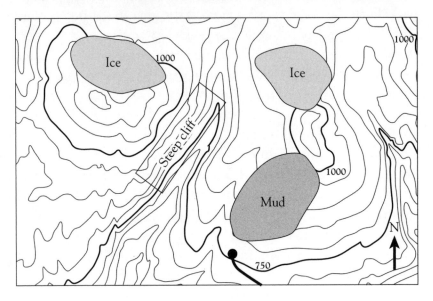

Engineers are trained, from early in their careers, to make choices and keep refining them until the result is good enough. Engineering mathematics depends on the calculus, and calculus is about calculating something approximately and—through a formal process called limits—narrowing the error in the calculation. Engineers have this approach drilled into them in college. Engineering design classes normally apply the same emphasis: pick a guess at a starting solution and narrow it until it is as good as it can be or is good enough.

This approach limits flexibility and maneuvering room early on. If something changes, the designer often has no information on whether a deviation from the selected path will work. A change often means starting over, sometimes from the beginning. In hiking, this is comparable to following a narrow trail and having no idea what is on either side of it. A point-based approach is efficient—if nothing changes to invalidate it—but it is brittle, not accommodating change well.

Set-based design approaches the situation from the other direction. First the designer looks for regions of the design space that will not work. A design region might be unworkable for any number of reasons:

- Violates the laws of physics, such as conservation of mass
- Violates the laws of geometry (two objects in the same space)
- Exceeds power consumption or power dissipation limitations
- Relies upon unproven technology
- Uses unapproved material or components (for example, possibly toxic materials for food packaging)
- Makes the product too difficult for customers to understand
- Makes the product too difficult to service or upgrade
- Exceeds current manufacturing capability
- Infringes on others' patents

Developers actively seek such constraints and impose them as they discover them, just as the hikers imposed the mud, ice, and cliff constraints in Figure 5.2. Figure 5.3 contrasts the two approaches graphically: In 5.3.a, a point-based designer homes in

Figure 5.3 Useful Ways to Visualize and Contrast Point-Based and Set-Based Design

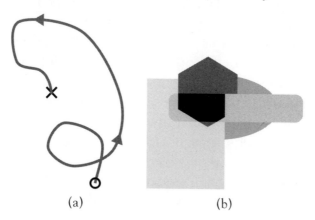

(a) (b)

on the best solution but may do so slowly due to lack of information regarding what lies off the path. In 5.3.b, a set-based designer keeps adding constraints (denoted by the different shapes in the Venn diagram), thus reducing the remaining design space (the intersection of the shapes) but retaining flexibility.

At Toyota, developers in all departments collect constraints from their own departmental view. Toyota formalizes these as checklists over time from all projects and maintains them as departmental documents. These checklists are simply lists of things developers have learned do not work. When a new project appears, they review these checklists and apply them as constraints. At the end of each project, developers review what they have learned and update their checklists for the next project.

Another source of constraints at Toyota is supplier information. Before making any decisions on a new model, Toyota invites suppliers to present what they know about upcoming technologies. From these presentations, Toyota obviously is looking for ideas to incorporate in the new model, but it is also updating its map of the design space and constraints.[3]

Set-based design differs from parallel development, as Figure 5.4 shows. Designs often start by using the set-based approach, where sets containing countless solutions exist. As work progresses, the developers narrow the design to a few distinct options, which are then developed in parallel.

Another way of distinguishing set-based from point-based work is in the tools designers use to consider possibilities. A popular tool used early in the development cycle is the "Pugh concept selection method" or related methods that arrange alternative concepts side by side and compare them using weighted criteria.[4] These are all point-based tools: they compare various discrete design concepts. The set-based equivalent is a "trade-off curve," which shows the constraints between certain design variables. Such a curve leaves an infinite number of options open, and a designer who moves to a nearby point on a smooth trade-off curve can rest assured that this solution will perform similarly to the preceding one.

Figure 5.4   Progression from Set-Based to Parallel Development on a Project

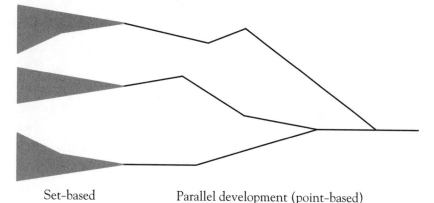

Set-based   Parallel development (point-based)

Source: A similar sketch was originally drawn by a Toyota general manager.

Of course, the exploration and front-loaded prototyping described in Chapter Four are an effective and common way of creating such trade-off curves, or more generally, establishing constraint boundaries and understanding the design space.

Supporting Technical Reports

Operating in the realm of constraints instead of choices requires new ways of communicating. Rather than saying, "This is what we can (or cannot) do," engineers offer, "These are the *kinds of things* we can (or cannot) do"—always keeping a range of possibilities open.

Although Venn diagrams are a useful way to think about the process, in reality, the relationships involved are often more complex than this two-dimensional portrayal can capture, because constraints are often trade-offs among multiple variables. For instance, a manufacturing capability constraint on the accuracy of locating a hole may be a function of the hole's diameter, location, and angle.

Toyota calls its deeply established system for describing such trade-offs "A3 reports," as they use one side of a sheet of A3 paper (roughly equivalent to an 11"×17" sheet in the United States).[5] This report's objective is to provide accurate information that anyone can understand quickly. The reports emphasize pictures (graphs or sketches) over words whenever possible, due to pictures' power to communicate. Toyota trains its people to condense almost any subject into this easily digestible standard format. The emphasis is much more on disciplined thinking than on writing, as clear thinking about the topic is essential to reducing it to one A3 sheet. Contrast this with technical communication in other companies, which is either a set of slides that fragment the information into many pieces impossible to see at once, or a technical report that is usually low in information density and difficult to comprehend.

Although A3 reports stand independently, Toyota goes further. The author of an A3 report, now the expert on the topic, makes a point of actually meeting—usually individually—with the key people this topic affects. The author sends the A3 report and then arranges a meeting to discuss it. Such meetings build a consensus around the approach taken in the report, ensuring that everyone moves in the same direction while taking other opinions into account.

Benefits of Set-Based Design

As mentioned, Toyota considers set-based design simply good engineering practice, but one of the benefits it brings is flexibility. In this book, I concentrate on the flexibility advantage.

First, set-based design reduces or eliminates the cost of change, because designers can pass forks in the road without having to commit to either branch—taking them both, as Yogi Berra might put it. Offsetting this, they may incur extra cost for the exploration necessary to map the design space. For the hikers in the example, some scouting might be necessary to locate the mud and ice, although the cliff would be obvious if they were simply sensitive to constraints. As usual, this is a matter of balancing the benefits of flexibility against the cost of building and maintaining options. When uncertainty is low, a point-based approach is more economical, but as uncertainty increases, the value of the flexibility gained can outweigh the mapping cost.

A second benefit of set-based development is that you will have better information for making a decision the later you wait to make it. Like the hikers looking at the map in Figure 5.2, you need not decide on your route at the trailhead (that is, far in advance). You can go to the point where the routes split and then decide among them, based on your more accurate current understanding of the challenges they present and on your current ability to deal with them.

However, Western managers, when introduced to set-based design, tend to fixate on the potential cost of creating and maintaining these options.[6] The ultimately unused solutions appear to be waste. However, these unused solutions must be compared with the waste that accumulates in a point-based approach when a group finds that it cannot use a solution developed by another group and must redesign it. Set-based design allows all groups to reach agreement together on what is feasible before one group invests labor in a detailed design that is outside the feasible region of another group. Perhaps more important from a flexibility perspective, the set-based approach also reduces the cost of redesign when change is imposed from the outside.

Managing Set-Based Design

The basic process involved in set-based design is *pruning*. At each step, one looks for the weakest solutions and eliminates them—by imposing constraints—and then goes on to prune the next-weakest possibilities in the next step. In the beginning, the things to prune are likely to be both numerous and obvious, but later the weak spots are not likely to be so clear, so more judgment is needed.

You can use many tools for pruning. Start with the simplest, least expensive ones: sketches, simple models, an easy test, a first-order analysis, and feedback from certain stakeholders, for example. If an option becomes too expensive to maintain, it becomes a candidate for pruning too.

Thus, the pruning process needs careful attention, as it can be done too quickly—eliminating options and thus flexibility too fast—or too slowly, prolonging convergence to a solution. Think back to Figure 1.4, which illustrated how maintaining a high level of flexibility—thus uncertainty—until late in the project simply increased the chaos as the product launch approached. The same applies here. At Toyota, a major responsibility of management is to manage the rate of convergence, balancing slow convergence (lack of progress) with fast convergence (lack of flexibility).

All the while, both the team and management watch to ensure that they always have at least one feasible solution, so that if they had to decide today, they would have something that works.

Managers at Toyota play a critical role in the convergence process. They ensure that developers consider a broad range of possibilities initially, and they guide the pruning process to make sure that the design space narrows appropriately. Simultaneously, they maintain a sense of urgency so that when the time comes for a decision, it is made and the team moves on. This is a complex process that requires considerable experience. Toyota's managers are all excellent engineers first, so they are well prepared for this role. In a company with weaker engineering managers, convergence might be choppy or delayed, thus jeopardizing the set-based process.

Another important aspect of managing the process is eliminating surprises, that is, making sure the pruning does not remove solutions into which someone has invested considerable time or upon which someone is depending for their part of the mission. Once the team imposes a constraint, all developers commit to staying within the remaining space so that others can plan their work accordingly. Clearly, this requires excellent communication among all players. Toyota has found that A3 reports provide this strong communication about constraints and feasible regions. The gradual, progressive approach to narrowing the solution space also aids in eliminating surprises and design rework.

The mathematical concept of sets supports this confidence-maintaining process well. An important property of sets is that if B is a subset of A, then anything that is true for A is also true for B, specifically, if solutions are feasible in A, then they will also be feasible in B. Consequently, a constraint on A produces a subset, B, and we know that any feasibility that existed before imposing the constraint will persist.

Another advantage of narrowing gradually through constraints is that as you proceed, you gain more information and more clarity regarding the final solution set, so that when the time for a final decision arrives, you are confident in your selection.

You can appreciate the importance of managing convergence well by considering what often happens with point-based design, especially for complex products such as automobiles, where design involves several departments. As the design moves from department to department, the receiving department often must modify it to achieve its goals. In doing so, it is likely to move to a solution that is unacceptable to another department, necessitating changes in that department, which in turn trigger changes in a third department, and so on. With a well-communicated set-based approach, changes occur within the feasible space for all departments, eliminating these cascading changes. This is why it is so important to communicate the constraints to all and to shrink the design space methodically.

Designers know this cascading change phenomenon well, and it encourages them to refrain from acting on information that may not be final. In a naturally circular process such as product development, this means that everybody is waiting on everybody else. Set-based design avoids this trap by allowing designers to do useful, durable work early by defining constraints and managing the design space.

Delaying Decisions

Thus far, I have covered the relatively formal process that Toyota uses. Typically, its developers only apply the set-based approach in the front end of development—up to what the industry calls the "clay freeze" or styling approval. However, the mind-set that underlies set-based design—delaying decisions—is a consistent theme of Toyota's development throughout.

Consider exhaust systems. Compared to some other components such as the transmission or suspension, which demand considerable engineering development and thus long lead times and a high cost of change, the exhaust system is quite easy to change—just bend the pipe differently or reconfigure the internals of the muffler to improve performance or to provide a more appropriate sound.

Typically, other automotive manufacturers do not exploit this freedom. They freeze all characteristics of the exhaust system relatively early in development—along with all other parts of the car—and then they produce one exhaust system in parallel with development of the other subsystems for final assembly in a functional prototype. This uniformity is easy to manage, but it sacrifices flexibility. Exhaust systems have an important subjective component: the manufacturer wants the car to emit a certain sound that has connotations of power, smoothness, or luxury, and such sounds can be assessed well only on a complete car.

Consequently, Toyota deliberately leaves exhaust system details open until the second prototype build. Its developers sometimes order as many as twenty exhaust system alternatives for a prototype, and they work closely with their exhaust system supplier, which also conducts laboratory assessments of each system to understand the trade-offs among them, like the one between emitted noise and back pressure as some parameter, such as muffler length, varies. Then during prototype build and testing, they make final decisions on the exhaust system—when they have the best information available on their choices. The cost of the prototypes they scrap is minor compared to the flexibility gained (although someone else might call this scrap *waste* and try to eliminate it!).[7]

More broadly, contrast Toyota's approach to prototyping with that of Chrysler, a typical competitor. Toyota builds a 1S prototype and Chrysler builds an F1 prototype, which are similar in that both are the first cars to employ all the new designs and components contemplated for the new model, both employ prototype tooling, and both companies build batches sufficient for extensive testing. However, Chrysler uses its F1 prototypes only for verification of design decisions already made, whereas Toyota considers this a systems integration step to try alternative subsystems on the target vehicle and decide which subsystem to use in production. That is, Toyota delays until this stage carefully selected decisions that its developers can make well only by using the target vehicle.

Perhaps the most counterintuitive example of delaying decisions at Toyota is body panels. These panels present great engineering challenges in simultaneously satisfying styling, quality, fabrication, assembly, and structural goals. The dies used to form the panels are large, complex, expensive, and difficult to change. Accordingly, other automobile manufacturers follow a natural course: at the clay freeze milestone, they fix all body dimensions, including final tolerances, and thereafter all work moves forward to achieve these goals without making any mistakes, which will be expensive to correct.

Toyota looks at this quite differently. At clay "freeze," they allow quite generous variations of up to 1 cm (0.4") on all dimensions. Body engineers can make changes within these allowances to improve function or manufacturability as long as they do not change the customer's perception of styling (everything at Toyota looks to the customer as the ultimate judge). Then at successive checkpoints, they close up these variations progressively. Notice that this process provides much more flexibility to make changes, a flexibility that decreases at a controlled rate. The alternative, in other companies, is that fixed specifications cause designs to move through different departments cyclically to make adjustments, resulting in late-stage engineering changes.

Toyota body engineers pass their drawings to manufacturing for fabrication of the forming dies with nominal dimensions only—no tolerances. These expensive dies are simply made as close as possible to nominal. Finally, at assembly of the second generation of prototypes, they look for areas of disagreement, and where these occur, they ask themselves which of the two mating parts would be easiest to change. After making these changes, they measure the final parts, and these dimensions—whatever they are—become the final specifications. The designers then adjust their CAD design database to match the parts. Manufacturing—rather than Design Engineering, as is customary in the industry—then sets the tolerances in accordance with manufacturing capability. In short, Toyota developers carry a diminishing amount of flexibility all the way to prototype assembly, which is far deeper into development than their competitors do.

Toyota is perhaps better than its competitors at delaying decisions, but the principle applies broadly across all types of products. Consider a photocopier. The primary measure of photocopier performance is speed: number of copies per minute. The tendency is to negotiate this key value and fix it in the product specification at the beginning of development. However, before starting design, developers know little about the technologies needed to achieve this speed and their cost. It's entirely possible that another speed value would yield a more profitable product, as shown in Figure 5.5. That is, the value of a photocopier depends directly on its speed, a relationship obtainable in advance from a market survey. But its manufacturing cost is known only after testing some technologies and doing some design work. Consequently, by delaying this decision, the developers can both gain flexibility and find a better design solution based on the improved information that becomes available later.

Progressive Decisions

You can remove much of the pressure of making a decision by making it progressively rather than all at once. Unlike other

**Figure 5.5   Delaying a Decision on Photocopier Speed
Improves Profitability**

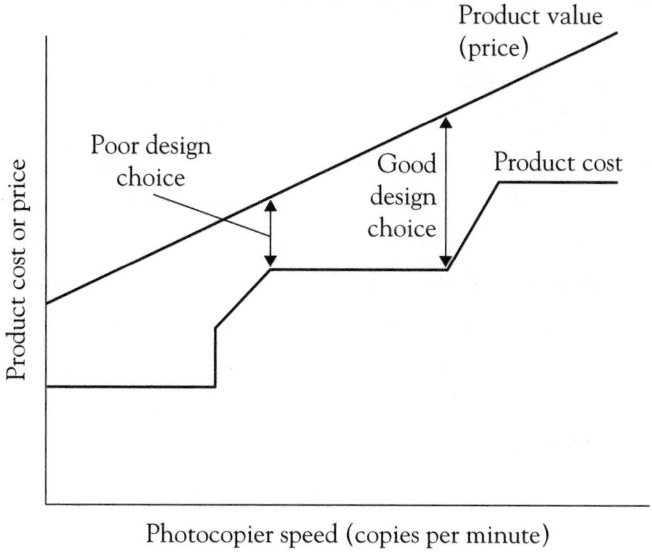

Used with permission from *Developing Products in Half the Time* (Second Edition) by Preston G. Smith and Donald G. Reinertsen (Wiley, 1997).

automobile manufacturers, which tend to freeze the whole design at some point, Toyota moves gradually, eliminating the weaker options or progressively tightening up tolerances. In this way, its developers gain experience and confidence as they go and maintain flexibility to make adjustments if necessary, in addition to lowering the pressure associated with a major decision. All of this lowers the cost of change.

This shows up in other ways Toyota staff operate. For instance, they do not adopt a new supplier in one step. Instead, they ask the supplier to make a few samples, next they might use it on a small project, and so forth, before committing this supplier to a major project.

Other companies use this progressive approach in the way they release drawings. Normal practice is to release a drawing for production all at once, but more sophisticated organizations have several release points for a drawing, one to procure the material, one to rough-cut the part, one to finish-cut it, another to apply the surface finish, and so on. Other organizations release product specifications progressively, the more certain items early and the more uncertain ones later, or they release initial specifications with large initial tolerances that narrow over time.

Another variation commonly used in making tools such as injection-molding dies is to start out "tool safe," that is, to leave a buffer of extra metal that can be removed later. Because removing metal is easier and less disruptive than adding it, this lowers the cost of change in uncertain areas. In other words, if an area is uncertain in either direction, err in the direction that is easiest to change.

Clearly, this principle has many possible applications. Create ones for your organization that delay your most uncertain decisions longest or keep the cost of change low as long as possible.

The Difficulties

Set-based design and keeping options open seem straightforward, but they go against the grain of human nature. First, most of us feel more comfortable in reaching decisions rather than having affairs remain in limbo. A decision is an accomplishment, an item of the project that you can chalk up as a step forward. Managers in particular are paid to make decisions, often being measured in terms of the decisions they have made. A manager who resists making decisions can be viewed as a weak manager. Consequently, training and reward systems may have to change to encourage managers to place value on decisions not made.

A major responsibility of Toyota's managers is ensuring that decisions are not made prematurely. Toyota entrusts managers with this important responsibility because their level of experience and wisdom is needed to keep premature decisions from occurring. Many companies do not have technical managers as seasoned as Toyota's, so these companies may not have the skill needed to provide this guidance.

Another psychological difficulty is that most people tend to justify any decision once made as the best decision. Someone who has just bought a house or a car is apt to spend a lot of time explaining to the world why this is the best house in the neighborhood or the best model of car made today. Just prior to making the purchase, they may have agonized over it, but afterward, they have a strong impulse to sell their decision and discredit other options.

This happens with development decisions too, and it is damaging to the project. Should the chosen path not work out, the developers have probably so discredited the alternative paths that they are no longer viable options. Consequently, not only are these potential backups somewhat stale from an objective standpoint, they also have to overcome the psychological burden that they have assumed.

Therefore, when choosing an alternative, document its pluses and minuses—especially ones that might change over time—relative to the alternatives not chosen and keep these on hand in case you must revisit the decision later. Then, at least, you will not have to pay a psychological cost of change in reversing your decision.

Set-based design at Toyota benefits from an excellent staff of highly competent engineers operating in a strong communication network (A3 reports, engineering checklists, effective technical meetings, and outstanding mentoring). This network synchronizes everyone on the constraints so that the design space narrows predictably. No one has enough experience with set-based design outside Toyota to know for sure how essential this communication network is. As Toyota globalizes its product development outside Japan and the relatively protected environment it enjoys there (long-term employment, for instance), it will be revealing to see if techniques like set-based design continue to be viable for the company.

For other companies wishing to initiate set-based design, one solution is to start set-based design in a strong subteam (dedicated, co-located, and with sufficient authority, as described in Chapter Six) developing only a single subsystem. If this team runs into difficulty combining or coordinating constraints, it is probably working on a piece of the system that is too complex as an initial project. Only when it has a smoothly working subteam should the firm move constraint management to a broader level that requires integration between subteams or subsystems.[8]

More broadly, Toyota has built over time a culture that supports exploring options and delaying decisions. It's easy to cite many examples of how Toyota operates differently—often oppo-sitely—from its competitors even in Japan.[9] Developing such a culture is a big investment. Again, this culture is being tested as Toyota expands its product development to other countries.

Finally, automobiles are a mature product area, so Toyota can partially reuse on future projects the effort invested in exploring the design space for one project, especially given the company's outstanding ability to preserve tacit knowledge (see Chapter Nine). In other product categories, especially new ones that are in flux, reuse might drop off enough to make set-based design prohibi-tively costly. However, even if set-based design itself were not cost-effective, developers could still practice many of the other delayed or progressive decision-making approaches offered in this chapter.

Summary

These are the high points of this chapter:

- At Toyota, set-based design is simply a part of good engineering practice, but others can use it to build and maintain flexibility.
- Set-based design involves imposing constraints in contrast to making choices.
- Think of imposing constraints as pruning the weaker options from the design space.
- Conduct this pruning methodically so that the design space narrows predictably, without invalidating anyone's part of the design.
- Besides formal set-based design, which Toyota uses only in early parts of a project, many similar approaches are available throughout the project to delay decisions and make them progressively.
- Set-based design works at Toyota partly because of its unique culture. It is hard to tell how difficult it would be to implement elsewhere, especially in companies whose products have not reached maturity.

6

DEVELOPMENT TEAMS AND PEOPLE FACTORS

> While methodologies, management techniques,
> and technical approaches are valuable, the most
> critical success factors are much more likely to be in
> the realm of people factors.
>
> —*Richard Turner and Barry Boehm*[1]

Richard Turner and Barry Boehm studied both agile and traditional software development projects in preparation for their book on the subject, and one conclusion that stood out was that people factors dominate the process.[2] This is surprising, as their main focus was on methodologies. They go on to mention "a long list of wake-up calls" and list several other studies dating from 1971.

These studies include Boehm's well-known COCOMO (Constructive Cost Model) work, which is the source of Figure 6.1. In this figure, notice the multiplier of thirty-three on people factors in determining the effort required to complete a development project, which means that the labor cost of developing a product can differ by a factor of thirty-three due to variations that relate to a project's people. COCOMO's people factors include programmer and analyst capability; experience with the product domain, with the computer platform used, and with the languages and tools used; personnel continuity; team cohesion; and team dispersion. Each of these individual factors can range independently, generally from the fifteenth percentile to the ninetieth percentile. That is, the labor cost for a project could range from US$10,000 to US$330,000 just due to these people factors! You can interpret the other bars in Figure 6.1 comparably.

Figure 6.1   Factors Influencing Labor Cost for a Development Project

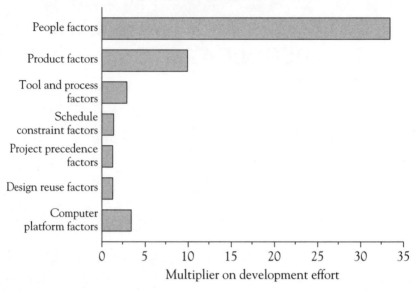

Source: Data from Boehm (2000).

The next most important factors—with a multiplier of ten—are those connected with the product: complexity, required reliability (for example, life-critical), rigidity of the requirements, formality of the documentation, and database size. Third, with a multiplier of only three, are the factors connected with the development process and tools used, including development process maturity, design review thoroughness, and development tool capability. The other factors at the bottom of Figure 6.1 are relatively minor (and the platform factors, such things as host computer memory and timing constraints, apply only to software projects).

Consequently, people factors—the subject of this chapter—are by far the most important ones in determining project effort and thus cost. Product factors are second, and processes and tools are a distant third—quite different from the normal emphasis on process and tools! These conclusions, from Boehm's 2000 study, mirror conclusions from a similar study done almost twenty years earlier,[3] even though there were vast changes in programming (object-oriented versus procedural) and computers (personal computers versus mainframes) over this interval. This emphasis on people fits with "individuals and interactions over processes and tools," which is the first statement of the Agile Manifesto (Exhibit 1.1).

The characteristic measured by Boehm is labor cost. My interest here is instead in the ability to be productive under rapidly changing conditions. These are different, so this chapter requires the addition of personal characteristics of comfort with change and chaos. However, the main measure is productivity, so I believe Figure 6.1 makes a compelling case for emphasizing people factors over process factors.

The overwhelming impact of people factors makes this the most important chapter in this book. You have probably read about teams before and have already improved in your teams over the years. However, this topic is so important to success in flexible development—indeed, in any type of product development—that I urge you to consider seriously some of the opportunities presented in this chapter.

Teams and Flexibility

Teams and people are important to flexibility in two ways. First, flexibility requires a higher caliber of people, principally because flexible processes are emergent (as discussed in Chapter Nine): they must be constructed and modified as you encounter the changes. The title of a recent book on dealing with change communicates this concept: *Building the Bridge As You Walk On It.*[4] Changing a process is a higher skill level than simply following an established process.

Second, to deal with change effectively, developers must be able to communicate the change—even the possibility of change—quickly and accurately to those who might be affected. Improved communication is a major benefit of an effective team. If you select the right people for the team, structure the team effectively, and provide effective communication tools, information will flow as needed to manage change well. This chapter addresses the people factors affecting flexibility first, and then the structural or organizational factors.

Having the Right People

Flexibility demands a lot from people. It's worthwhile to consider this, so that you know what to look for in your people and what sort of people to assign to a project likely to experience change.

The main issue is that a project subject to change is unpredictable, so it is not possible to apply fixed, established processes to it at a top level (see Chapter Nine for more detail). The process must be emergent. This calls for individuals who are comfortable working in a fluid environment and who have enough experience with such environments that they know how to respond—rather than simply freezing. Two elements enter: temperament and experience. Some people crave structure and prefer to have rules to follow. They are likely to do poorly in an environment subject to change, even if they have experienced it often. Among those who would be comfortable in an environment undergoing constant change, however, some simply do not have the experience to know what to do when things change, so that aspect is worth further discussion.

Useful Experience

Chapter Two outlines Alan MacCormack's studies of the Internet software development industry, where he found that success in a fast-changing environment depended heavily on team members with broad experience in delivering new products, what he calls "generational experience."[5] Interestingly, he found no connection between the normal measure of experience—tenure in a position in years—and success. Instead, he found that productivity was highly correlated with the number of earlier product generations a developer had worked on.

Although specific knowledge can atrophy quickly in high-tech fields, working on many generations of products helps a person build certain patterns and problem-solving skills that make it possible to deal with change smoothly. When people have resolved many other problems, they know where to look for clues, how to plan experiments that locate the cause, how to sift through experimental data quickly, how to structure alternatives and workarounds, and when to move on. To MacCormack, a "generation" means a new generation of a product, not just a minor upgrade. Such new generations provide the richest problem environment and offer the greatest experience with change. As developers move through them, they assimilate the problem-solving skills to handle new changes quickly.

Others concur that in a fast-changing environment, the number of years of experience in a field is less helpful than the amount of hands-on experience in dealing with change. In fact, traditional experience can get in the way by leading people to believe that the situation will remain static, as it has before.[6]

Mastery Levels

In addition to this technical problem solving, flexible developers must adjust—or even invent—the development process while they are in the midst of it. Alistair Cockburn, an author of the Agile Manifesto (Exhibit 1.1), suggests three levels of process mastery, and Boehm and Turner contribute another one, which I combine as shown in Figure 6.2.[7]

Level 1 developers need a process to follow. They cannot even select among several processes. By temperament or lack of experience, they would be confused and likely to judge poorly if given a choice of methods. They want explicit instructions. Unfortunately, some contemporary management approaches, such as "best practices" and bodies of knowledge, reinforce this mentality and persuade people that there is one best way to complete an activity. Although systems such as ISO 9000 do not specify or even require a single process, by auditing relative to *a* process, they imply that

Figure 6.2   Levels of Process Mastery

Level 1 (following): Able and willing to follow a single specified method	Level X (uncooperative): Unable or unwilling to collaborate or follow the team's specified method
Level 2 (detaching): Able and willing to consider multiple specified methods, comparing strengths and weaknesses	
Level 3 (fluent): Able and willing to adjust and improvise without reference to specified methods	

an organization should have *one* documented process. To enhance flexibility, we encourage people to grow out of Level 1, but these management systems (and management's desire for order and predictability) can send opposing signals.

Level 2 individuals are seeing some cracks in the dike. Their experience and observations suggest that the standard process has flaws. They are seeking alternative processes, but they still need a process for guidance. They might adapt part of a process. As suggested earlier, how far they go with this depends on the encouragement they receive from management. (Deviation also depends on other factors, such as government regulation of the industry and the life-criticality of the system they are designing.)

Level 3 people are the masters. They have been through this exercise so many times that the steps are automatic to them. They mix and match to fit the occasion. They invent a process when an existing one does not fit. They might be bewildered or amused if you asked them which methodology they were following; they are simply doing the job and haven't named the process.

Clearly, Level 3 people are best for a flexible project, but they are scarce. Thus, it is a matter of having an adequate mix of levels and ensuring that some Level 3 people fill key roles.

Figure 6.2 shows another level, Level X, added by Boehm and Turner.[8] My consulting experience supports this addition. Fortunately, Level X developers are rare, but when they are on a team, they can cause great damage. Typically, they have the knowledge and expertise of Level 3 people, but they insist on being sole contributors. They will not cooperate with others, and often they operate by withholding key information. They will not follow the agreed process. Level Xers present a dilemma for management: because they alone hold key information or expertise, they seem indispensable, but they also poison the team and its process. My experience and that of Boehm and Turner is that management should identify such individuals and remove them from the team quickly, as painful as this may be.

Some corporate cultures breed Level Xers, and some repel them. I once asked a senior executive of Intel about Level Xers, but he could not comprehend the question even after I explained the term to him carefully.

Great Teams from Average Individuals

Ideally, you would have all Level 3 people on your team, but the reality is that, because they are scarce and in high demand, you will have to create an effective team from a mix. How do you proceed?

First, ensure that you have at least a Level 2 person in each facet of the project: someone who is good at adapting the process, someone who is good at applying the technology you are employing, someone who is good at seeing and overcoming people and communication problems, and so forth.

Then, for a flexible team, identify the areas of the project where change is most likely and place a Level 3 process person there. For instance, if the market or how customers might use the product is complex, put a Level 3 market research person on the team. If the team might have to explore many technologies and test their limits to find an adequate technical solution, look for a Level 3 experimenter. If your search for a workable technology might lead you to collaborating with many suppliers in your search, include a Level 3 purchasing person. When you assign these people, explain to them that you expect Level 3 process leadership from them, that this project should not be done "by the book."

Finally, build for the future. Establish migration paths up through the levels. Watch career paths and provide generational experience. Recruit, train, and retain your people to expand your cadre of Level 3 and 2 people for the future. A large part of this depends on the way you reward them and the signals that management sends about the value of process flexibility—at the extreme, in praising those who break the rules and stretch the system.

Desirable People Qualities

Through years of consulting to a broad variety of businesses on accelerated product development, I have observed that certain individual characteristics can enhance team effectiveness greatly. What follows is not new, but before you write it off and skip to the next section, you might look back at Figure 6.1 and ask yourself if you would like to capture a larger part of that top bar.

Skills

Clearly, developers need an impressive array of skills to develop a new product, especially a truly innovative one. These skills are of two kinds, technical and social. Technical skills depend on the individual's role on the team; the project may need expertise in radio frequency amplifier design, in purchasing polymers, in conducting effective focus groups, and a host of other specifics. These are the easy skills to deal with, because they are well recognized, and individuals are usually hired and categorized according to their technical skills.

Equally important—perhaps even more important—are the social skills: speaking up with contrary views when necessary, communicating what you are doing, respecting others' views, and many others. People are rarely hired for such skills, training in them is generally meager, and pay grades often do not correlate with them. However, without them, your team will not have the glue needed to function effectively, especially in a chaotic environment. Do not ignore the social skills.

Dedication

Dedication means placing an individual on the team full time. The objective here is to capture your team members' mind share so that they think about team issues even when not doing team work. In reality, you will not have them 100 percent of their time at work—sickness, training, consulting to past projects, and similar activities are bound to intervene—but about two-thirds of their hours at work is reasonable and sufficient.

Clearly, this overcomes many issues of priorities. When a project is undergoing a great deal of change, people who are on multiple projects are inevitably missing during key periods on the subject project, so they are continually out of date, and others waste time bringing them back into the project. Beyond this, assigning an individual to more than two projects is simply wasteful of human resources, as Figure 6.3 shows.[9] Here you can see that a second project assigned to individuals allows them to fill any gaps in the primary project, but after this, they run out of gaps to fill. Additional projects contribute to inefficiency, by racking up project-switching losses—if only the time needed to put down one task and get back up to date on another one. If you switch frequently or if the tasks are undergoing rapid change, the losses are higher.

Figure 6.3 shows that assigning more than two projects to an individual is outright wasteful, but even with only two, you gain some efficiency but lose the focus, commitment, and accountability that accompany concentrated attention. If a project is undergoing a great deal of change, you should dedicate key members of the team full time so that they can keep up with it.

Figure 6.3   The Inefficiency of Working on Too Many Projects

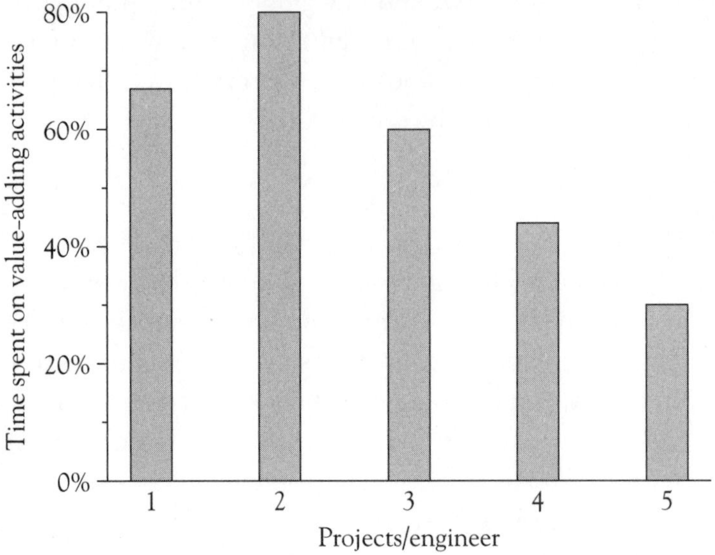

From Wheelwright and Clark (1992, p. 91). Used with permission.

An even better way to interpret Figure 6.3 is to assign individuals to two projects (provides maximum efficiency), but tie the projects together. That is, the "second project" should be to look around for unassigned but needed work on the first project. With this sort of secondary assignment, a team member who is idle scans the project to see what is on the critical path that could use attention, who could use some help, or which upcoming task would benefit from attention now.

Most teams need some types of members you usually cannot hope to keep on board full time—people from Marketing or Purchasing, for instance. However, rather than asking for a certain percentage of their time, which is unlikely to be fulfilled, ask for a certain portion of the work week, such as every Tuesday from 11 AM until 5 PM. This is much easier to monitor and thus is more likely to happen.

Dedication to one team strengthens accountability to that team. Some individuals feel uncomfortable with this level of accountability and prefer to split their efforts and maintain a fog about their commitments to their teams. Watch for and correct these situations. Better, prevent them by dedicating as many people as possible.

Commitment

Teams have become popular in the corporate lexicon, to the extent that employees might not be considered "team players" unless they are members of several teams. Although this may have advantages, it dilutes commitment to each team. The work done by product development teams is demanding—even more so when the project is subject to frequent change.

Those who participate on teams with the best of intentions but are only partially involved can be more trouble than benefit for their team. The typical partial participant is a manager who attends an occasional team meeting and makes some suggestions that the team feels obliged to pursue, because of the manager's rank or authority. Some of these suggestions may be helpful, but many are a net waste of the team's time.

In my experience, this situation varies greatly from organization to organization, so you will have to decide if it is a problem for your team. If it is, there are several things you can do. One is to name the players. I like to use Figure 6.4, which illustrates three levels of commitment by analogy to the typical U.S. breakfast of bacon and eggs, with a glass of milk. The pig is fully committed to the team, having given its life for the breakfast. The chicken is involved but not committed, having donated life from the next generation. And the cow is a bystander without any life invested in the project. Arrange your team to have as many pigs as possible, and be careful about how the cows participate.

Another approach is to restrict input from the less committed participants. Agile development typically uses daily stand-up meetings (more about these later), and agilists run these using

Figure 6.4   Who Has Skin in the Game?

Illustrator: Lyn Doiron.

strict rules, which usually include a rule that those outside the dedicated team are welcome to observe the meeting at any time, but they cannot actively participate in it.

Often, the chickens and cows possess a great deal of experience that could benefit the team. I have seen them shifted to helpful roles by coaching them to offer guidance and suggestions on a purely discretionary basis without implying any assignments or compulsion to follow through.

Finally, observe that dedicated team members go a long way toward achieving commitment, because whatever is getting most of people's time is going to show up as most of their performance evaluations as well.

Generalists

Teams tend to fill up with specialists who excel at doing one thing well. If you need a different skill, no problem: just add another specialist for it. Such team staffing solves the immediate problem, but it leads to fragmented teams of part-time, uncommitted members who come and go as needed.

This revolving door makes it more difficult for a team to move quickly when change occurs. Members do not truly understand the project, what is driving it, or what might change. Specialists work efficiently from a script, as long as the script does not change.

Consequently, generalists dedicated to the project, who stick with it throughout, provide much more flexibility when change is likely. Try to staff your teams with a few people who have a broad range of skills. Then if something changes, not only are the people on the spot in a better-informed position to react, the team is also more likely to have the skills needed without switching players.

However, two factors militate against the unlimited use of generalists. One is the law of diminishing returns. Although a few generalists provide a great deal of flexibility, the benefit tapers off if generalists dominate the team. The other is that, most likely, your competitive advantage results from specialists who provide an edge in certain areas of strategic strength. For instance, if you produce photocopiers, a paper-handling specialist may give you a competitive advantage in reduced paper jams. Do not try to replace these essential specialists with generalists.

Generalists do not just appear on your teams. They must be recruited, trained, rewarded, and supported in their roles. Thus this is a long-term human resource issue. Like the preparation of a senior manager, preparing a generalist requires the cultivation of a variety of experiences.

Better yet, cultivate team members who are both generalists and specialists. I call these people "T-shaped individuals": they are broad on the top and have one (or more) specific areas of depth.[10]

Team Qualities

Now I move from the individuals on the team to the techniques for assembling them as an effective working group. Nevertheless, individual skills and attitudes still reign supreme in team performance, as teamwork expert Christopher Avery makes clear in *Teamwork Is an Individual Skill*.

Self-Organizing

Self-organizing means that the team arranges itself as needed to meet its immediate challenges best. The principles behind the Agile Manifesto state that "The best architectures, requirements, and designs emerge from self-organizing teams."[11]

Observe that if the team is operating in an atmosphere of frequent change, it is likely to change its structure and—indeed—even its leadership (from within) frequently. In fact, a measure of a self-organizing team is how frequently the leadership changes. This contrasts with the normal team that initially defines roles and responsibilities and sticks to these definitions so that everyone knows when a member is "falling out of line." Comforting as it is to define each member's role, it also leads to rigidity.

Also notice that the aforementioned individual qualities of dedication, commitment, and generalists are important prerequisites for a self-organizing team. The pieces do indeed fit together in a mutually supportive, interlocking way!

Cross-Functional

Cross-functional means that team membership includes all the key functions involved in the project, usually Engineering, Marketing, and Manufacturing, at a minimum. Given the complex nature of today's products, engineering staff could include mechanical, electrical, software, and perhaps other types of engineers. Beyond these, members often come from Industrial Design, Purchasing, Quality, Technical Documentation, and Finance.

This breadth of viewpoint and expertise provides assurance that the team can maintain effective balances regarding product requirements, new technologies, architectural choices, suppliers, and manufacturing capability as changes occur. Observe that most organizations turn such important cross-functional decisions over to a management group, but this arrangement is usually slow to react in a turbulent environment. Such groups do not convene often enough or quickly enough to deal with constant change. In addition, these managers, although they are experienced decision makers, do not have information at hand regarding decisions the team faces today. The team would have to brief them, which wastes precious reaction time. When a team is encountering constant change, it needs the capability to make cross-functional trade-off decisions internally, which means that it needs an internal cross-functional composition. Anything less simply increases reaction time in a situation where reaction time is paramount.

Adequate Authority

Similarly, to make responsive decisions, the team needs adequate authority. After all, to function at all, let alone smoothly, a team must make many kinds of decisions—and some of these decisions are normally the responsibility of management. It can be unclear whether the team has sufficient authority to make a given decision. Sometimes the team waits for management to make a decision while management is waiting for the team to make it.

Consequently, I suggest that the team and management reach agreement beforehand on the areas of authority the team has and the situations where it must go to management. A list such as the one in Table 6.1 is useful here. This table presents about fifty areas of authority needed to develop a new product. (This list is necessarily general. Please translate it into the activities and terminology of your organization.)

Notice that each of these items is an area of authority potentially held by either management or by the team. You can use this table in two ways to streamline team decision making. The first is to draw clearly the line between the team's authority and management's so that when a decision arises, there is no confusion about who makes the decision. This can save time when change occurs frequently. Simply go down the list, delineating the boundary

Table 6.1   Areas of Authority

Financial Control

Prepare project expense budget

Modify project expense budget

Prepare project capital budget

Modify project capital budget

Use project capital budget

Authorize travel

Pay for manufacturing variances

Establish delegation limits

Cancel project

Management of People

Prepare staffing plan

Modify staffing plan

Select team members

Hire team members

Remove team members

Evaluate team member performance

Determine team member compensation

Determine team member bonuses

Provide recognition to team members

Management of External Relationships

Select key business partners

Manage key business partners

Select key technology partners

Manage key technology partners

Select outside contractors

Manage outside contractors

Select vendors and suppliers

Manage vendors and suppliers

Operational Control

Select product features

Modify product features

Determine product architecture

Set reuse objectives

Make reuse decisions

Make design outsourcing decisions

Prepare project schedule

Modify project schedule

Select development location

Determine layout of team work area

Determine agenda of team meetings

Select development methods

Modify development methods

Select engineering tools

Select test procedures

Modify test procedures

Determine test criteria

Set documentation standards

Select manufacturing site

Select manufacturing processes

Set quality standards

Set manufacturing yield targets

Set management reporting
requirements

Table copyright © 2003, Reinertsen & Associates. Derived 7/21/03 from Figure 6–4 of *Managing the Design Factory* by Donald G. Reinertsen (New York: Free Press, 1997).

between the authority granted to the team and that reserved by management, for each item. Then discuss your rationale with management so that everyone agrees to the same boundaries.

The second use of the list is to do a triage on it. You will find that some areas are definitely under the team's control and thus not in dispute. Likewise, some are clearly management's prerogative and not open for discussion. However, you are likely to find a few that are under management's control now, but the team feels that it could be more flexible if it had at least partial authority here. For example, selecting and managing prototyping suppliers could be vital if you plan to practice the front-loaded prototyping suggested in Chapter Four. Once you have short list of additional areas of authority that would improve the team's responsiveness, negotiate this list with management.

Co-Located

My definition of co-location is that the primary members of the development team (at least the ones from Engineering, Manufacturing, and Marketing for a non-software product) are located within ten meters (thirty feet) of each other, preferably with visual contact while sitting. This is a strict criterion to meet, but it enhances communication greatly.[12] Often, it enables members to overhear each other's telephone conversations.

Although other degrees of co-location are possible, the principal alternative is a dispersed team.[13] A dispersed team might be distributed throughout a building or across the globe, and it might be dispersed by time zone, country, language, or culture as well. Dispersed teams are quite popular today—especially with multinational corporations—as they allow management to draw talent from wherever it exists. Sometimes this means tapping low-cost labor, but it also allows a company to assign developers who are more familiar with a local market. Dispersed teams employ modern electronic communication—from fax machines to multimedia team rooms—to overcome, at least partially, the difficulties of operating at a distance.

Regrettably, those who advocate co-located teams and those who espouse dispersed ones operate in different realms with very little interaction between them. Co-located team believers assume they have the correct solution and are unwilling to dilute it. Advocates of dispersed teams view co-location as antiquated and unworkable in today's world, and many of them believe that technology overcomes distance—or that it will soon. Consequently, if you study a book or article on co-located teams, you are quite unlikely to find any references to dispersed teams, and vice versa. I intend to bridge this gap, but my bias will be clear.

Until recently, the only evidence for co-location was in some comprehensive studies done in 1977 (before fax machines, voicemail, or personal computers) that showed clearly how team communication degraded depending on various obstacles, such as separation, a stairway, or a transition to a nearby building.[14] However, three new areas of support have appeared in the twenty-first century.

Donald Reinertsen has led product development seminars for thirteen years at the California Institute of Technology (Caltech) as well as elsewhere, including many in the United Kingdom. In these, he asked his students two questions about co-location:

- Have you ever worked on a product development team that had Engineering, Manufacturing, and Marketing members all located within twenty meters (sixty feet) of each other?[15]
- Of those who answered yes to the first question, if you had to bring a new product to market quickly, would you choose to co-locate the team?

He reports that less than 15 percent of product developers can say yes to the first question, but of those who can, their reply to the second question is *unanimously* yes. Over the past four years I have conducted a similar experiment with classes in the United States, Southeast Asia, and China with the same result: of those who have tried it, they would use it again if they had to rush a product to market, unanimously!

Notice that neither Reinertsen nor I asked, in the second question, if people *liked* co-location. It can be unpleasant. If your neighbor did not take a bath, you will be aware of it. It can be difficult to take a telephone call from your physician or psychotherapist, and Monday mornings can be distracting as everyone settles down from the weekend. However, there is no substitute for the way it enhances communication, and this is what those who answer the second question positively have experienced with co-location.

Those who answered no to the first question (that is, those who have never been co-located), on the other hand, have countless reasons why it will not work. However, none of these reasons is based on the personal experience of actually having worked on a co-located team. In short, it is just one of those things that you must experience to appreciate.

The second type of evidence comes from a group of university researchers, principally Gary Olson and Judith Olson at the University of Michigan. In an extensive survey article titled "Distance Matters," they conclude not only that distance really does matter but that "distance will continue to matter."[16] In some interesting research, professor Olson and her colleagues ran six projects using "radical collocation" (what I simply call co-location) and compared them to comparable traditional projects. They found that co-located teams were twice as productive as traditional ones. Their conclusion:[17]

> Our study of six teams that experienced radical collocation showed that in this setting they produced remarkable productivity improvements. Although the teammates were not looking forward to working in close quarters, over time they realized the benefits of having people at hand, both for coordination, problem solving and learning. They adapted to the distractions of radical collocation, both by removing themselves to nearby hotelling areas when they needed privacy, and by zoning out, made possible because of the distance between people in the larger rooms. Of the nine kinds of

activities the team engaged in, only two were best done individually and separate from the rest of the team.

Regarding the possibility of achieving this with dispersed teams, they conclude:

> What does this say about trying to support remote team members in a way that produces the same kinds of productivity enhancements? This will be difficult. One of the main drivers of success was the fact that the team members were at hand, ready to have a spontaneous meeting, advise on a problem, teach/learn something new, etc. We know from earlier work that the gains from being at hand drop off significantly when people are first out of sight, and then most severely when they are more than 30 meters apart.

Finally, the third type of evidence for co-location comes from the many teams that use it regularly as a part of agile software development. This is especially unexpected for software development, because programmers frequently claim that they need the lack of distractions that accompanies isolation to maintain their creative train of thought. However, a common thread of agile development is co-location, and agilists often push this to pairing (see a description of pairing and its benefits in Chapter One).

Whether or not they practice pairing, agile teams usually sit together in one room. They generally put their desks in the middle of the room and use the wall space for their living project documentation: project schedule and status, product requirements, personnel assignments, defect tracking, metrics, and architectural diagrams. These visual controls, called "information radiators" by Alistair Cockburn, can be whiteboards, bulletin boards, or collections of sticky notes.[18] They lend themselves to informal but complete documentation by simply having a digital camera handy to snap shots of the panels as they evolve.

As pairing "turns the knobs up to ten" on co-location (see Chapter One), there are many lessons to be learned from it. For instance, Laurie Williams and Robert Kessler have published a book on pairing that provides advice, in the form of short chap-ters, on many possible pairings.[19] Here's a short sample:

- *Expert-expert:* Great for completing the most complex tasks well, but the key to making this pairing work is mutual respect.
- *Expert-novice:* Accomplishes a task while training the novice, but the expert must be willing to teach in a master-apprentice relationship, not just take over the work and do it all.
- *Extrovert-extrovert:* Can provide very creative solutions, but the partners must have the discipline to stop talking and get on with the task.
- *Introvert-introvert* (very common among technical people): Excellent solution to the task, but partners must find a way to overcome a natural tendency not to communicate.
- *Gender combinations:* A nonissue, except that men and women tend to communicate differently, men more about things and women more about feelings.

The conclusion is that almost any combination can work, but each type fits a certain objective best. Because co-location—especially pairing—is designed to enhance communication, the benefit is realized only if lots of communication actually takes place. Consequently, anything that inhibits communication will reduce performance—failing to keep talking, feeling supe-rior, feeling inferior, being unwilling to share. This last item goes back to the Level X person mentioned in Figure 6.2; such people inevitably degrade a co-located team, no matter how brilliant they may be.

Pairing might be an interesting idea, but does it apply out-side software development? Yes. One co-located team I advised was developing a robot for electronic assembly. They placed the mechanical engineer next to the manufacturing engi-neer, because many of the designs they'd tried in the past had turned out to be unmanufacturable. It took awhile to get into a rhythm, but these two engineers established a norm that before the mechanical designer went to his workstation to start a new part, he grabbed the manufacturing engineer, and the two of them went to the whiteboard to discuss alternative concepts—mix, match, and compare them—which is pairing. Once they agreed on a manufacturable concept and its critical features, the mechanical engineer went to his workstation to detail it.

It is noteworthy is that both the Olsons and Williams and Kessler found, as did Reinertsen and I in our surveys, that participants are reluctant to try co-location at first, but after experiencing it, they readily see its advantages.

Partially Co-Located

Co-location enhances team performance greatly, and I strongly recommend it whenever you can assemble a team from the same metropolitan area. The more innovative the product and the more the project is subject to change, the greater the rewards of co-location. If you cannot justify some members, such as those from Marketing, being on the team full time, provide a desk for them in the team area and make sure that they occupy it when they are scheduled to be with the team.

However, in today's global workplace, it is becoming a luxury to draw a team all from one city. In this case, you can realize many of the benefits of co-location by recognizing what enables it and providing these features to the extent possible. Because dispersed teams are so common today, many books have appeared to help you obtain the most from your dispersed team. I divide these books into two groups. Some portray dispersed teams as the "modern solution" and suggest that contemporary communication technology can completely overcome distance (in contradiction of the Olsons' research discussed earlier) and even allow teams to flow around the world continuously working twenty-four hours a day. Others present a more realistic picture and provide tools and approaches for making the most of the situation. Deborah Duarte and Nancy Snyder provide an excellent book in the latter category; they are quite candid about the complications of running a dispersed team (quotations from this book):[20]

- These stories of lessons learned are based on firsthand knowledge of problems that occur in a virtual world that did not occur in the real world. The rapid maturing of virtual teams has created a new and different set of problems and opportunities for digitized disasters [p. xv].

- There are seven critical success factors for virtual teams, of which technology is only one. The others are human resource policies, training and development for team leaders and team members, standard organizational and team processes, organizational culture, leadership, and leader and member competencies [p. 10].

- [A myth] The added complexity of using technology to mediate communication and collaboration over time, distance, and organizations is greatly exaggerated [p. 79].

- Although [dispersed team members] may correctly calculate the difficulty of the technical task of the team, they may underestimate the extra time and effort that they need to spend in coordination and collaboration activities [p. 125].

- Leaders of virtual teams, however, report that recognizing conflict and performance problems is one of their most difficult management tasks [p. 204].

You can take steps to gain much of the benefit of co-location even if you cannot do it completely. And although disagreement on co-location is rife, everyone agrees on one item: if you can co-locate the team for any part of the project, do it initially. Mike Griffiths of Quadrus Development puts it this way: "I am happy to spend 70 percent of a project's travel budget up front to get people working face to face early in the project; it pays dividends later." Initial co-location builds trust and understanding at the outset. This is a wonderful time to establish common work methods for the team, given the sheer number of possible ways and styles of developing a product, some of which conflict with others. It also brings the team together for the part of the project where high-quality communication—including some hand-waving—is needed most: discussing rather fuzzy alternative product features and concepts. No need for special team-building exercises—you can do productive work while building the team. For example, any group will find plenty of challenging team-building material in defining the product and the project. However, include some natural social occasions, such as a dinner together, for more informal interaction and bonding.

Often, you will find the team split among a few widely separated areas, perhaps some members in Melbourne, some in Birmingham, and some in Dongguan. Try to co-locate each of these groups within its facility rather than having members spread across that facility. A related approach is to divide the product into relatively independent modules (see Chapter Three) and assign a co-located team to each module. This takes advantage of the high cohesion within a module and weak coupling between modules that is characteristic of modular architectures.

Another approach is to analyze communication patterns for the team, as in Figure 6.5. This figure shows who spoke to whom on a certain day. The heavier arrows signify more numerous conversations. Technically, these are called directed graphs, and you can obtain software for drawing them and automatically rearranging them to place the heavy communication in the center. From this diagram, it is clear where the bulk of the communication occurs, and you can make co-location of this portion of the team a priority.

When doing this type of analysis, sample the team at various times over a period. On a particular day, communication might be biased heavily by a particular problem being resolved that day. Base co-location arrangements on long-term communication patterns.

If most of your team is within walking distance, a daily stand-up meeting can help greatly to keep the team focused. This is standard fare for agile software development teams, and they have

Figure 6.5   Team Communication Patterns

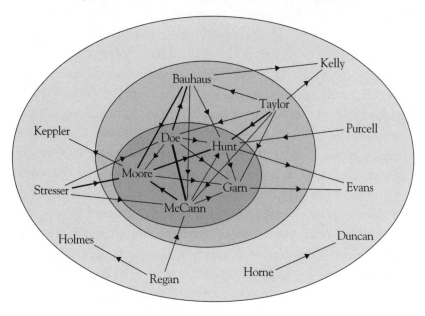

developed norms to make such meetings especially effective:

- Maximum length: fifteen minutes.
- Same time and place each day.
- Stand up in a circle (no chairs).
- Pigs only; cows may observe.
- Three questions answered at each meeting by each team member:
    What did I do in the last twenty-four hours?
    What do I plan to do in the next twenty-four hours?
    What obstacles stand in my way?
- Team leader notes and resolves obstacles.
- No problem solving; if problems arise, they are noted and resolved offline.

If a member or two of your team is remote, they can participate by speakerphone.

Consider how C-Cor, a provider of broadband network equipment and management software solutions, uses stand-up meetings for a broadly dispersed team. Most of the team is in their Connecticut (Eastern U.S.) headquarters, so this is where the stand-up meeting occurs, following the norms just listed. However, some team members are in Pennsylvania (about three hundred kilometers, or two hundred miles from Connecticut), Oregon (Western U.S.), Mexico, the Netherlands, and Serbia. Monday through Thursday the meeting occurs at 9:00 AM in Connecticut, and it is videotaped. This file goes on the company network for others to watch. On Fridays, the meeting shifts to 1:30 PM to allow other members in the United States and Mexico to participate by speakerphone, and although it is late there, even the Netherlands and Serbian members can participate. Also, the Netherlands member spends half of his time in Connecticut. Observe how C-Cor has honed a solution carefully to suit its needs. Jim Callahan, PMP, the senior program manager, notes, "Now issues are brought up in less than twenty-four hours, which means they are resolved quicker. When members resolve issues, complete a task, or take an initiative, the team celebrates immediately in a small way."

Electronic Communication

Electronic means of communication are commonplace today, and, as just noted, are vital for dispersed teams that must rely on them. Although what follows applies in general to any means of electronic communication, I focus on e-mail here because it is so common. In fact, it is too common, to the extent that it is probably today's most overused technology, according to Deborah Duarte and Nancy Snyder.[21]

Managers often receive a hundred e-mail messages per day, so sentences—and complete messages—are lost and response times are excessive, especially when the project is changing quickly. Consequently, anything the team can do to improve its e-mail communication will help greatly. I suggest that you do this by agreeing, as a team, on some norms that everyone uses for team e-mail. I will provide a few examples, but you should examine some recent failures in your e-mail communication and then create norms to correct these defects.

A common problem is not receiving a reply or an excessively slow reply. Here, you can stipulate that any team e-mail will receive a reply in N hours or N days (the team decides what is reasonable for N). The reply might be only that the e-mail was received but that the recipient is overloaded now. Or the norm can go beyond this and stipulate when a substantive reply will be sent. Again, the team decides on how to structure these norms, based on past e-mail failures balanced against members' tolerance for rules.

A similar problem is that, despite replying, the recipient does not take the action that the sender requests. This often happens because the sender buried the action desired in a long e-mail message, and the recipient simply didn't notice it. In this case, the norm might be that any requested action always appears in the last paragraph or in the subject line.

Sometimes the team e-mail is lost in a mass of other messages. Here the norm could be to put the project name or number in the subject line so that other team members can filter their mail on this item.

Finally, sometimes an issue bounces back and forth several times via e-mail without resolution. The norm here might be that if an issue is unresolved in one round, the sender must pick up the telephone and call. (Such breakdowns are often due to differing underlying assumptions, which can usually be resolved in seconds on the telephone.)

The possibilities are countless, but this illustrates the concept. Sometimes you can apply these norms on a broader scale. For instance, one company noticed that the "Reply all" button was causing e-mail proliferation in the natural desire to keep everyone informed, so the corporate Information Technology Department removed the "Reply all" buttons from everyone's computer.

Summary

Here are the important points on teams:

- Individuals and their interactions are a far richer area for improved performance than are process and tools improvements.
- Seed critical positions in the team with Level 3 (fluent) individuals, and remove any Level X (uncooperative) ones immediately.
- Seek to place dedicated (full-time), committed individuals on the team (send the cows out to pasture); encourage generalists, who are naturally flexible.
- Determine, at the outset, what authority the team has and what authority would be most beneficial.
- Do not write off co-location, even for a global team.
- If you are heavily dependent on electronic communication, analyze your communication failures and establish team norms for communicating.

7

DECISION MAKING

Hang on to the agony of a decision as long as possible.

—*Robert Spinrad*[1]

Decisions are at the heart of the product development process, whether your process is a formal, structured one or an unwritten and ad hoc one. If you dissect this process, you will find that it reaches down to decisions at its core—decisions made every day, thousands of them altogether. This is the inner loop of the development process. In contrast, most authors emphasize the major, formal decisions made between stages of a phased process.[2]

It follows that if you wish to improve product development, you should concentrate on improving decision making. This inner loop is where programmers concentrate to improve the performance of their code. They make this loop run faster, often by programming it in a low-level language, which takes more programming effort but results in faster execution by using a minimum of machine instruction cycles.

However, what you do to improve decision making depends on your objective for development. You have several choices:

- To make your development process faster, use approaches that will speed up every decision loop, such as co-located, cross-functional teams, low-level decision authority, and an empowered team leader (see Chapter Six).

- To make the process more certain (for life-critical system development, for example), use methods that double-check each decision, such as sign-offs on many defined kinds of decisions.

- To make the process more efficient (more new products per unit of human or financial resources), make decisions to minimize rework—do-it-right-the-first-time.

- Finally, to make the process more flexible, emphasize flexibility in making decisions by keeping options open, not making decisions until necessary, collecting information on a decision early to help you make it faster later, and related techniques.

Such flexible decision-making approaches are the subject of this chapter.

Improving Decision-Making Flexibility

Chapter Five (on set-based design) aims at improving flexibility in decision making by building and maintaining options, by not making decisions prematurely, and by making decisions progressively. There the emphasis is on managing the design space to preserve options, and here it is on the actual process of decision making.

The Last Responsible Moment

The most important point about making decisions flexibly is *not* to make them until they must be made. As Robert Spinrad puts it, stay with the agony of a decision. This may seem rather obvious, but it tends to oppose what is normally regarded as good management. For example, phased development processes attempt to specify everything as completely as possible before development starts, as this minimizes skipped tasks and items left to chance. Unfortunately, such completeness also limits options unnecessarily at the outset, as shown in Figure 7.1. Chapter Five included several examples from Toyota, showing how the company deliberately maintains considerable flexibility until late in development—in contrast to competitors, Japanese and foreign. This is not normal for management, and Toyota management works hard to delay decisions.

Figure 7.1   Creating a Flexibility Opportunity

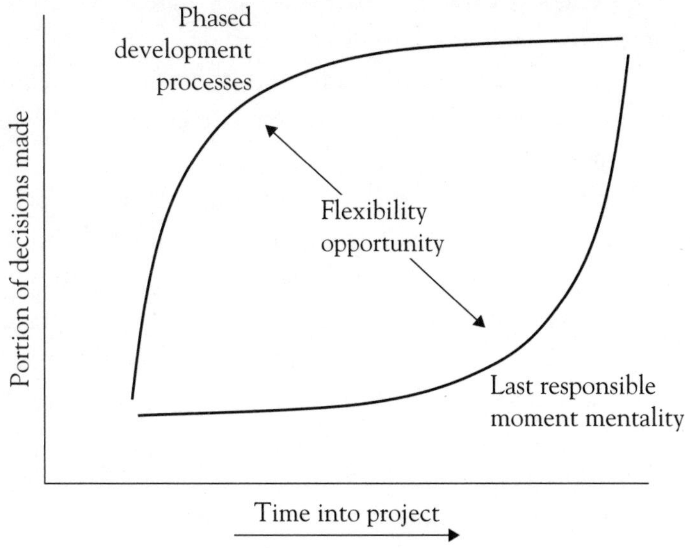

Source: Figure suggested by Jon Marshall and Innovation Frameworks LLC.

An aid for helping you delay decisions is the concept of *the last responsible moment*.[3] The last responsible moment is the earliest of the following occasions:

- An important option expires, leaving you with less attractive options.
- An important source of information or assistance in making the decision becomes unavailable.
- The decision goes onto the critical path, delaying the whole project.
- The risk to the project is about to increase as a result of further delay.
- The expense of carrying the decision rises greatly.

There may be other triggering conditions, but these are the ones I have observed.

Sometimes a decision links with something critical that will expire at a certain time. For instance, perhaps a design option needs prototype testing before you can decide on it one way or the other, and you know that Angela Brown, the test technician, will go on maternity leave in August. You have to complete the testing by August or you lose her availability.

The critical path of a project is defined by those tasks that, if one of them slips by one hour, the completion date of the project automatically moves out by one hour. Slippage on the critical path is costly, and usually it is not worth delaying the project by allowing a decision that affects it to slip. However, until a decision reaches the critical path (that is, while it still has some slack), there is often no penalty for letting it slip.

Rising risk is a common situation that triggers a decision. Suppose that you plan to use a new, unfamiliar technology, but you do not have an engineer free to assess it. The longer you delay your decision to assess this technology, the higher the risk to project success becomes.

More generally, an option can have a cost associated with it that is nonlinear: it remains low for a period, and then jumps. For example, say you need to have a mockup built, and you know that Walt Thompkins could fit it in now for next to nothing. But if you wait for two months, the upcoming Omega project will consume Walt's time and you will have to go to an outside model maker, paying market rates.

Observe that delaying a decision helps in two ways. First, it adds flexibility, because the cost of reversing (changing) a decision is nearly zero until it is made (as long as you have not passed the last responsible moment). Second, decisions usually require information, and your information becomes better over time. If you delay a decision, you can usually make a better decision, because it draws on fresher, more complete information.

Here is an example of using the last responsible moment, supplied by Mike Cohn of Mountain Goat Software. He was leading a team developing a desktop client-server application where time to market was essential. For several reasons, Java was the preferred language for the application, but most of the developers were experienced only in Visual Basic. They faced a decision: go with the preferred Java and train the developers in it or stay with Visual Basic where their experience resided. Instead, Cohn's team started with some of the middle-tier portions that would be written in C++ in either case for performance reasons while they collected information on how quickly their developers could learn Java. This gave them six weeks in which to learn and make a better decision on the primary language.

The ultimate in waiting, of course, is that in waiting, the decision will be made automatically—the procrastinators' dream. However, in waiting this long, you may have passed the last responsible moment, allowing an important option to expire and leaving you with a poor default option—the procrastinators' curse.

Applying the Last Responsible Moment Responsibly

It is quite important to distinguish the last responsible moment from procrastination. Procrastination is being lazy about a decision; applying the last responsible moment is instead an active process. First, you determine when the last responsible moment will occur, that is, you establish a deadline for the decision and schedule it. Then you determine the information needed to make a good decision and proceed to obtain this information. Often, this information is not free, so suspending a decision requires a commitment of money or time, which again is quite different from procrastination.

To use the last responsible moment effectively requires discipline about scheduling decisions and collecting information so you can make the decision when its time arrives. For a major decision, this might entail adding tasks and resources to the project plan, but even for minor ones, the decision's deadline and the information needed to make it should appear on someone's to-do list.

Also, using the last responsible moment is not an excuse to vacillate on a decision. Once a decision has been made, all parties commit to sticking with it—unless, of course, a significant change forces you to reverse the decision. As discussed in Chapter One, the last responsible moment is not an excuse for sloppy planning, hoping that improved flexibility will compensate for any lack of rigor.

However, it is acceptable, and even advisable, to make a decision progressively, as covered in Chapter Five. This allows you to extend the last responsible moment concept even longer, gaining even more of its benefits. That is, if you do not make a decision progressively, its last responsible moment is determined by the earliest last responsible moment for any part of it. Working progressively also allows you to work iteratively on the decision, building experience and confidence from an early part of it and adjusting before moving into a more costly phase. Finally, approaching a decision in steps removes some of the pressure from making it, because the risk at any single decision point is lower.

Finally, the last responsible moment is not always the best strategy. In some cases, it is better to make a decision early and put it behind you. For example,

- Sometimes the decision is clear and not likely to change, and then it is best to remove it from your agenda.
- Sometimes the decision can be reversed easily (that is, it has a low cost of change).
- If too many decisions are close to the critical path, overall schedule risk increases, because the likelihood of one of these decisions going awry rises as their sheer number rises.

People and Decisions

It hardly needs stating that people make the decisions, but this is important to remember. The uncertainty inherent in decision making and the differing interests of various parties turn decision making into a complex and difficult social activity. This is why this chapter follows the one on teams and people factors. A strong team structure is essential to making effective, sustainable project decisions.

Decisions made within the project team are usually better ones than those imposed from the outside. People internal to the project have the freshest and most complete information from which to make the decision, and they will be more motivated to carry it out if it is their decision. However, to make the decision, they must have the authority to do so, as covered in Chapter Six.

In addition, team members must have a willingness to share information and be willing to consider the larger good of the whole team, placing it above their own personal interests. The qualities of dedication and commitment discussed in Chapter Six play heavily in building a collaborative atmosphere. Clearly, Level X people interfere with collaboration.

Reaching Consensus

Whenever a group makes decisions, the question of consensus arises. Consensus does not mean that everyone agrees with the proposal. Arriving at such unanimity would take too long and is not necessary. What is necessary is complete agreement that the team can move forward together. Conversely, what a team cannot tolerate is people who do not agree with the decision, withhold participation, and come back later saying, "I told you so."

The concept of a *decision gradient* is helpful for polling a group to see if there is a sufficient degree of consensus for moving ahead.[4] A decision gradient has three essential levels:

- I agree and commit to the proposal.
- I am neutral but will commit to the proposal so that we can move forward.
- I cannot support the proposal (veto).

Another level between neutral and veto can be helpful:

- I have reservations but will commit to the proposal
so we can move forward.

The way you use these levels is to poll everyone. If there are any vetoes, you do not have consensus, and you need more work before moving forward. Even with no vetoes, if there is a preponderance of votes for the neutral level and especially for the reservations level, this is a red flag to have more discussion or to explore other options; your consensus is likely to unravel before long.

Experienced consensus builders sometimes use one other level (which would go at the top of the list):

- I am not ready to decide yet, because I lack enough information.

This level can be very helpful, because when it draws a response, it can indicate missing information that, when provided, turns some of the neutrals into strong supporters, thus solidifying the consensus.

Following the advice in Chapter Four (on experimentation), I suggest taking a consensus poll on a proposition early and often (that is, front-load it). You may have attained consensus already and discover that you can save time by moving on rather than debating matters further. Also, taking a poll early may indicate where discussion is needed or what information is lacking.

Your votes can be written or by a show of hands. A fast way to handle the three basic levels is with a show of thumbs: thumbs up, thumbs sideways, or thumbs down.

Consensus voting ensures that the proposal is attractive, that the process is fair, that the outcome is sustainable, and that the group is confident that it has done as well as it can. Sustainability is the key item here. Note that this degree of solidarity is not needed for every decision. This is a relatively heavy-duty tool for use only on decisions that are important, complex, or politically sensitive.

These are the basics of building consensus. Some corporate cultures are quite dysfunctional about reaching consensus, with passionate (or tedious) continuing discussions about technology alternatives, a right of infinite appeal, or any number of other possibilities. These are beyond the scope of this book.

Uncertainty and Decisions

A hallmark of decisions is uncertainty. In a situation with no uncertainty, a decision is usually clear—and thus uninteresting.

Because of this, decision making is not perfect and cannot be expected to be perfect. A good decision can result in a bad outcome, and a bad decision can yield a good outcome. For instance, if you are concerned about rain today, you can use a thorough decision-making process: looking out the window, consulting the latest weather forecast, and calling the friend you are going to visit to ask if it is raining there before deciding not to take an umbrella on your journey. Nevertheless, you might encounter a thunderstorm and ruin your new suit. On the other hand, you can ignore all of this and head off without an umbrella, escaping the downpour because you happened to be indoors eating with your friend when it happened.

Consequently, it is not a matter of eliminating bad outcomes but rather one of using good practices that will reduce the chances of bad outcomes. Flexibility makes it possible to recover more easily from the bad outcomes.

Note also that because flexibility aims at dealing with uncertainty, decision making is a core flexibility tool in that it deals directly with managing uncertainty.

Reducing Uncertainty

Change and uncertainty go hand in hand, so uncertainty is likely to be a big part of any project where you wish to apply flexibility tools. Thus it is valuable to find ways of reducing uncertainty. Again, these tools will not eliminate uncertainty, but they can reduce the chance of bad outcomes significantly.

Product development employs two predominant ways of reducing uncertainty, and I cover these in Chapters Two and Four. Much uncertainty comes from customers and their changing or poorly understood needs. By keeping in touch with customers, as suggested through many examples in Chapter Two, you can "walk in their shoes" and appreciate where they might be likely to want change.

Experimentation (Chapter Four) is more of a general tool that allows you to understand customers, markets, technologies, design choices, and manufacturing difficulties better, thus reducing uncertainty. Consequently, when you notice an area of uncertainty in a project, train yourself to ask, What kind of experiment could I run to understand this uncertainty better?

In some industries, especially high-tech ones, a significant amount of uncertainty stems from evolving industry standards. One way of dealing with this uncertainty is to volunteer to serve on the industry board developing the standard. This provides insight into where the standard is likely to go—as well as an opportunity to steer it in your direction.

Finally, much change in industry today is organizational uncertainty: changes in the players and their roles. Managers receive new assignments, and top management changes strategies. Ongoing networking, chatting at the water cooler, and so forth are your best sources of information on such changes. Also, make sure your project has an executive sponsor who is watching for shifts in management direction.

Decision Trees

Now I move from general guidance on making decisions that maintain or enhance flexibility to a specific tool called a *decision tree* (sometimes called decision analysis), which is especially helpful and easy to use for understanding decisions involving uncertainty.[5] With decision trees you can explore a decision's possibilities so that you understand the options and their consequences and likelihoods. Such trees are especially helpful for understanding linked decisions, so that if you make one decision, you appreciate the decisions that it opens or closes for you. All this is valuable for maintaining flexibility in the midst of change.

Always remember that decision trees offer only a model of reality, and as with most models, they can be pushed past their limits. A model only partially represents the reality being modeled. If you mismodel a key part, the tree can lead you astray. Garbage in yields garbage out. As the statistician George Box put it, "All models are wrong. Some models are useful."

It follows that a decision tree is more useful for the insight it provides and the questions it raises than it is for actually helping you to make the decision. Consequently, actually creating a decision tree or analyzing it is more instructive than looking at one created by someone else.

Figure 7.2 illustrates a simple tree for a decision of whether to use a new technology or keep the existing one. If you decide on the new technology, it might be ready on time (20 percent

Figure 7.2 Simple Decision Tree, Showing Nomenclature

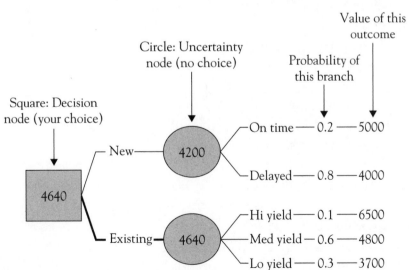

chance estimated) or it might be delayed by engineering problems. But if you choose to keep the existing technology, you have a chance of low manufacturing yields (30 percent) or medium yields (60 percent) because you will have to push this older technology to obtain the performance that your new product requires.

The conventions for drawing decision trees are well established. Referring to Figure 7.2, a square denotes a decision that you can make, whereas a circle represents uncertainty over which you have no control. Uncertainty nodes always have probabilities associated with each branch, and these always sum to unity for a node. Both decision nodes and uncertainty nodes may have two or more branches. The tree reads from left to right as time advances. At the final (right-hand) end are the outcomes, sometimes called the *leaf nodes* in keeping with the tree metaphor.

The values shown on the leaf nodes and in the circles and squares should be a consistent set in the same units. Often, they are profit or a similar financial measure. They could also be units manufactured or sold over a certain period or another measure of goodness or utility. To make this example more concrete, assume that the values in Figure 7.2 are all project profit in euros.

Although the tree reads from left to right, the calculations proceed from right to left. For an uncertainty node, the value of the node is the sum of the products of the outcomes and probabilities feeding into it, for example, $0.2 \times 5000 + 0.8 \times 4000 = 4200$ at the top of Figure 7.2. For a decision node, its value is the best (largest or smallest, depending on which is good) of the values feeding into it, in this case, 4640; I have drawn the 4640 line heavier to indicate that this is the preferred choice. The value of this tree is 4640, as shown in the root node on the left.

You obtain values for the outcome or leaf nodes by building a profit (or similar) model for the decision situation and adjusting the parameters in it to agree with the assumptions of that leaf node, thus calculating each leaf's value from the common model. More generally, you can use a more general measure of utility if different leaves employ different measures, for instance one leaf could be measured in savings while another reflects customer satisfaction, while the common measure that ties them together is utility.[6]

Figure 7.3 is an expanded and more interesting version of Figure 7.2. Now if the new technology is delayed, you can decide whether to act by adding more people or to do nothing. If you decide to add more people, it might bring the project back on schedule or it might not. Similarly, if the yield is low, you could decide to redesign the offending parts or do nothing, and if you redesign, it could improve the yield or not.

Figure 7.3 shows how a decision tree can illuminate a decision and enable discussion of it, although decision trees can be much more complex than this (the complexity of a tree is limited only by what you can print on a sheet of paper or see on a screen). Another way to use a decision tree is through sensitivity analysis, as shown in Figure 7.4, which also originates from Figure 7.2. On the left is a sensitivity table for the new-technology uncertainty, and at the bottom is a sensitivity table for the three-branch uncertainty. Either can be created quickly in spreadsheet software.

You can use these tables in two ways, to determine how sensitive a decision is to a specific uncertainty or to understand the value of improving a probability. To understand the former, observe the table on the left of Figure 7.4. It shows that the probability of being on time would have to rise to about 0.6 before the decision would shift to the new technology. The latter use of the tables is apparent in the one at the bottom of Figure 7.4. It shows that if you could raise the medium-yield probability to 0.9 (by eliminating the low-yield possibility), the value of the decision would rise by 330 to 4970, that is, it would be worth investing up to 330 euros to shift the low yield to medium yield. In addition, it quantifies the additional potential of shifting the medium yield to high yield. With this kind of information, you are in a better position to decide whether to pursue the existing technology or move to the new one.

These decision trees all relate to a technology decision. Figure 7.5 is another example exploring a strategy and marketing decision. Suppose that your company is located in the United

Figure 7.3 Expanded Version of Figure 7.2, Showing Downstream Decisions and Uncertainties

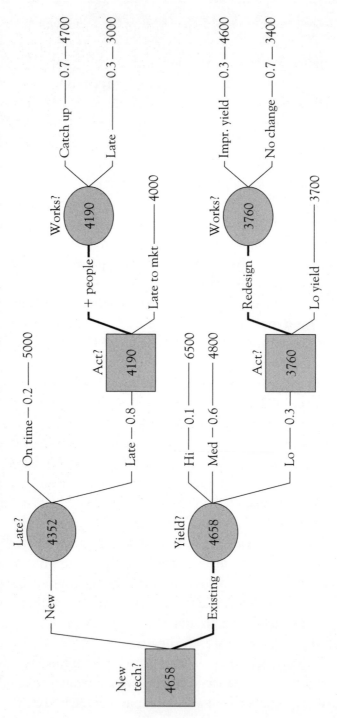

Figure 7.4   Sensitivity Tables for the Uncertainties in Figure 7.2

On-time sensitivity

0.2	4200
0.3	4300
0.4	4400
0.5	4500
0.6	4600
0.7	4700
0.8	4800
0.9	4900
1	5000

New — 4200
- On time — 0.2 — 5000
- Delayed — 0.8 — 4000

4640

Existing — 4640
- Hi yield — 0.1 — 6500
- Med yield — 0.6 — 4800
- Lo yield — 0.3 — 3700

Yield sensitivities

		High yield				
		0.1	0.2	0.3	0.4	0.5
Medium yield	0.6	4640	4920	5200	5480	–
	0.7	4750	5030	5310	–	–
	0.8	4860	5140	–	–	–
	0.9	4970	–	–	–	–
	1	–	–	–	–	–

States (where 110 volts is the common electrical service), and you are starting a project to develop a heating pad. The Marketing staff might continue with their domestic market or decide to pursue a global one. If they remain domestic, they might produce a 110-volt model aimed mostly at those who do not travel internationally, although there is a small chance that some international travelers will buy it, either because they only travel to countries using 110 volts or because they are unaware that most of the world uses 220 volts. Or Marketing staff might decide on a dual-voltage model. This would be ideal for a minority who travel abroad, but its extra manufacturing cost would put it at a disadvantage against the competition for the non-traveler.

If the Marketing staff decide to go global, they estimate a 70 percent chance that they will find an acceptable partner to handle the foreign part of the business. If not, they will build a dual-voltage

Figure 7.5 Decision Tree: Marketing and Strategy Decisions for an Electric Heating Pad

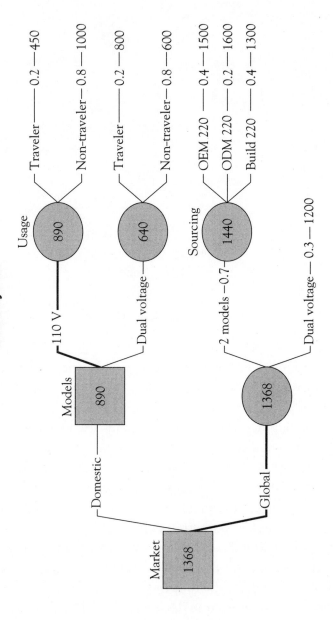

model themselves and attempt to distribute it globally. Should they find a partner, they would produce a 110-volt model in the United States for the world market, and the partner could proceed in one of three ways on the 220-volt market:

- OEM (original equipment manufacture), providing drawings and specifications from which an overseas manufacturer could produce it
- ODM (original design manufacture), providing only product requirements from which the overseas firm would both design and manufacture it
- Design and build the 220-volt model in the United States for export

At this point, you might be thinking, "Why didn't they do [this]?" Or, "Isn't there a chance of [that]?" There is, and I invite you to redraw the tree as you see the situation. You will find that decision trees are quite flexible and are an excellent means of communicating and prompting a discussion about decisions involving uncertainty. They uncover options and question assumptions.

The Value of Perfect Information

I have advised you to start collecting information about a decision early (but delay making the decision itself), and I have suggested that this information both has value in making the decision and is likely to cost you something. How do you know how much to pay for information that will help you make a decision?

Sometimes sensitivity tables like the ones shown in Figure 7.4 can help you place a value on information that will improve your decision or its outcome. The value of the information in this case is the amount that the shift in probability raises the value of the node. In addition, decision trees offer a powerful way of calculating the value of having perfect information about a decision involving uncertainty.

By removing the uncertainty analytically, you can see how much it would be worth if you had perfect information about the uncertainty.

For example, think back to the Black & Decker cordless screwdriver shown in Figure 3.3. I have no information on how Black & Decker actually decided on the two-cell model, but they could have used decision trees as follows: Assume that the developers created the decision tree in Figure 7.6. This tree looks at the situation negatively. For each of the two model options, the tree shows the sales dollars to be lost from unhappy customers, so high (less negative) numbers are good. Suppose that they formulated three forecasts for the sales lost for each model, a high forecast that was relatively pessimistic, a medium (most likely) forecast, and a low (optimistic) one. With the numbers shown in Figure 7.6, you can see why they were having trouble deciding: it was simply too close to call.

Recall that you read a decision tree from left to right, so in this case, B&D had to decide on the number of cells first, and then find out which forecast was correct after they started selling that model. What if they could reverse the situation so that they knew which forecast was correct before deciding? This would make the decision easy. Fortunately, decision tree software can actually *flip* trees, or reverse their levels, analytically. Figure 7.7 shows this tree flipped. This says that if the high forecast prevails, they should launch the three-cell model, but for the medium or low forecast, they should

Figure 7.6   Decision Tree for Black & Decker Electric Screwdriver Batteries

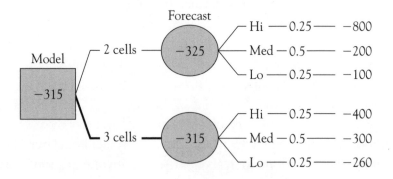

Figure 7.7 Flipped Version of Figure 7.6, Illustrating the Value of Perfect Information

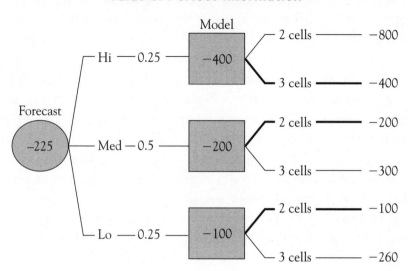

proceed with the two-cell model. Consequently, their next market research should concentrate on how likely the high forecast is. Furthermore, this information is worth US$90 (−US$225 minus −US$315) to them, because the value of the flipped tree increases by this amount.

You can't flip every decision tree. The tree must be symmetric, which means that everything except the values of the leaf nodes is symmetric. However, in many cases, a tree can be expanded by adding some dummy nodes to make it symmetric, or it can be simplified to a symmetric form. In a tree with more than two levels, you may have choices as to which levels you can flip, that is, which uncertainties you can "see" before you must decide at that level.

Decision Trees in Practice

As Figures 7.3 and 7.5 suggest, many development decisions are linked, that is, one decision leads to another. Decision trees are useful for discovering and emphasizing such linkages, and the linkages are important for managing flexibility. Often, the way in which you make one decision affects your downstream ability to make other decisions or pursue certain options. Anticipation is important for flexibility, and decision trees help you anticipate future events or at least their possibility.

That said, do not overdo anticipation. If you are in a volatile environment, the future will change and may become cloudy quickly. Nevertheless, a certain amount of anticipation is very valuable, and decision trees facilitate anticipation.

I mentioned at the beginning of the chapter that decisions are the "inner loop" of product development, and thousands of them occur. Many are simple decisions that must be made almost instinctively. Decision trees are overkill for these. Use decision trees for more important decisions and for more complex or controversial situations where you need extra clarity. Some decisions warrant a formal decision tree, created by software; sometimes a simple tree sketched on a napkin will resolve the decision, and sometimes even this is too much analysis.

As with most modeling tools, remember that the benefit of decision trees comes not from obtaining the right answers but from helping you formulate the right questions. This is why it is important not to be satisfied with reviewing someone else's tree but to try building one yourself.

I conclude this section on decision trees with a list of the many benefits this tool offers:

- Clarifies your thinking about a decision or a sequence of decisions
- Makes the general structure of a decision apparent
- Uncovers unknown factors and alternatives
- Shows flaws in your logic
- Illuminates future events
- Surfaces subjective or controversial factors (in advance)
- Suggests information you could gather to make the decision

- Quantifies how much this information is worth to you
- Displays your reasoning to others and documents it

Real Options Thinking

Flexibility in decision making raises the topic of real options with some people. If this includes you, you will enjoy this section. Otherwise, you may skip to the Summary section without missing anything essential to understanding the remainder of the book.

Real options stem from financial options, and the two are closely related. I describe financial options first, because they are easier to understand, and then proceed to real options.

An *option* is a contract whose purchaser has the right—but not the obligation—to exercise the contract (the option) on or before a future date. A financial option applies to publicly traded investments, such as stocks, bonds, or pork bellies. The type of option of interest here is a *call option*, which applies to buying the security (in contrast, a *put option* relates to selling it). Here's an example to illustrate the concept.

Suppose you are considering buying shares of a stock whose share price today is ¥100. However, you can't afford to make this investment today, although you believe the stock will appreciate considerably over the next year. So for ¥6 you purchase an option to buy this stock anytime in the next year for ¥110 (called the strike price). Then, say, the stock's price rises to ¥125 in the next year. You buy it at ¥110 with your option, and your return of ¥15 on your investment of ¥6 represents a pleasant gain of 150 percent. Should the stock never reach the ¥110 strike price (or should it decrease any amount in value), you simply let the option expire, and you are out only the ¥6 that you spent on it, a 100 percent loss on your investment.

An important observation related to financial options is that the riskier the underlying stock is, the more the option is worth. This occurs because your downside risk is limited to what you spent on the option (the 100 percent loss above), but your upside opportunity is unlimited. You will pay more for a call option on a junk bond than you will for a comparable option on a blue-chip stock. This characteristic is also important for real options.

A *real option* applies the same reasoning to a business investment, such as a new factory or a new product. Although the reasoning is the same, each business investment is unique—unlike financial options, which have a uniform framework—so you must calculate each one by going back to basics.[7] This quickly enters Ph.D.-level math. Due to their uniformity, the values of financial options (the ¥6 above) are calculated readily by using the so-called Black-Scholes formula, for which the 1997 Nobel Prize in Economics, in part, was awarded. The Black-Scholes formula depends on some assumptions that work well for financial securities but may not apply to business investments. For instance, it assumes that the underlying asset (the price of the stock for a financial option) cannot have a negative value.

The primary lesson from real options is that a future decision—an option—has more value the further into the future you can push the decision and the riskier it is. Real options theory quantifies these situations, but the qualitative relationship applies to most product development decisions.

A prime candidate for real options is an R&D (research and development) investment in a new product, and there is much literature and some controversy about this application.[8] All the discussion seems to focus on project valuation, that is, on deciding which development projects a company should undertake and whether they should continue pursuing them once started.[9] The basic model is that you do some R&D and then decide whether you will commercialize the product, which is usually a larger investment than the R&D one. in contrast, in the context of development flexibility, it would be helpful to apply real options at a lower level to reach decisions on how to proceed within R&D. Unfortunately, the literature seems to ignore this more frequent application.

One strong message from the real options literature is that riskier projects and decisions further into the future have greater value, just as a longer-range financial option on a riskier security is worth more. However, because this conclusion is dependent on some assumptions, such as the underlying asset (the potential profit from the prospective new product in the case of R&D valuation) being non-negative, which may not always be the case, it's necessary to be careful here. In most cases, however, real options thinking will lead you toward risky but attractive options at the project and at the subproject level.

Fortunately, real options are equivalent to decision trees for problems that are amenable to the latter, and decision trees employ far more comprehensible mathematics and more useful visuals than do real options.[10] Consequently, decision trees are convenient for running a flexible project, but real options thinking might be useful as an alternative way of understanding what you are doing.

Summary

Here are the important points covered in this chapter:

- The key objective in making flexible decisions is to make them at the last responsible moment.
- Holding out for the last responsible moment is far from procrastination, because it involves identifying and collecting information now that will help you make a better decision when its last responsible moment arrives.
- Consensus-building tools allow a group to make sustainable decisions.
- Because flexibility concerns dealing with uncertainty and decisions are intimately connected with uncertainty, decision making is a core flexibility-management tool.
- Try to make decisions progressively, which allows you to make each part of a decision at its own last responsible moment

while easing the pressure and risk of making the complete decision.

- Decision trees are a simple graphical technique for exploring a decision and the links between decisions; available software supports them well.

- Decision trees help you calculate the value of information that would help you make a better decision so that you know how much to spend on obtaining this information.

8

PROJECT MANAGEMENT

If you don't know where you're going, you might
not get there.

—Yogi Berra

In recent years, the project management profession has become
much stronger. Membership in the Project Management Institute,
the leading body of the profession, passed 200,000 in 2005 and is
growing strongly. This organization has published a guide to the
profession's body of knowledge, and it and others have published
countless pieces on project management practices.[1] Despite some
notable exceptions, such as Doug DeCarlo's *eXtreme Project
Management* and Jim Highsmith's *Agile Project Management,* as well
as the Agile Project Leadership Network (APLN.org), much of the
existing knowledge aims at what I will call "mainstream project
management," which emphasizes project predictability.[2] Predictability is an attractive objective, but unfortunately it stands in the
way of flexibility. My goal is to present project management techniques that enhance flexibility and help you understand how some
of the mainstream techniques can restrict flexibility, especially
when applied in a heavy-handed way.

Mainstream project management is ideally matched to projects
where change occurs relatively gradually. As the rate of change
increases, it becomes less suitable. It is not true that mainstream
project management is "bad" and flexible project management
is "good." Mainstream project management has a long history of
success in relatively stable and gradually changing environments
and is the most economical approach in these cases. But in highly
turbulent environments, it encounters several barriers—described

in this chapter—that make it less effective than more flexible approaches. As with much of the other material in this book, your best route will depend on the degree of uncertainty and change you face. You can use mainstream approaches in certain parts of your project and more flexible ones in other parts.[3]

In any case, project management is critical to flexible development. As Yogi Berra observes more colorfully than I can, without it, you might not get where you are going. It is not a matter of skipping project management—or even parts of it—but rather of employing alternative approaches that work better under rampant change or, in the best case, actually taking advantage of change. In a flexible project, you will probably be doing more project management than in a mainstream project, but it might not look like project management.

Flexible versus Mainstream Project Management

To set the stage for this chapter and highlight the distinguishing features of flexible project management, I make some contrasts in this section between mainstream and flexible project management. I do this not to downplay the mainstream approach but to sensitize you to the differences so you will understand the adjustments needed as you require more flexibility. Following this contrast, I provide approaches and tools for managing a project flexibly.

The root contrast is in the implicit view of change. Often, the mainstream project manager is motivated strongly to bring the project in on time and budget, so change is unwelcome. If possible, it should be avoided. In contrast, flexible project management is more likely to view change as normal, expected, and even as a source of competitive advantage; it thus emphasizes management methods that accommodate and even embrace change.

The Project Plan Is Not the Guide

Often, mainstream project management puts heavy emphasis on the project plan, including the schedule. Much work goes into creating and negotiating the plan. It usually covers the entire project and provides considerable detail. It essentially becomes a two-way contract with management: the team commits to achieving its plan, while management commits to providing the resources needed to achieve it. Project management software contributes to this plan-centric view of project management by making it easy to build schedules too complex to print on a single sheet of paper, even A3 (11"×17") paper.

This is acceptable and preferred when stability prevails; in many cases, you can establish a schedule for the entire project at its outset and follow it to completion with good results. However, in an environment of rapid or constant change, this kind of plan becomes an anchor that inhibits needed change. In this case, the project manager—and the team—often pay greater allegiance to the plan than is healthy. This occurs because of the sizable investment in the plan, its contractual nature, and the fact that management often measures and rewards the project manager in terms of adherence to the plan. So without a plan, what is there to guide us? Scary stuff.

An alternative scenario is that, facing considerable change, the project manager spends too much time maintaining the plan, continually on the computer keeping the project management model up to date and meeting with others to renegotiate commitments and resources. This leaves little time for actually running the project.

The primary problem here, as suggested, is excessive allegiance to the letter of the plan. Later, I suggest how you can plan a flexible project. But in an environment of turbulence, overemphasizing the plan is dangerous. The agilists have shifted the balance in the other direction: the Agile Manifesto (Exhibit 1.1) rebalances it as "Responding to change over following a plan."

As an illustration, consider how you might handle "corrective action." Say that changes have caused your project to follow a path different from the one specified in the plan. The mainstream response is "to bring expected future performance of the project work in line with the project management plan."[4] Notice that the presumption here is that the plan is correct and "corrective action" is needed against the "project work." Agilists instead replace *corrective action* with an emphasis on *adaptive action* that could change project execution *or* the plan, as appropriate.

Redefining Project Completion

Mainstream project management, centered on the project plan and its list of deliverables, tends to view project completion primarily in terms of delivering on this list. Thus the list of deliverables becomes the criterion for completion.

In contrast, agile software development has moved away from this concept. It executes the project in iterations, which are self-contained units of completion. Between iterations, the remaining project essentially is replanned, and the remaining list of deliverables (called the *backlog* in agile development) can be completely reorganized. Consequently, the original list of deliverables is only a starting point, never a commitment or a measure of project completion.

This leaves a vacuum: how will we measure completion and progress toward completion? The agilists have an answer: they turn to the customer and ask if the customer is receiving sufficient value yet. Because they do this on an iteration-by-iteration basis, the project can complete ahead of the original schedule by providing sufficient value with fewer features delivered than originally envisioned (see the discussion accompanying Figure 2.2), or it can go beyond the original plan by delivering more features than anticipated.

The essential difference is that the criterion for completion now becomes customer value rather than a list of deliverables. This shift in emphasis has much merit, but the difficulty is in defining customer value in a workable way. Many agile development projects involve information technology, where the customer is nearby and can be consulted relatively easily for satisfaction. Assessing customer satisfaction is more difficult for commercial off-the-shelf software or non-software products. Nevertheless, this is a reasonable goal, and iterative development helps achieve it.

Reorienting Quality

Likewise, the quality of the product and the development process must be reoriented for a flexible project. Mainstream projects often define product quality as a part of the product requirements. In addition, they may have corporate quality standards to satisfy. Although the corporate standards are likely to remain stable, the product requirements are likely to change in a volatile environment, so again, quality becomes more a matter of satisfying the customer. This is why I emphasize ongoing customer contact in Chapter Two.

In agile software development, product quality improves in another way. Mainstream development tends to be sequential (a waterfall process) in which quality problems in the code are hidden until a late stage when all of the code transfers to testers. In agile development, developers test a feature immediately after coding, finding quality problems far sooner and closer to the source. This makes it much easier to isolate and fix problems. You can apply this lesson to non-software products also: How can you test your designs earlier and closer to the source?

Mainstream project managers tend to measure development process quality in terms of following the plan, which creates measurement problems if the plan changes. It also inhibits change by penalizing teams and managers who do not follow the plan. Recall the MacCormack studies in Chapter Two: the project managers of the (commercially) successful projects did not believe they had been successful, because they did not follow the plan. In this case, rewards were not involved; these managers simply were unhappy with their work because they had been conditioned to follow the plan.

Again, development process quality, for a flexible project, depends on satisfying the customer, which is exactly the basis that MacCormack suggests. It is true that customer satisfaction measures are softer and more difficult to monitor than mainstream measures, but they are far more stable and meaningful in a changing environment.

Individuals Over Processes

Process is the framework of activities followed to complete a project. Mainstream project managers describe their job in terms of process. For example, the guide to the profession's body of knowledge, mentioned earlier, is organized around forty-four processes. Another popular book on project management builds the subject on a process framework: phases of conceive, define, start, perform, and close.[5] In contrast, the first value of the Agile Manifesto (Exhibit 1.1) is "Individuals and interactions over processes and tools." I emphasize this critical shift in emphasis in both Chapter Six and Chapter Nine.

The Role of Tacit Knowledge

In Chapter Nine I describe tacit (know-how) knowledge, contrasting it with explicit (know-what) knowledge. Explicit knowledge receives greater emphasis in mainstream project management, because it is easier to collect, communicate, and control. But tacit knowledge is more critical in a flexible project. In Chapter Nine I show that tacit knowledge fits with the emphasis on people over process and suggest ways of strengthening tacit knowledge.

The Role of a Flexible Project Manager

In product development, project managers go by various names. *Project* could instead be *team*, and *manager* could be *leader*, thus resulting in team leader (or other combinations). These distinctions bear some consideration, as they influence the emphasis placed on the role. Are you more interested in the project or in the team accomplishing it? The project may create business value, but

if the team lacks motivation, the project is unlikely to succeed. Is the role to manage or to lead? That is, should the incumbent focus on the tasks and data involved or on motivating and guiding the people accomplishing the work? For consistency in this chapter, I stick with *project manager,* but I urge you to choose the terms that fit your objectives best. Remember that the terms you choose will influence how these individuals approach their jobs and what others will expect of them.

Over years of observing project managers in action, I have reached conclusions about what makes for excellence, especially in a fast-moving project. Because most of the project management literature is structured around processes, the leadership qualities a project manager needs for executing those processes effectively are inevitably deemphasized. The following sections list what I believe to be the qualities of a superb manager of a flexible project.

Out in the Team Space

The software available for managing projects seems to hold a magnetic attraction for some project managers—especially when the project is in flux, unfortunately. The manager has invested a lot in building the project model and understandably does not want to see it decay as change makes it obsolete. Thus the compulsion to keep the model up to date is huge.

Admirable as keeping up the model may seem, it steals time from the foremost duty of a good project manager: spending time with team members to guide them and obtain a real-time, unfiltered view of what is really happening on the project. This is what Bill Hewlett and Dave Packard, founders of Hewlett-Packard, institutionalized as part of the HP Way: management by walking around (MBWA). It is simply a matter of visiting team members regularly to see how they are progressing and what difficulties they are encountering. Any level of management can practice it.

A big advantage of MBWA over updating the project model is that MBWA is a leading indicator of problems, whereas the model is a lagging indicator. Keeping in touch with the troops will tell you about problems when they start: a designer's child in the hospital, for example. The project management model will tell you about the consequences: a missed deadline on that designer's work.

In recent years a new villain has accompanied project management software at the computer: e-mail. We can spend the bulk of each day at the computer and in meetings, which makes time for MBWA that much more precious. I have actually helped managers schedule apparently random MBWA sessions on their calendars to make sure that they happen.

Supporting and Protecting the Troops

In Chapter Six, where I describe the daily stand-up team meeting, I mention that the project manager's role is not to run the meeting but to take action against any obstacles encountered by team members. This fits perfectly with the style of MBWA, as its goal is to keep team members working effectively on their tasks.

In some cases, for team members to work effectively, they must be shielded from distractions. The effective project manager buffers people so they don't get pulled away by old projects encountering difficulties, managers from other projects trying to recruit people from this one, or executives (the cows in Chapter Six) making "small assignments" or suggesting things they "might consider."

Clarifying and Enforcing the Product Vision

Chapter Two covers the product vision and its power to focus the team in the midst of change. The project manager is the owner of the product vision. This means preserving the vision, clarifying it, communicating it, and applying it repeatedly as a filter of new ideas that bombard the project. When new ideas or possible tasks appear, the project manager applies the vision filter, accepting them if they fit the vision and rejecting them otherwise (thus protecting the team).

Project Planning

Project planning presents a dilemma in a volatile environment. If you do not plan enough, you will not arrive at your destination, as Yogi Berra observes, but if you plan too much, you squander your planning effort on plans that become obsolete. So how do you go about avoiding this dilemma?

Planning versus Anticipation

Planning attempts to lay out in advance what *should* happen. Its objective is to create a plan: "A formal, approved document" that defines how the project is to be "executed, monitored and controlled."[6] When events change, you lose the effort that went into this planning. An alternative is a more open-ended process that might be called anticipation.[7] *Anticipation* is a matter of speculating about what might happen and collecting information about possible options so that you can respond effectively when change occurs.

Anticipation is also a wasteful process, because most of the scenarios considered will never happen, so a large portion of your work is for naught. However, if change dominates, your anticipation is more likely to be useful than your planning. Planning works best when change is unlikely; anticipation is the better choice when change is likely.

Anticipation involves collecting information about your options early, and often this information has a price in money or labor. Thus you must apply judgment as to how much the information is worth and be willing to pay relatively more for information about your most likely options. The alternative is planning, which also requires a labor investment. You make the trade-off between planning and anticipation based on your current judgment of the possibility of change, which can vary by subsystem or by project phase;[8] for instance, some parts of the system might employ more anticipation, while others might rely more on planning.

Anticipation is not procrastination. Instead, it is a forward-looking process willing to invest in the future, albeit with a diverse set of bets.

Rolling-Wave Planning

Rolling-wave planning resolves the paradox that we need plans to progress effectively, but long-range plans will require revision—constant revision in a constantly changing project. The solution is to combine a detailed short-term plan with a shallow top-level plan. Then, when you have exhausted the detailed plan, you roll the planning forward a step, planning in detail the next segment but leaving the remainder planned only in broad terms.

In practice, you might work with three levels of planning rather than two. Then you have a short-term detailed level, a moderately planned next segment, and everything else left in broad terms. As this wave rolls, the moderately planned segment receives detailed planning, and you plan the following segment moderately.

Figure 8.1 shows how this works for developing a bicycle. You decide to develop the drive train first, the frame and fork next, and leave the remainder of the bike until later. So the drive train receives detailed planning, you plan the frame and fork moderately, and the remaining subsystems appear only as a summary line on the chart. When you start the frame and fork, you do detailed planning for them and moderate planning for the brakes, leaving the wheels as only a summary line, and so forth.[9]

Rolling-wave planning has a natural bias to keep in mind. In doing shallow planning, it is easy to be too optimistic—to use sunny-day planning and miss the details and problems that consume time. Guard against this as you build the long-term shallow plan or provide a buffer on it to protect yourself.

Even though the top-level plans are intentionally shallow, it is always wise to spend time at the outset of a project understanding the key factors of success and the principal project risks so that you can monitor them throughout. Also observe that a great advantage

Figure 8.1   Rolling Wave Planning for a Bicycle: Detailed, Moderate, and Summary

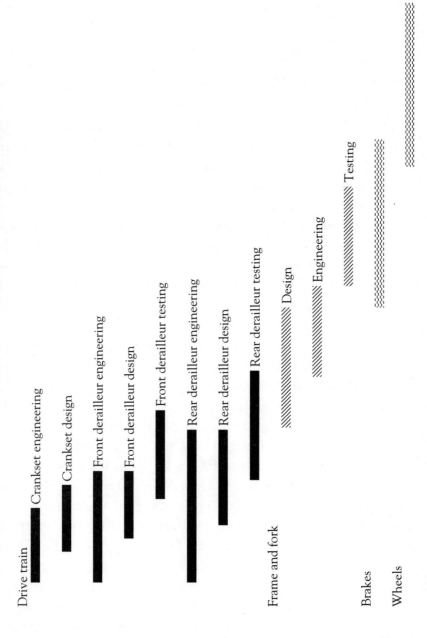

of rolling-wave planning is that it defers decisions on planning details, as covered in Chapter Seven. Consequently, it offers the benefits of deferred decisions: keeping options open and having fresher information when you make the decision.

Loose-Tight Planning

Agile software development takes a different approach to planning. Developers alternate periods of tight but short-term planning with open periods where they replan the remainder of the project freely. Their short iterations and tight customer involvement facilitate this, but their approach can be adapted to non-software projects.

At the beginning of an iteration, the team has available a so-called backlog, which is an unprioritized list of undeveloped product features. The marketing and customer members of the team prioritize this list based on customer value. Then the technical members estimate the effort required to develop the top items on the list, comparing it to the resources available for the iteration. When they have consumed their resources, they draw a line on the backlog list and develop the features above the line into working code in the next iteration.

This process, called the "planning game" in Chapter One, repeats in each iteration. Observe that the developers make no commitment to anything below the line on the backlog, so they can reshuffle it completely or add new items at each iteration. The process ends not when the backlog is exhausted but when the team judges that it has provided enough customer value or that the cost-benefit ratio of the remaining features suggests going to market instead.

Notice the interplay between the customer and marketing members and the technical members of the team. The former choose what is developed and the latter determine how much is developed in an iteration, based on their professional judgment.

However, they support this professional judgment with established estimating processes. Basically, the initial iteration is a guess, but from there on, the team keeps records of what it accomplishes per iteration, calculating what agilists call "velocity." They update their velocity in successive iterations, using it to establish how much they can seek to accomplish per iteration.

Although the marketing and customer members normally choose what is developed based on customer value, there is an important exception: risk. To manage well in an environment of uncertainty, the team must address high-risk items early. Consequently, especially in early iterations, they may place more emphasis on risk than on value. This requires more interplay between the technical members, who normally have a better understanding of technical risk, and the marketing and customer members, who will be prioritizing primarily on value.

Observe the overall pattern here: very tight planning without change during an iteration (typically one to four weeks) alternating with open periods where anything can change. Some agilists are so strict about this that they will abort an iteration rather than make any change in the feature set being developed within the iteration, while they encourage change between iterations.[10]

This loose-tight approach was also used by Boeing in designing its 777 aircraft. That development process alternated design and stabilization cycles. During the design cycles, the design was relatively open to change, and then it was frozen during the stabilization cycles to identify and correct design defects.[11] Although Boeing planned these change-freeze cycles into its process and they were discernable, the project's openness to change (say, in product features) was far more limited than observed in an agile software project, due to the huge investment involved, the enormous development team, the complexity of the product, and the regulated nature of the industry. However, this example illustrates that alternating cycles of change and stability do apply to non-software projects.

Timeboxing

A related technique from agile development is *timeboxing*. The idea is to specify a certain amount of work to be done in a fixed time box, such as an iteration, and to expect that this work be finished. By bringing the planning down to a detailed, predictable, measurable level, by prohibiting change within a box, and by being honest about what can be accomplished in a box of time and resources (such as by calculating the velocity, as covered in the preceding section), you can make the amount accomplished quite predictable. In this way, you can maintain control over the schedule and budget even when the content of the project changes.

Timeboxing is really about prioritizing, not about time. As Jim Highsmith, an author of the Agile Manifesto, puts it, "In my early years of iterative development, I thought timeboxes were actually about time—making sure things were accomplished within the specified timeframe. What I came to realize is that timeboxes are actually about forcing tough decisions."[12]

Although an agile iteration, as described in the preceding section, is a time box, you can generalize the time box concept to portions of an iteration or to other situations beyond iterations. For example, you could timebox what you will do from your to-do list in the next two hours, not allowing any change in the list until the two hours is over.

Expectations Management

The planning and timeboxing techniques are means of maintaining control of a project even in the face of great change. However, for many organizations, you might have noticed a cultural hurdle hidden in them. They require an honest assessment of what you can do with a given unit of resources. Too many organizations consistently try to put ten kilos into a five-kilo bucket, and the result is lost control of the schedule and budget. If such control is important to you, even in the face of rapid change, these techniques offer a great opportunity to improve. However, they will require

that you honestly estimate what you can reasonably do, based on your history, and stick to it. The challenge is not in the arithmetic; it is in changing a culture that consistently asks for more than can reasonably be expected.

Project Risk Management

As uncertainty and change rise, the importance of managing risk in a project rises correspondingly. In fact, for a fast-changing project, risk management *is* the means of managing the project. Here again, this differs greatly from the mainstream view that risk management is just one of several project management processes going on simultaneously.

As with other techniques covered in this book, your approach to project risk management depends on the level of change you face. As change and uncertainty rise, add the techniques covered here to mainstream risk management approaches. It is not a matter of simply replacing mainstream techniques with more flexible ones, because mainstream risks will still appear. However, you are likely to apply mainstream techniques in a shorter-cycle, more iterative way in changing environments.

Integrated versus Intrinsic Risk Management

You can approach project risk management in two ways. For a mainstream project with limited change, the Project Management Institute and numerous authors, including myself, provide multi-step processes for identifying, analyzing, prioritizing, and resolving your most serious risks.[13] When managed well, these planned risk resolution actions become additional tasks in the project with assigned resources, due dates, responsible individuals, and metrics, just like any other project task. I call this "integrated risk management": the risk management process is integrated with all other project management processes.

In the context of earlier parts of this chapter, there is a misfit here. Earlier I suggested that mainstream project plans with tasks planned for the length of the project will decay as change occurs. The same applies to risk resolution tasks integrated into mainstream project plans.

For a fast-changing project, risk management must move beyond simply being integrated to being intrinsic. In intrinsic risk management, running the project and managing its risk are identical. Everything you do in project management aims at managing risk:

- Using short iterations
- Keeping in close touch with customers
- Isolating change through architectural choices
- Emphasizing front-loaded prototyping
- Keeping options open through set-based design
- Enhancing team communication
- Making decisions at the last responsible moment
- Making decisions progressively
- Remaining aware of decisions beyond the current one
- Building consensus
- MBWA
- Seeking money-for-information opportunities (Chapter Nine)
- Building tacit knowledge (Chapter Nine)
- Managing your queues (Chapter Nine)

Risk Management and Iterative Development

I mentioned in the Introduction that one important topic does not have a chapter of its own: iteration, because it is so central to flexible development that it pervades the whole book. Iteration is also a core tool for managing risk. It cuts risk up into small, manageable pieces and provides early feedback on how the risks are progressing. Iteration allows you to sample customer feedback early, to do front-loaded prototyping, to give management confidence of making progress, and to calculate your velocity in completing work.

In short, it is very risky not to iterate when you face constant change.

That said, recognize that phased development processes do not fit well with iteration. Agilists faced the same obstacle with waterfall processes, where steps of a project flow sequentially with no opportunity to backtrack.[14] Many software developers have paid lip service to agile and iterative development but have not been able to break out of the waterfall process rut. Moving to iterative processes will be even more challenging for non-software development, simply because the cost of building and testing the product in each iteration is higher.

Managing Unknown Risks

Project risk management specialists speak of unknown unknown, or *unk unk*, risks. These are risks you simply will not know about until they happen to you. By definition, they are unidentifiable, so they fail the first step (identification) in a conventional risk management process. Until recently, the project risk management community discussed but did not have means for addressing unk unks.

However, a recent book addresses unk unks and provides approaches for addressing them.[15] This is a breakthrough for the field, because unk unks are quite likely in a project facing great change. I provide the basics here, but please see that book for details.

By definition, you cannot identify unk unks, but you can circumscribe them. This is a process of discovering where your knowledge of the project is the weakest; the unk unks are likely to be in areas where you know the least. Iteratively, you dig deeper into these areas to understand them better.

Once you have circumscribed the unk unks, you can use two methods to narrow your search. One is an iterative approach to home in on them and the other is simultaneous exploration, which you use when you are so uncertain that it is safer to try several

Figure 8.2   Two Ways of Approaching Unknown Risks

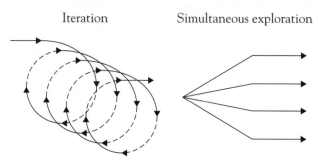

Iteration   Simultaneous exploration

independent approaches to improve your chances of avoiding dead ends. Figure 8.2 illustrates these two approaches, which are similar to those discussed in connection with Figure 4.5.

Dealing with unk unks requires a mind-set quite different from normal. Here a related book on managing the unexpected is useful.[16] This book describes a type of mindfulness the authors observed in those who deal with the unexpected professionally: air traffic controllers, military field commanders, and nuclear power station operators, for instance. These are the characteristics of this mindfulness:[17]

- A preoccupation with failure, which means immediately investigating any deviation from normal, because it might be a harbinger of bigger problems ahead
- Resisting simplification, because simplifying draws on old patterns and the unexpected is apt to be a new pattern
- Returning to basics, because existing procedures and standards might have assumptions built into them that hide unk unks
- Maintaining readiness, which recognizes that the unexpected will happen and constantly stays ready for it
- Pushing decisions down, where there is more specific expertise, a variety of views, and quicker response

This list, in sum, reminds me of a book that appeared several years ago by Andrew Grove, a founder and former CEO of Intel: *Only the*

Paranoid Survive. I am not recommending that book, but its title succinctly summarizes this mind-set—and it comes from someone who has demonstrated flexibility for years.

This type of risk management—managing unk unks and the unexpected—is radical and warrants application in its pure form only to projects that face huge amounts of uncertainty, but it indicates the direction that managing risk in a flexible project must move, which is a major departure from the procedural approach commonly practiced today. (My intention certainly is not to increase paranoia in the world!)

Project Metrics

Engineers and managers love to measure things, and metrics have moved from their roots in finance and manufacturing into product development. As the old saying goes, you can manage only what you can measure. The challenge is to extend metrics into the realm of the changing project in a helpful way.

Strategic versus Tactical Metrics

I find it useful to distinguish between strategic and tactical metrics, as they have different objectives and must be handled differently. A *strategic metric* is a long-term performance trend. A popular one in product development is a firm's percentage of sales stemming from products introduced within the last N years. Hewlett-Packard posted a chart of this metric, plotted against time, in its annual reports for several years. It showed management and stockholders how well HP was keeping its product line fresh, a vital sign for a high-tech company.

In contrast, a *tactical metric* indicates how well you are managing your development project. In the best case, it is a leading indicator of problems downstream.

Notice that, to be effective, a strategic metric must persist unchanged over a long period. HP's new-product percentage would have lost its power if the company had changed it every year, say by choosing a different value of N. In contrast, tactical metrics are usually transitory. Often, they arise to measure a problem you have discovered, such as long queues in the integration-testing lab. If you notice that your bottleneck is this queue, you might measure it daily until you fix it; then you abandon this metric, because it has served its purpose. (See Chapter Nine for more on bottlenecks and queues.) In other words, tactical metrics are part of your problem-solving tool kit and exist only as long as the associated problem exists.

A Flexibility Index

At the beginning of Chapter One, I defined flexibility as the ability to make changes in the product being developed or in how it is developed, even relatively late in development, without being too disruptive. It is admittedly difficult to measure against this definition, as every change is different and results in a different kind of disruption. Nevertheless, a strategic metric for flexibility would be useful to see if flexibility is improving over time. Here is such a metric.[18] Suppose your development process is divided into two phases, concept and implementation, as shown in Figure 8.3. The concept phase starts at the beginning of the project and ends at concept freeze, which is when further design changes are prohibited or highly discouraged. The implementation phase starts when you begin making models or

Figure 8.3 Phases Used for Calculating the *Flexibility Index*

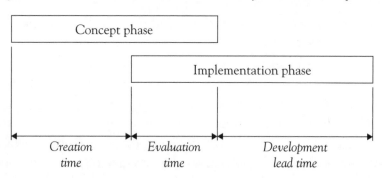

prototypes of the product and ends at market launch. Observe that in a normal phased development process, these two phases would be sequential (not overlapped).

From this figure, the metric, call it the *Flexibility Index*, is

$$Flexibility\ Index = \frac{Evaluation\ time}{Development\ lead\ time}$$

Note that the *Flexibility Index* is zero when there is no *Evaluation time* (no overlap), is unity when *Evaluation time* equals *Development lead time*, and reaches infinity as *Development lead time* tends to zero.

This metric will be useful only when you can define the time points involved. Defining the concept freeze point or the beginning of the implementation phase may be difficult. In particular, this index will not work well for a highly iterative process, such as those used in agile software development.

With a development process as shown in Figure 8.3, flexibility over the project would look like Figure 8.4 (compare Figure 8.4 with Figure 1.4). In connection with Figure 1.4, I emphasized that

Figure 8.4 Project Flexibility for a Project with Two Overlapping Phases

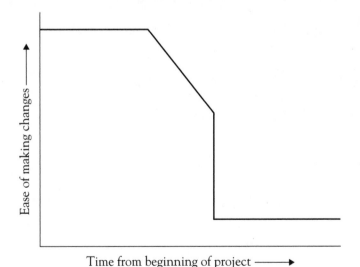

more flexibility was not necessarily better and have reinforced since then that flexibility is only valuable if you face change; otherwise it is costly. Consequently, although the *Flexibility Index* measures flexibility, the goal is not always to increase it but to compare your current state of flexibility with that required for competitiveness in your business.

Burndown Chart

A popular tactical metric used in agile software development is the *burndown chart*, which measures the amount of work remaining versus time or iteration. Figure 8.5 is a burndown chart used to write this book. After I had written the initial part so that I could estimate its size and content, I estimated the remaining word count (65,000), and every Friday afternoon I counted the words I had written in total and plotted the estimated words remaining to write. Such a chart clarifies how you are doing against plan.

Figure 8.5   Project Burndown Chart for Writing This Book

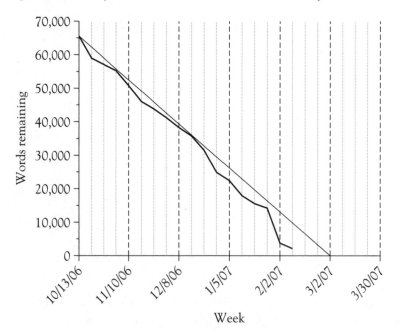

If you use a burndown chart, it is important that it measure *work* remaining. Agile developers normally use product features or story points (from the user story technique described in Chapter Two). You can also use labor hours if they relate to estimated hours of work actually remaining and not to the original planned hours minus the hours expended to date (which can be misleading if you are not accomplishing work at the rate originally planned). To use labor hours, you generally must estimate each task initially by hours and then sum these initially estimated hours for all remaining tasks to be completed.

Although the chart in Figure 8.5 fell continuously, it can also "burn upward" if the project's scope increases, for instance if I had added a chapter to the book. In fact, this is an advantage of burndown charts: scope increases are usually quite apparent.

Team Mood

Teams often assume that they can measure only objective, quantifiable characteristics, but this precludes their use of some genuinely useful metrics. One subjective metric I have found useful is team mood. There are various ways to monitor how the team feels about what it is doing.[19] One is to poll all team members regularly on, say, a five-point scale regarding such questions as these:

- How do you *feel* about the progress we made this week?
- Do you *feel* that you could bring up any problems you observe?
- How do you *feel* about how we cooperate?
- Do you *feel* that we understand what the customers need?

Compose the question that reflects your current team challenge best. This is a tactical metric, so feel free to change the question as needed to track the current best indicator of team mood. After polling the team, tally the results as a histogram and post it along with prior team mood histograms so that everyone can assess how the team's mood is shifting.

Even simpler, draw multiple copies of some happy faces, sad faces, frowning faces, uncertain faces, and the like, and have team members post their current feeling (drawing) about the team in a designated corner of a white board; they can do this every day, say, as they return from lunch.

These measures are leading indicators. If they turn sour, you have some repair work to do or you will have bigger problems—missed milestones, product defects, or resignations—tomorrow.

Sharing and Acting on Metrics

My experience suggests two important rules to follow if you collect metrics. First, share the metrics with those from whom they were collected. If you collect metrics and do not share them, employees will become suspicious and even cynical: "Will they use this information against me?" Then they will clam up or distort the data they provide. Also, individuals have various perspectives on what the data mean. By sharing results and encouraging discussion of them, you obtain richer interpretations and potential solutions.

My other rule is that if your metrics consistently indicate that something needs fixing, fix it. If you ignore it, you will also build cynicism about the information-gathering process, undercutting the value of your metrics in the future.

Project Retrospectives

Retrospectives are simply a means of looking back at what you have done, learning from it, and taking definite steps so that you can do it better in the future. James Morgan and Jeffrey Liker believe that such retrospectives and the culture of learning and improvement that accompanies them are among Toyota's greatest strengths as a product development company.[20]

Retrospectives are a good idea for any project, but they are especially crucial for a flexible one, for two reasons. One is that as you adopt flexibility, you will be conducting development differently. Some activities will need adjustment or even complete redirection. Retrospectives will help you identify and improve these. The second, more important, reason is that flexible processes are inherently emergent, that is (as mentioned in Chapter One), the process emerges from the nature of the work to be done. (See Chapter Nine for still more on emergent processes.) The process you use will be different for every project. In this situation, you have a continual need for learning about the process you are using.

Retrospectives are another area where the non-software development community can learn greatly from software developers. Despite years of talk about retrospectives, non-software projects do not receive them consistently—and when they do, it is often because the project has failed and management wants to know why, which is hardly being proactive! The non-software community often calls these events *postmortems* (look this up in the dictionary), or *postpartums*, to put a more lively spin on them.

In contrast, software developers have found a good name for them—*retrospectives*—and they offer two excellent books on conducting retrospectives, Esther Derby and Diana Larsen's *Agile Retrospectives* and Norman Kerth's *Project Retrospectives*. As a project is a project, these books, which presume a software development audience, are equally applicable to non-software projects. The main difference between them is that Kerth wrote before the agile movement had gathered strength, so he concentrates on multi-year phased development (waterfall) projects using large and often-dispersed teams, while Derby and Larsen aim directly at agile development with smaller teams and much shorter iterations (every two weeks, say), so their technique can be applied more frequently. Thus, a Derby-Larsen iteration retrospective might take two hours, but count on perhaps three days for a Kerth project retrospective.

Actually, there are three quite different types of retrospectives. One might best be called a *product audit*. It occurs after you launch the product—sometimes a year or so later—and it assesses how well the product satisfies its associated plan: does it have all the features specified in the requirements document, is its manufacturing cost on target, and are actual sales tracking forecast sales? The next type is a *project retrospective*. It also occurs after project completion, but it focuses on the project, not the product. It too may be an audit: did we follow the process and submit all documentation acceptably? But a real retrospective is a learning exercise, not a conformance-to-plan one. The objective is to learn what went well, what went not so well, and to take steps to improve the latter. The third type comes from agile software development and is called an *iteration retrospective*. It occurs regularly with each iteration and is basically a scaled-down project retrospective. It is considerably shorter and focuses more directly on the development team, whereas a project retrospective expands to interacting functions, such as Purchasing and Finance. Another important difference is that an end-of-project retrospective helps the next project, whereas a within-project retrospective improves the current one.

I recommend that you consider both project and iteration retrospectives. If you do not develop in iterations, you can simply conduct retrospectives periodically throughout the project, for instance, once a month, or at the end of each phase. Either project or periodic retrospectives normally include five steps:

1. Open the retrospective, stating its objective and giving each person a chance to check in. This is important to set the expectation that everyone contribute.

2. Collect some data (related to the stated objective) as a team. This need not be a formal process, but you will proceed much better by making this a shared view of what happened,

3. Generate insights from these data. What are the data telling you that you need to improve?

4. Create action plans. How will you improve the situation you have discovered? Without definite plans, nothing will change.

5. Close the retrospective, thanking participants for their contributions.

For each of these steps, Derby and Larsen offer numerous activities to help you both tailor the retrospective to your needs and keep it fresh, which is especially important for periodic retrospectives. Kerth provides other exercises more suitable for longer retrospectives.

Regardless of how you conduct retrospectives, keep a few points in mind. The most important is that these sessions are aimed at learning and discovery, not blame (this is one reason why *audit* is entirely the wrong name for them). Thus the facilitator must maintain an atmosphere where everyone feels comfortable raising and discussing difficulties. It is important that everyone participate, so the facilitator's job is to limit the more vocal members while drawing out the more reticent ones. Once an idea is stated and becomes the group's property, however, it also remains the initiating individual's responsibility. Thus if it starts to die after first being mentioned, its owner should keep it alive until it receives a fair hearing.

Finally, when you conduct retrospectives, remember to balance the difficulties with celebration of the successes to maintain a high energy level. Also, as with metrics, make sure to act on discovered weaknesses to maintain interest in the process.

Summary

These are the high points of this chapter:

- A useful way to appreciate project management for a flexible project is to contrast it with project management for a mainstream one:

    Because the project plan will most likely change, it is less reliable as a road map than in mainstream project management.

    Project completion cannot be judged in the same way.

    Product quality is measured more in terms of satisfying the customer than in meeting requirements.

    Tacit knowledge becomes more important as turbulence increases.

- The flexible project manager should spend more time with the troops than on documentation and updating the project plan.

- Project planning becomes more fragmented as plans change, but a flexible project can still be planned effectively.

- As uncertainty rises, project risk management becomes intrinsic to running the project rather than being a separate process.

- For emergent development processes, project retrospectives are essential; fortunately, wonderful guidance for conducting them is available from the software development community.

9

PRODUCT DEVELOPMENT PROCESSES

It depends.

—*Anonymous*

This chapter is at the back of the book because it is less important than some others. This is not to say that development processes are unimportant, but they are less important than people and their interactions. The Agile Manifesto says this, and you will find it repeated throughout the agile literature, as well as between the lines in the non-software development literature. See Figure 6.1, for example. This is important, because the tendency is to equate product development with the process used and to devote considerable time to creating and documenting development processes and training people to use them. Have you ever asked someone from another company how they develop their products? They are likely to start by describing their process: a phased one, an NPI (new product introduction) one, or something similar. In contrast, have you ever heard someone say, "We hire the best, make sure they have product development experience, give them what they need, and turn them toward their own judgment"?

Nevertheless, there is much you can do with processes, so it's worth looking at what makes a process flexible.

Emergent Processes

Basically, flexible processes are *emergent*, that is, they emerge during the project according to its needs. Guiding this emergence requires skill and experience with development processes to appreciate what is essential and what can be eliminated or modified under the circumstances. This is where the Cockburn mastery levels discussed in Chapter Six are important. You should have some Level 3 people in key roles, especially where you expect change, as well as a liberal proportion of Level 2 people throughout. A preponderance at Level 1 will freeze you into following the book.

Standardize in the Lower Layers

Development processes are built in layers, from fine detail layers at the bottom for routine activities you do often up to the top overarching layer for the whole project. One way to enhance flexibility in processes without opening everything to an ad hoc style is to standardize processes in the lower layers and leave the upper layers open for creative adjustment and emergence. This means having standard, established ways of running a certain kind of test, preparing a drawing, procuring a prototype part, determining tolerances, and so forth. Then developers can combine these basic processes in creative ways.

This low-layer standardization shows up in the way humans build languages. At the most basic layer of letters or characters, standardization is high. No one invents new letters. At the next layer up—words—standardization is prevalent but not complete. Languages tolerate variations in spelling, such as *co-location* or *collocation*, *judgment* or *judgement*, *manifestos* or *manifestoes*, and *organize* or *organise*. People invent new words or borrow them from other languages: *telecommute*, *podcast*, *wiki*, *blog*, *recyclable*, *biofuel*, *siesta*, *loco*, *ciao*, *shalom*, *kaizen*. Going up a layer—to sentences—in English, they are normally in subject-verb-object sequence, but other arrangements also appear, as in, "The faster I go, the dizzier I become." And although some grammarians tell us not to start a sentence with a coordinating conjunction or end it with a preposition, sometimes I am not sure where they are coming from. Up a layer from sentences—paragraphs—even fewer rules exist.

It is nice to have a topic sentence near the beginning of a paragraph and to cover only one topic in a paragraph, but apart from this and reasonable limits on length, paragraphs are largely at the discretion of the writer. On the top layer, documents are even more free-form, with few rules. Observe that this structure, from strictly standardized at the bottom to wide open at the top, simultaneously provides effective means of communication and virtually unlimited freedom of expression.

The quality of a product development project often depends on doing basic activities in proven, consistent ways, but you can enhance flexibility more by being able to rearrange these parts in varying combinations and adjust their lengths, frequencies, and levels of effort—that is, by maintaining upper-layer freedom. In contrast, traditional product development processes, such as phased development, often attempt to specify the upper layers in detail, for example, by defining which activities will occur in which phases, who will work on them, for how long, and what form the output should take.

Quite differently, agile software processes are specific in lower layers with coding standards and insisting on pairing (see Chapter One), as well as daily stand-up meetings in a fixed format (Chapter Six). In the upper layers, the only structure is strict timeboxing of iterations (Chapter Eight). This allows great flexibility between iterations to replan activities and adjust effort to deliver greatest customer value.

Toyota does the same by standardizing lower-layer activities, for instance, the style and procedure for A3 reports and engineering checklists, how meetings are run, and how information is communicated.

Build, Do Not Scale Down, Processes

Except for immature companies that lack a formal development process, product development processes tend to be overly burdensome for most projects. Often, staff experts or process development teams create the process by focusing on the firm's major projects and adding items that other projects conceivably might need. The result is overkill for all but the largest projects the company undertakes—a one-size-fits-all approach.

Actually, in defense of those who create such processes, they usually intend that these processes be scaled down. That is, they tell developers to look at the process in light of the current project and remove parts that are unnecessary, which sounds quite simple.

Unfortunately, it is not so simple. Although those who created the process are fluent in it (Cockburn Level 3) and capable of making such judgments, those who use the process daily find comfort in it and are ill equipped to make these tough decisions. Cockburn Level 1 people *need* a process. They find security in knowing that the process will be their safety net. Also, many managers feel more comfortable knowing that they have plenty of process in place for protection against unknowns. Too often, managers regard a heavy-duty process as "best practice"—and removing items from it as cutting corners. Observe that when one examines a process item by item, each item can be justified by imagining a circumstance for which it might apply.

Consequently, much of the advice and literature on product development processes suggest having a comprehensive process and encouraging developers to scale it down by removing unneeded items. The problem is that real life does not work that way.

In my opinion, the roots of this problem are in a natural human tendency toward greed, or to put it more nicely, security. Attending an all-you-can-eat buffet, many of us eat more than we should because it all looks so "necessary." We keep things in our attics that we might need "someday." We travel with items in our suitcases we never use. The penalties for such behaviors might not be severe, but in product development, excess baggage inhibits flexibility greatly.

As a result, the agile software community and software methodology researchers have found that the best approach for a flexible project is to start with a minimal process and add items to it as you discover that you need them, what the agilists call a "barely suffi-cient process."[1] Although this yields a lighter, more flexible process than you get by starting large and removing items, the difficulty is that it requires Cockburn Level 3 people in key roles, and they may need to comfort the more timid Level 1 people. One could consider this as a burden on the project, but it has the long-term advantage of bringing people up through the mastery levels faster.

The Essentials of Flexible Processes

Recall that Chapter One lists the practices of Extreme Programming and its underlying values. Actually, some basic principles are even more essential to agile methods—so important that without them, you are quite unlikely to become flexible. I consider these here.

Iterative and Incremental Innovation

Iterative means that the product is developed in several short loops rather than in one linear sequence. Good practice is to pro-vide a working sample of the product at the end of each iteration, but for physical products where builds can be expensive or time-consuming, a model or simulation might be substituted for early iterations. Note that iteration is at odds with phased development processes, which typically do not provide a working product until late in the project.[2]

An *increment* is one release to the customer. Thus, a product can pass through several iterations within an increment and have several increments before it becomes mature.

Iteration and incremental releases provide opportunities to resolve uncertainties with customers, who are the final judge of a product's value. Consequently, when there is no uncertainty, one iteration (phased development) and even one increment may suffice. However, flexible development deals with uncertainty, and here iteration and incremental development are essential to resolve uncertainty to the customer's satisfaction.

Normally, a blend of iteration and incremental development is most effective, the choice depending on economics. If the cost of a release is not too great and customers gain value from it, an incremental release has advantages, in part because it shortens time-to-market by reducing development effort.

Less obvious but probably more valuable, incremental development makes better use of development resources. Say that you are developing a product with twenty features, six of them must-haves, as shown at the top of Figure 9.1 (called a predictive process in the figure). Normal tendency is to develop as many of the twenty features as you can. But if you only developed the six must-haves in the initial increment, you could presumably bring the product to market in roughly a third of the time (assuming the same resources and effort proportional to features developed). Rather than having about one-third of the features must-haves, they would all be must-haves, so your resources would be concentrated more heavily on satisfying the customer. Now with the product in the marketplace, you receive the most valuable type of customer feedback—from a real product they have purchased—and you will discover exactly which of those remaining features are also highly desirable. Or others—the

Figure 9.1   Comparison of Predictive and Incremental Processes

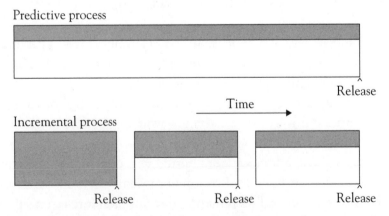

Note: Must-have features are shaded and not-so-certain ones are white.

new "highly desirable" list might well include some not even on your original list! You find that you must have three more features, so in your second increment you develop these three plus three other strong possibilities. Notice that in this release you are devoting 50 percent of your resources to must-haves, and you are making selections now from fresher information. You repeat the same strategy for the third release. After three increments, you are at the same time that you would have been with one long increment, but you now have a much richer product based on more accurate customer information.

In short, iterative and incremental development allow you to sample customer and other feedback frequently, which is essential when you face uncertainties.

Another advantage of iterative and incremental innovation is that it emphasizes working products relative to documentation (in contrast to traditional or phased processes, which rely more on documentation as a measure of progress). This is a value stated in the Agile Manifesto. Working products do not lie, whereas documents can mislead you about how much has actually been accomplished and how much work remains.

However, iterative or incremental development has a price: the cost of completing an iteration or the cost of releasing a product, respectively. To enjoy the benefits of these styles, you must find ways of reducing cyclic costs, either through automation or simplification. For instance, the iteration cost for an electronic product often includes expensive and time-consuming testing for electromagnetic emissions, electrostatic discharge, temperature and humidity, and drop and vibration resistance. If you suspect you will be passing through several iterations as the design changes, you might defer some of these tests until the final iteration to reduce the cost of an iteration. Or you could do engineering-level checks on the items with large costs of change and defer compliance testing until the end. Another approach is to standardize a robust hardware platform early and plan to make most changes in software where the cost of change is lower.

The agilists have applied such thinking by automating their building and testing activities so that they can build and test almost continuously and at essentially no cost. In addition, however, they have made supporting changes to make automation effective. For instance, they create all tests in a simple pass/fail format so that they can accumulate tests during development, running them continuously while watching for a single failure.

Balancing Anticipation and Adaptation

Throughout this book, I have provided only two basic ways to improve flexibility. One is to anticipate the future better, and the other is to adapt more readily when circumstances change. Alistair Cockburn proposes a useful way to consider and connect these approaches.[3] Many of the tools or approaches available to improve flexibility involve spending money, which can be spent in two ways, either to gain information or to gain adaptability. In money-for-information (MFI), we spend money to gain more information about a situation so that we can proceed with more certainty, that is, to remove uncertainty. This is relatively straightforward, and the main issue is how much the information is worth and thus how much to pay for it. The money-for-adaptability (MFA) option invests in gaining adaptability for those situations where the route is so unclear that either there is no way to use MFI or its cost is prohibitive.

Some development activities are relatively predictable, and you can invest directly in advancing design and development. Conducting a project similar to an earlier one falls into this category. Others involve some uncertainty, but this uncertainty can be resolved through MFI. In these cases, what you would normally spend directly on development is better spent as MFI to understand your uncertainties better. In some areas that are quite uncertain or where a great deal of innovation is occurring, the path is clouded but MFI is not an option for resolving the uncertainty. Go for MFA, which allows you to handle the uncertainty faster.

This book provides both MFI and MFA tools and approaches. For instance, Chapter Two addresses understanding customers. Traditional voice of the customer (VOC) techniques involve market research (MFI), so the techniques in Chapter Two provide increased flexibility through MFA when the uncertainty is irresolvable with MFI. Chapter Three—on product architecture—mostly aims at MFA techniques, whereas Chapter Four—on experimentation—involves principally MFI. Chapters Five and Six are primarily MFA. Chapter Seven—on decision making—uses MFA to delay decisions while it uses MFI to collect information for making the decision.

Observe that either MFI or MFA involves spending money to deal with uncertainty, money that could have gone directly toward development, so in either case, it will be more expensive than in the certain (inflexible) case. In short, flexibility is not free. Whether to use MFI or MFA is mostly a matter of economics: use whichever one buys you flexibility most inexpensively. However, observe that MFI is proactive while MFA is reactive, so MFI is preferable when the economics are close.

There are cautions with both MFI and MFA. MFI can become expensive quickly; see Figure 1.2. MFA can become a catchall and a crutch for sloppiness. When you can resolve an issue directly or with some inexpensive MFI, this is more proactive and probably less expensive than leaving uncertainties unresolved and waiting for adaptability to rescue you.

Tacit Knowledge

Knowledge management has been a prominent topic recently as management has harnessed the power of information technology (IT) to capture the knowledge that is the essence of product development.[4] Such knowledge is of two kinds, explicit knowledge and implicit, or tacit, knowledge. *Explicit* knowledge is know-what knowledge, such as project plans, product requirements, drawings, bills of material, and defect registers. It is relatively easy to capture and manage with IT, and this is the focus of current product development software.

In contrast, *tacit*, or know-how, knowledge is much softer and is usually carried in the heads of developers—and walks out the door when the developers leave. It includes information such as which tests work with which materials, how accurate the test results are likely to be, which suppliers are best and most responsive at running these tests, and what kind of follow-up checks to make to verify the test results. The knowledge management community has not pursued tacit knowledge much because of the technical and cultural difficulties in capturing it. Tacit knowledge is important to product development and critical to flexible development. This is what distinguishes Cockburn's Levels 1, 2, and 3. Tacit knowledge is what allows developers to adapt processes, to know how quickly to narrow the design space, which alternative solutions are currently viable, when customers need to be consulted or ignored, and when a series of experiments should be started and what their fidelity needs to be.

Unfortunately, with the exception of Toyota, most organizations are poor at managing tacit knowledge—and tacit knowledge may be Toyota's principal competitive advantage in product development. Toyota manages tacit knowledge through long-term employment, extensive training and mentoring, developing those who are superb at handling tacit knowledge into managers, and institutionalizing A3 reports and engineering checklists maintained by departments.[5]

However, you can do a great deal to improve your management of tacit knowledge. One is to recognize that since much of it resides in employees' heads, reducing turnover is important— except when you can increase your tacit knowledge explicitly by hiring it. In these days of corporate downsizing, it is often possible to hire highly experienced people from competitors. The extra these experienced people cost (compared to newcomers to the field) pays off greatly by expanding the tacit knowledge your organization can bring to bear on its products. Furthermore, feeding tacit knowledge into employees' heads by exposing them to a variety of experiences, as MacCormack observes, helps. Cross-training and cross-experiences also help by improving redundancy; this is an advantage of pairing. Mentoring spreads the knowledge too.

There are also things you can do to capture tacit knowledge in your IT systems, as Toyota does. I have seen companies in the United States place rich tacit knowledge on their intranets by providing recipes there for basic tasks, such as how to conduct an endurance test, how to prepare for a design review, how to order a prototype part quickly, and the like. Observe that this not only captures tacit knowledge but also helps to standardize in lower layers, as discussed earlier.

Balancing Structure with Flexibility

In the earlier section, "Standardize in the Lower Layers," I discuss a significant difference between mainstream product development practice and what is needed to be flexible: process flexibility in the upper layers. There is another important difference between prevailing product development processes and the needs of flexibility: the freedom to use flexible processes where needed and more structured processes where they are more advantageous, as well as the ability to concoct appropriate blends when indicated.[6] Thus the guiding theme for the chapter, as quoted at the outset: "It depends."

Balancing Opposing Risks

Extreme programmers suggest "turning the knobs up to ten," but ten is not appropriate for most situations requiring flexibility. Thus, the real question is where to set the several "knobs" associated with each project. Following is an approach from Boehm and Turner that balances risks.[7] This approach recognizes that an activity in a development project often faces risks both from being too flexible and from being too structured. Thus the best management approach is not to swing too far in either direction where the

Figure 9.2 Balancing Opposing Risks of Being Too Flexible and Being Too Structured

risks are high. However, each activity is different and requires an independent assessment of its opposing risks to set its knob correctly. Figure 9.2 illustrates this by showing the first two risks from each of the lists in the following paragraph.

Consider the categories of risk associated with a development project. I break them into two groups, first some that are specific to flexible approaches, then some specific to structured approaches. Notice that product complexity appears on both lists for different reasons.

Risks specific to a flexible approach:

- Project team size (flexible approaches may not work well with a large team)
- Product criticality (products that are life-critical need more structure and documentation)

- Product complexity (imposes constraints on the organization and the product architecture that may restrict a flexible approach)
- Technology complexity (very complex technologies might require heavy staffing that would tax a flexible approach)
- Organizational complexity (complex, multi-organizational teams thwart the co-location that facilitates the flexible approach)
- Team turnover (flexible methods depend more on tacit knowledge built within the team, so if members leave, flexibility is compromised)
- Skill with flexible methods (flexible approaches are emergent, which require some Cockburn Level 2 and 3 people)

Risks specific to a structured approach:
- Market changes (structure implies replanning and reapproval that thwarts following fast-moving markets)
- Customer usage uncertainty (effect similar to that of market changes if customers change the way they use the product)
- Technology flux (effect similar to that of market changes if the product or manufacturing technology is changing)
- Emergent requirements (effect similar to that of market changes if new customer requirements appear during development)
- Product complexity (encourages specialization and compartmentalization, which hampers project communication)
- Skill with structured methods (developers and managers might lack training, experience, or patience with structured procedures, especially in a changing environment where they might be taxing)

This list is intended to be general for a non-software development project, but it probably lacks some risks or distorts them compared to the way you experience them in your projects. Thus I encourage you to expand and modify the list to suit your projects.

Some projects clearly fall into the flexible domain because they are subject to a great deal of change; you can complete them with a small team co-located in one organization; they are relatively simple and do not threaten human life; and they can be staffed with stable, seasoned members. On the other hand, some are clearly best for a structured approach because they have little uncertainty in markets, customers, and technology; you need a big team or to involve several organizations; the product is life-critical; and your culture and skills do not support a flexible approach. These are the easy ones; you can turn all the knobs to ten or one, respectively, and start developing.

Most projects fall in between and require a mix of flexible and structured approaches. For instance, suppose that you wish to use a new infrared technology developed by NASA (the U.S. National Aeronautics and Space Administration) together with some algorithms available from university research to measure the internal temperature of meat and thus know noninvasively and for certain that cooked meat is safe to eat, whether it comprises little chunks or a whole roast.[8] You intend to develop this technology into a consumer instrument to capture the largest possible market.

Scanning the lists of risks outlined earlier, you see that this project mostly fits the flexible approach due to likely changes in markets, customer usage, and technology, as well as the possibility of emergent requirements. However, the product could threaten the health of millions of people, especially when used by amateurs (consumers rather than professional chefs). There are also concerns that the technology is beyond the skills of your organization.

Consequently, you decide to use a flexible approach, which is dictated by the great changes likely during development as this concept morphs into a product that will be a cook's godsend. However, you must manage the risks of malfunction in a more structured way, and you must find ways to augment your co-located team with expertise in infrared technologies and the algorithms you will use. Accordingly, this is what you would do (in addition to a general flexible approach):

- Although encouraging front-loaded testing under field conditions, establish strict protocols that either all meat tested must be destroyed or a professional meat chef must be present to approve what is served to humans.
- Although encouraging wide public assessment of prototypes for user friendliness, either ensure that these prototypes are functionally inert or follow strict audits to assure the recovery and destruction of all of them.
- Voluntarily follow FDA labeling protocols to ensure that instructions supplied with the product are as clear as possible.
- Arrange in advance to retain an infrared specialist and an algorithm specialist to be on call and have them visit the team in advance to build effective working relationships and acquaint the specialists with project goals.

Each situation is different, so you must adapt this approach to your business. For instance, many companies are OEM (original equipment manufacturer) suppliers who develop subsystems for their customers' overall product. They may need to control changes to product requirements tightly (or arrange an equitable means of allocating the cost of such changes to control their design expenses) while allowing great flexibility in implementing the design.

You can also balance risks on an activity basis. Say that your current activity is planning a field trial of the cooked-meat instrument, and you want to ensure that you cover the spectrum of meat types and sizes (bite-sized chunks to roasts) for which customers might use the instrument. The structured approach to this activity might suggest doing market research to assess customer groups, types and sizes of meat purchased, and items that appear on restaurant menus and ready-to-eat food in grocery stores. Then you might plan a series of field trials to cover all of these groups. The flexible approach, instead, might choose a few likely customer groups and

Figure 9.3   Balancing Opposing Risks for a Field Trial

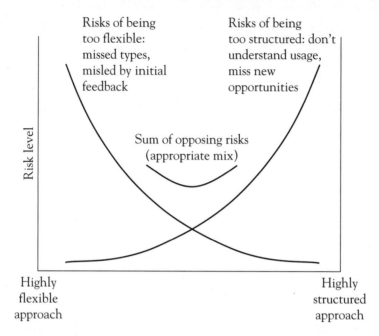

put the instrument in their hands as early as possible (remember the MacCormack studies in Chapter Two). Figure 9.3 is Figure 9.2 modified to show the opposing risks specific to this activity. The risks of flexibility include missing types and sizes of meat that customers might cook and being misled by following early results from a biased sample, while the risks of structure include failure to understand how the instrument is actually used by customers and missing new opportunities that would have appeared in early field trials.

Observe that once you have identified the opposing risks in an activity, as just done, you may not have to live with them. Once you understand them, you might be able to adjust your process to overcome them. For instance, if you go with the flexible approach for running the field trial, you can log the types and sizes of meat customers choose in the early trials and compare this against ongoing research into the meat market to overcome the risk of a biased sample. On the other hand, if you proceed with the structured approach, you can separately put some instruments into customers' hands early solely to observe how they use them, regardless of the types and sizes of meat they choose, so that you do not miss new features that this early feedback might suggest.

Shifting the Balance

Now that you understand how to balance risks to find the best blend, recognize that you will be doing this often. Each project will have its own objectives and operate under its own conditions, suggesting a unique balance each time. Even within a project, some portions will be influenced more heavily than others by certain project objectives and conditions, which suggests a tailored balance for these portions. For instance, in the cooked-meat instrument, the software for the temperature-calculating algorithm is a life-critical subsystem, so it will require more structure and documentation than the user interface software. On the other hand, the user interface software needs subjective user feedback, so the flexibility to change it easily is valuable here. Consequently, these two parts of the instrument's software should have different structure-flexibility balances.

Furthermore, you can expect these balances to shift over the life of the project. In the beginning, little has been invested in the project (low stakes), many uncertainties are likely in the untested technologies and uncertain and emerging requirements, and the development team is small, all of which suggest a more flexible approach. Later on, the stakes (cost of change) are higher, the technology is tested, the requirements should be reasonably stable, and other organizations may be involved, all of which point toward more structure. See Figure 9.4, and observe that this shift fits with Figure 1.4. Figure 9.4 portrays a general phenomenon for projects; it is not specific to the meat temperature instrument.

Bottlenecks and Queues

As covered earlier in this chapter, flexibility stems either from anticipating changes or from adapting to them when they occur. Adaptation requires that you be able to respond quickly.

Figure 9.4   Process Shift Over Time

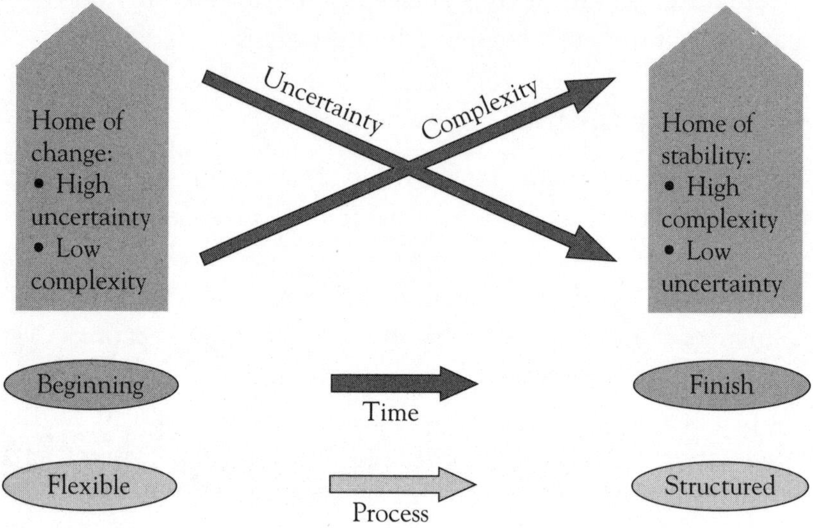

In turn, this requires that you have unencumbered basic development processes that can turn work around quickly. Clearly, you will not be very flexible if, wherever a design change occurs, the new design must sit and wait its turn for redesign and again for retesting. Consequently, to be flexible, you must scan your development operation for long queues, that is, bottlenecks, and remove them.

There is a methodology, called *theory of constraints*, for doing this scanning.[9] This theory says that there is usually a single key constraint (bottleneck) limiting the performance of a system. Once you identify the constraint and resolve it, another one is likely to appear elsewhere. Consequently, this is a repetitive process of finding and improving the specific spots that limit your performance most.

You can identify bottlenecks in a couple of different ways. One is simply to watch for them: the bottleneck in your development process is where you see the longest queue (measured in time, not in number of items in queue). For systems of machines, as in a factory, this works well. However, for product development, where people are involved, it is messier, because people will camouflage short queues that might suggest idleness.

Consequently, you can use another method. Propose a change to the design and ask for a quick turnaround. Then listen carefully to the responses you receive, for example, "We cannot possibly finish it by next Monday because the test stalls are all booked for the next three weeks." You have just discovered that test stalls are your current bottleneck (repeat this test a few times to check for consistency). Remove this bottleneck by adding testing capacity and rerun the experiment to see where the bottleneck has moved. Continue this process until you have a sufficiently responsive system.

The Myth of Capacity

Most of us carry the illusion that the capacity of a person or a facility is not a problem until it is fully used. For example, the test stalls are not a bottleneck until they are all occupied. Figure 9.5 is the typical picture of capacity.

In this figure, waiting time is the total amount of time that you wait for an activity to complete; it includes service time—the

Figure 9.5   The Myth: Service Is Prompt Until the System Reaches Full Capacity

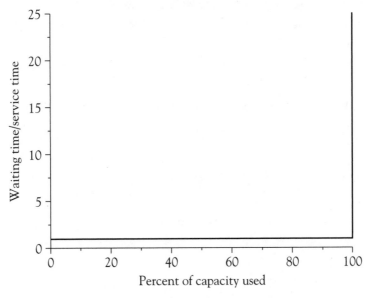

time actually needed to complete the work—and queue time—the time spent waiting for the work to start. For instance, think in terms of a test that requires a test stall. Figure 9.5 says that, up until all stalls are occupied (100 percent capacity in the figure), there will be no queue to enter a stall, and total waiting time is only the time required for the test. In other words, waiting time and service time are one and the same until all the stalls are occupied. This makes perfect sense, because if a stall were vacant, you could slip right into it and start testing immediately.

Unfortunately, "perfect sense" is wrong in this case, because these numbers are averages, and sometimes the bank of stalls will be busier than it is at others. If the world were perfect, designs to be tested would arrive uniformly, say at exactly one every thirty minutes, and they would be serviced uniformly, say, in exactly three hours for each test. If this were the case, Figure 9.5 would be correct.

In the real world, items arrive for testing randomly, sometimes close together and sometimes with long intervals between arrivals. Likewise, they receive service randomly, sometimes quickly (say, the test fails immediately) and sometimes slowly (say, the test requires supplies that just ran out). A branch of probability theory called *queuing theory* deals with processes like this, where arrivals are random and service is also random. It makes it possible to predict queue lengths with substantial reliability, and such queues are much longer than you would guess from Figure 9.5.

The basic queue is called an M/M/1/∞ queue. This means that

- The arrival process is Markovian with an exponential distribution.
- The service process is Markovian with an exponential distribution.
- There is one server (one test stall in our example).
- The queue can be infinite (no one becomes frustrated and leaves).

Figure 9.6 The Reality: Wait Times Rise Long Before Reaching Full Capacity

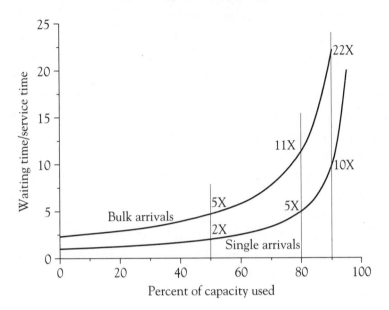

This simple case has a simple formula for the solution, as illustrated in the lower curve (single arrivals) in Figure 9.6. Accordingly, when the system is operating at 50 percent of capacity, you spend twice as long in total—as long in queue as you do waiting for service. And at 90 percent of capacity, you spend nine times as long in queue as for service—for a total of ten times the delay. Because these processes are random, the numbers are averages: sometimes the wait will be longer, sometimes shorter than this.

One assumption used in the simple $M/M/1/\infty$ queue model does not apply well to product development queues. It assumes that arrivals are isolated, that is, no clumps arrive simultaneously. In product development, it is common to submit multiple specimens to be tested, to request several variants of a prototype at the same time, or even to start multiple projects at once. This so-called bulk arrival queue, $M^{[x]}/M/1/\infty$, where arrivals are not only random but also clumpy, is shown in the upper curve of

Figure 9.6. Here the total wait averages twenty-two times the service time at 90 percent of capacity.[10]

Figure 9.7 portrays the same situation differently. It shows time-in-queue (excluding service time) over time for an M/M/1/∞ (single arrivals) queue loaded at 25 percent and 75 percent of capacity. As you can see, at 25 percent of capacity, there is often no queue, but it sometimes reaches seven times service time, for a total wait of eight times the basic service time. At 75 percent of capacity, an empty queue is quite rare and total waiting time can exceed twenty times the service time.

Queues are an important and common impediment to flexible development. Most organizations greatly overload their development resources, creating long queues that essentially prohibit flexibility. If you intend to be flexible, you should look carefully at your queues and shorten the long ones, which usually means increasing capacity of the associated systems so that they operate well below capacity.

Useful Concepts from Agile Software Development

I have borrowed unashamedly from agile software development throughout, and here are two more concepts from the agilists relating to development processes.

Refactoring and Technical Debt

I introduced refactoring in Chapter One as an Extreme Programming practice. It is widely used in other agile methodologies also. The idea is to modify the code (or the product design) to render it simpler or more comprehensible without changing its functionality. That is, developers refactor solely to improve flexibility or sustainability, not to add any new features or to fix bugs.

Agilists know that, over time, computer code gradually gets messier. Often developers are under pressure to add new capability so

Figure 9.7 Actual Queues, Which Can Be Much Longer Than Their Averages

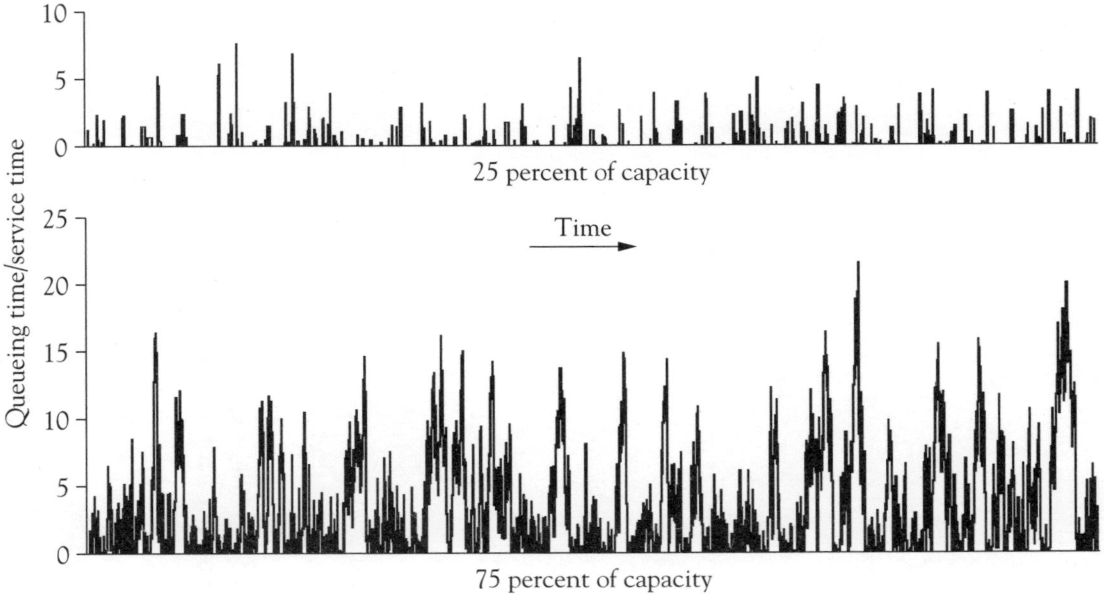

Queueing time/service time
10
5
0
25 percent of capacity
25
20
15
10
5
0
Time
75 percent of capacity

Figure 9.8   Technical Debt

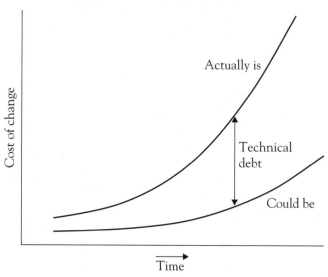

they skimp on programming cleanly. Also, they sometimes notice a better way of doing something later. Refactoring cleans up this messiness. Without regular refactoring, the cost of change gradually increases as the code becomes more and more error-prone and difficult to modify.

Technical debt is the gap between what the cost of change actually is and what it could be with routine refactoring, as shown in Figure 9.8. In other words, "Technical debt is the unfinished work your organization owes your product."[11]

Technical debt is like financial debt: the more of it you accumulate, the more difficult it is to maneuver or to escape from it. As with financial debt, it eventually becomes overpowering, making it impossible to make any changes in the product without huge consequences. At this point, the product has reached a dead end.

You Aren't Going to Need It

Extreme programmers have turned the knobs up to ten on avoiding anticipation with the phrase "You aren't going to need it" (YAGNI). Although this is a radical thought, like many others from XP, it provides valuable insight. YAGNI says not to provide anything in the code (product) that you do not need right now; do not add anything based on speculation that you might need it later. The motivation behind this is twofold. First, when the situation is chaotic, what you anticipate needing now is likely to change before you can use it, thus rendering any preparation useless by then. If you are refactoring and keeping your technical debt low, anything you need later can be added easily then. Second, if you resist adding excess baggage on speculation, you keep the design lean so that it can be changed easily.

When change is rampant, YAGNI embodies considerable wisdom; when relative stability prevails, ignoring the future is foolhardy, especially when high cost-of-change items, such as architectural choices, are at stake.

The opposite of YAGNI might be IMNIL (I might need it later). This might be the wisest choice in certain cases, such as electronic products where electromagnetic emissions and electrostatic discharge (which depend heavily on the physical layout of parts) issues are paramount and time-consuming to correct. However, you will know only by comparing the costs of change against the more subtle advantages of keeping the design simple for future changes.

The natural tendency of managers and engineers is to plan ahead and provide for contingencies, especially when such provisions are inexpensive. This keeps your options open, as advised repeatedly throughout this book. However, the wisdom of YAGNI is that these options may not actually be worth much at maturity in a volatile environment, and more important, they complicate the design, which raises the cost of change. Consequently, what YAGNI is telling non-software developers is to question automatically providing for future possibilities, because they may cost more in lost flexibility than they provide in possible benefit.

Ask yourself both these questions:

- How likely is it that this option will be useful in the future given the current rate of change?
- How much will this complicate the design, making any change more difficult in the future?

Summary

These are the main points of this chapter:

- Flexible processes are emergent: they emerge from the needs of the project.
- Standardize in the lower layers, leaving the upper layers of process open to adaptation.
- Start with a barely sufficient process, because it is more difficult to remove from a process than to add to it.
- Iteration yielding working products is at the core of flexible development: develop a little and try it out early.
- Tacit knowledge is critical to flexible development, but few organizations are good at managing it.
- Development processes can be balanced by comparing the risk of not enough structure against the risk of too much.
- Such risk balancing can be done on a broad basis, such as technological difficulty, or more narrowly on an activity, such as when to build a prototype.
- Processes should shift from flexible to structured over the life of the project.
- Overloaded resources create long queues, which paralyze flexibility.

10

IMPLEMENTING FLEXIBILITY

Structuring an organization for change is much
harder than designing a system for change.
—*Frederick Brooks*[1]

I have described this book using a tool kit metaphor, but this is misleading. As the agilists have warned themselves and the rest of the world repeatedly, tools are tangible and easy to learn, but it is the underlying values and principles that are critical to becoming flexible. You can be quite flexible by using tools other than the ones described in this book, as with Toyota, but without the values and principles of flexibility deeply instilled, no tools will provide sustained flexibility.

I have covered plenty of tools and approaches in the preceding chapters. At this point, I hope you have flagged some that you would like to try in your organization. This chapter guides you through the implementation phase for whatever tools you have chosen.

I believe this implementation is critically important. Without it, all you will have from this book are some interesting ideas. To obtain any business value from this book, you must make some of these ideas work in your organization so that it becomes more flexible. In short, unless your flexibility improves, you have wasted your time reading this book.

The first step is to recognize the nature of the task ahead. It can be a daunting one, as Frederick Brooks suggests. It is difficult because underlying the obvious tools and approaches are existing organizational values that will have to change, and changing an

organization's values is hard. Here are some of these new values:

- Accepting that the customers' requirements will emerge
- Responding to feedback rather than following a plan
- Regarding architecture as a business decision rather than a technical one
- Learning from and thus valuing failure
- Allowing experiments to drive the process
- Using experiments early for learning rather than later for verification
- Appreciating that chaos in the lab means success in the marketplace
- Investing in early exploration and maintaining options to reduce the cost of change
- Keeping options open while collecting information about them
- Being comfortable with making decisions at the last responsible moment
- Making dedicated, committed, co-located teams the norm
- Using project economics to support decisions, even at the lowest levels of the organization
- Being comfortable sending and using partial or incomplete information
- Letting the process emerge rather than trying to prescribe it
- Running each project differently, depending on its unique flexibility requirements

Organizational change is a complex process with many faces, each of which deserves a book on its own. Consequently, I cover it here as overviews from a few perspectives. At one time or another, you will probably need each of these perspectives. First, from my experience as a consultant in guiding many companies toward improving their development systems, I describe some of the paradoxes that I have observed. Then I consider how change actually

occurs through some critical transitions. Next, I describe a popular top-down strategic change-management process, assuming that you are at the top of your organization and in a position to put such a process in place. Finally, in case you are less fortunate in your position, I offer a kit of tactics for grassroots organizational change—working up from the bottom.

This overview from various perspectives is a good starting point, but my intention is simply to paint the big picture here and encourage you to dig further into each perspective using the suggested references.

Five Paradoxes

In assisting companies to make changes such as the ones covered in this book, I have observed several paradoxes. I describe each of them in the following sections, along with the trade-offs involved and some of the boundary conditions that apply. In each case, the proper balance depends on many factors that differ in each situation, so you will need a knowledge of the organization and some management judgment to find the right balance.

Top-Down or Bottom-Up?

In preparation for writing this chapter, I surveyed about fifty product development managers globally about their experience with and favorite techniques for making improvements in their product development. A dominant theme in the responses was that a senior manager (who controls the principal resources involved in the change) must lead, support, or otherwise be involved positively in a change initiative for it to be successful. This immediately creates a problem here, because such a manager is unlikely to have read this book. The value of flexibility may not be as apparent to senior management as the effort required in establishing the values needed for flexibility to work.

When I talk with senior managers, they often express their frustration that some changes they would like to see simply do not happen. They are not powerful enough, by themselves, to make these changes happen either. Later I discuss Kotter's eight-step process for organizational change. Step 2 is to empower a *team* to lead the change: "Even an extremely talented person does not have enough time, skills, connections, reputation, leadership capacity, and energy to lead change alone except in small groups."[2] Organizational change is not a one-person endeavor.

On the other hand, the typical employee is unlikely to have the resources, influence, and connections to make change stick. Without these, the effort is likely to fizzle.

The reality is that, regardless of the level of the person initiating the change, the job is largely one of converting others and enabling them to convert even more. If the person initiating change is near the top of the organization, Kotter's model is a good one, and if they are lower down, the Manns and Rising approach I discuss later is likely to work better.

Start Small or Start Big?

When one finds a better way of doing business—in this case, a better way of developing products—the natural reaction is to roll it out to the whole organization as soon as possible to realize the benefits quickly. However, many organizations fail in a change program by overextending themselves.

In contrast, organizational change programs also fizzle out by limiting their scope and failing to capture a critical mass sufficient to sustain the program.

Clearly, pace is important to manage. It is essential to keep pouring on the fuel to keep the temperature up. Balancing this, certain ingredients in a change program are in short supply, and proceeding too fast will overextend your supply lines. One such item is people's time, which will be easier to obtain if the program is led from the top, where management can redirect people on a large scale. Even so, the number of hours in a day is limited to twenty-four. Another ingredient is skills. Generally, people must

excellent judgment and knowledge of the situation. Strive for a shift substantial enough to reset the desired values, a change where business as usual will not suffice. Often, a visible change, such as a move to a new location, will facilitate this resetting.

Exposed or Sheltered Project?

To encourage further adoption, you would prefer to use groups now undergoing the change as demonstrations for others to watch so as to build their confidence in the new approach. Successful examples are important for demonstrating that the new techniques will actually work in your environment.

However, those trying the new approach are probably uneasy about it themselves, and they will be uncomfortable having others watching them possibly making mistakes. They need privacy to survive.

Later, typically, they will be proud of what they are doing and will welcome visitors and the recognition that this brings. Thus you must carefully modulate the exposure the group undergoing change receives. Usually, the group itself is in the best position to judge when it is ready to be exposed. I have seen this with many groups. One installed a door to their team area, including a combination lock to which only team members knew the combination. After a few months, the door remained open continuously. Another team put a "keep out" sign at the entrance to their area when they formed, then switched it to a welcome mat when they were confident enough to receive visitors.

Transitions Are the Crux

People speak of organizational change, but William Bridges draws a useful distinction between *change*—shifting from one situation to another—and *transition*—a more psychologically oriented viewpoint that emphasizes what happens in the interim. When we concentrate on change, we look forward to the desired state, but when we emphasize the transition, we look backward to see that the first step is letting go of the past. "The single biggest reason organizational changes fail is that no one has thought about endings or planned to manage their impact on people."[4]

Bridges describes three phases of any transition: an ending or letting go, a neutral zone, and a new beginning (see Figure 10.1). In the letting-go phase, it is important to appreciate who is losing what and acknowledge what is being lost. In the case of flexible development, managers are likely to lose some trusted tools, such as a known list of product requirements and even the project schedule. Even though these may be much less helpful in a changing environment than imagined, they nevertheless provide security. Observe that this approaches the what's-in-it-for-me issue, which many other experts also believe is critical, from a different angle.

Figure 10.1   Three Phases of Transition: Letting Go of the Past, Neutral, and New Beginnings

Illustrator: Lyn Doiron.

The neutral phase is a period of limbo when the old is gone, but the new is not established yet. It is even harder to manage than the letting-go phase, and worse, management may be getting impatient for results just when productivity is at a nadir. Nevertheless, it is also a period ripe for creativity. With the old gone and the new not yet firm, processes and methods can be adjusted or even invented.

Although a change management plan can specify when the new way will start—for example, it can call for a July 17 move to the new facility—new beginnings run according to an internal clock that senses when the time is right to move on. Still, you can do a lot to encourage and support this transition to the new way by providing a purpose, an image of the new state, and a plan for getting there. In this phase, Bridges provides four rules:

- Be consistent, which establishes a clear direction out of the neutral zone.
- Create quick successes (even small ones), which maintain momentum and diminish doubt.
- Provide symbols of the new, such as a map of the new process, that make it more tangible.
- Celebrate successes: do not miss an opportunity to cement the new path and thank participants for making the journey.

Top-Down Change

Change is a messy matter; imagine having a systematic process for it. John Kotter provides such a process, based on years of study of successful and unsuccessful change efforts in nearly two hundred organizations. He discovered two things, one predictable, and the other not—even by him. The predictable conclusion is that a flow of eight steps characterizes most successful changes. The second finding, which struck him in his most recent research, is that although the core of successful change is in changing behavior—what people do—changing behavior is less likely to occur through analysis and thinking than by presenting people with a vision that influences their feelings. As Kotter puts it, see-feel-change is more powerful than analysis-think-change.[5] Keep this in mind, because typically product development organizations are loaded heavily with engineers and MBAs (people with master's degrees in business administration) who thrive on analysis and are inclined to dismiss feelings as incidental. Notice that Kotter's finding fits with Bridges', which says that feelings such as grief are a key part of the transition process.

These experts are not saying that you should rely on feelings alone. Engineers and MBAs, in particular, will want facts to substantiate what you are saying; fluff will not do. But they, like everyone else, are more likely to be swayed toward change by emotions that accompany the analysis than by the analysis itself.

Kotter's eight steps provide a road map for managing change. Step 1 is to create a sense of urgency. Because change is uncomfortable, it must start with a jolt establishing its importance. Hewlett-Packard provides an interesting example.[6] In 1978, John Young became chief executive officer (CEO), replacing founder Bill Hewlett. Quickly, he recognized that the poor reliability of HP's products was a detriment, so he initiated a corporate change program to improve product reliability. Such corporate-wide change programs were uncommon at HP. Several months later, he noticed that it hadn't ignited, and, in fact, reliability metrics mostly had slipped even more. Clearly, Young hadn't established the urgency yet.

However, the Loveland division alone had made great progress, so Young visited Loveland, meeting for several days with various players to see what they were doing and how they were doing it. He took plentiful notes. A few months later, when the HP division general managers met, he addressed them in a thirty-minute talk about reliability. He described what was happening at Loveland, and he explained why reliability was important to HP's customers. Behind him for the entire period was a slide listing HP's divisions, the names of their general managers, and the change in each division's reliability rating over the past year, sorted by reliability rating (Loveland at the top). Interestingly, Young never mentioned the slide, but it was impossible to ignore. It provided undeniable evidence, and it was the emotional trigger. Without it, his description of what Loveland was doing would have been simply an interesting case study. The slide followed Kotter's see-feel-change pattern perfectly.

Step 2 is to create a team to guide the change. Apparently, Young did not appoint a team, but a change program is a bigger, more diverse job than any one person can handle, as noted previously. More important, the program will need the diversity of skills, credibility, connections, and formal authority that only a team provides. This not only divides up the work but shows people that those they trust are committed to and leading the program.

Step 3 is to build a credible vision of the intended change. This happens after establishing the guiding team, because the vision must mesh with this team's objective and style. A good vision is much more than a plan. It connects with people emotionally and paints a memorable picture of the future. Another example from HP: the company has been a leader in producing high-quality printers, but recently the market has shifted to cutthroat pricing on the printers. HP's printers were overdesigned for the current market. Hence the story I told in Chapter Two of a development manager who jumped onto a printer, proclaiming that they make printers, not footstools (see Figure 10.2). "Not a footstool" became a vision of intended change that was etched into developers' minds. A colleague of mine was at HP when this happened. Although she didn't actually see this demonstration, she heard about it from several others, and the event is still very clear in her mind six years later! Note that this is another example of Kotter's see-feel-change pattern.

Step 4 is to communicate the change and build ownership in it. Everyone must understand why the business must change and how they fit into it. This communication can be oral or written—or

Figure 10.2   "We make printers, *not* footstools!"

Illustrator: Lyn Doiron.

conveyed by actions or demonstrations. Repetition and consistency are critical. People often do not accept or believe a message when they first receive it. Belief, understanding, and commitment build slowly. Moreover, in the beginning, they are skeptical, looking for reasons not to believe. Consequently words and actions must match; management must "walk the talk."

Although Kotter does not address it explicitly, training in the new methods fits somewhere in steps 4 or 5. For flexible development, development teams and management (using a shorter, management-specific session) will need training in using the techniques.

Kotter calls step 5 "empowerment." It is a matter of identifying and removing barriers for those who are starting to make the change. Note that *empowerment* actually has it backwards. This is not a process of giving power to those undergoing change so much as one of removing obstacles in their way to lubricate the change for them. This kind of empowerment fits with the team leader's role mentioned for the stand-up meeting in Chapter Six.

By now, some small successes are likely. Step 6 is to celebrate these. Management and the guiding team should watch for movement in the right direction and make it apparent to others. This builds momentum, confidence, and credibility for more change. Change is a bootstrapping process, and celebrating even small successes is the mechanism that makes bootstrapping work. This momentum-building process is at the heart of the organizational change process that I have advocated for years.[7] Notice that the changes celebrated needn't be large or perfect—only moves in the right direction. Also notice that the steps needn't appear in this order: John Young celebrated the success at Loveland very early in the process, simply by visiting the division and talking with those who had started to change. Given his stature in the company, his presence and admiration were enough to provide the boost of celebration.

Step 7 is simply to keep it up. Many organizations declare victory and assume that the change will not only stick but continue to develop on its own. The reality is that behavior is like a rubber band: it likes to return to its former shape. You will need continued effort to mold the organization into a new shape having permanence. After John Young got his general managers' attention about product reliability, it was ten years before reliability reached the level that was his goal.

In other words, the journey is never over—even at Toyota, which I've been describing as a sort of paragon. Of all Toyota's advantages, such as its well-trained, long-term workforce, the company's strongest asset is probably that its people never believe they are good enough: "We do not recall a single incident where a Toyota employee, at any level, communicated a sense of complacency."[8]

The last step is to institutionalize the change. Once the change is apparent, supporting corporate systems must change to mesh with it. This includes recruiting criteria, new-employee orientation, personnel reviews, reward and motivation systems, promotions, and metrics. Management actions continue to be important; they must be consistent with the new style. Management must initiate discussions and ask questions that fit with the new style. Regarding development flexibility, for instance, in a project review, management should question why a certain decision must be made now, rather than quizzing the team on why it hasn't solidified all the product requirements before starting the design.

These pointers to the new behavior made by senior management are critical to the change process throughout. Senior managers have limited time but great opportunity to influence others through seemingly small things they do that greatly influence many people—in other words, high leverage. Perceptive managers look for and exploit such opportunities. For example, I remember one consulting engagement several years ago where design engineers were reluctant to make decisions, always deferring to management. Management got tired of solving engineers' problems for them. So one day when this happened, the senior vice president of product development called the engineer in question into her impressively grand office. The two of them sat down on her sofa, and she led him through a problem-solving session step by step. Then she had him formulate his solution and agree to execute it. That engineer didn't need any more encouragement to solve his own problems, nor did any of his colleagues who heard about the incident. Not only is it senior management's responsibility to take such a leadership role, it is their opportunity to play a pivotal role in change. Clearly, however, to execute this role well, they must be totally aligned with the change objective.

Bottom-Up Change

The top-down approach fits best when the person initiating the change is near the top of the organization. Often, this is not the case. Even if the top person eventually will lead the change, or at least support it, it may take considerable effort to make this individual aware of the opportunity—flexible development in this case. You will need a bottom-up approach for this.

I have described top-down and bottom-up as an either-or situation, but this is misleading. Perhaps it's best to combine them, using the Kotter steps as an overall framework and conducting daily activities using the tool kit from the bottom-up approach described next.

Throughout this book, I have borrowed liberally from software development, so it seems appropriate to continue in this vein. Software developers have created a means of effecting grassroots organizational change that they call *patterns* (or *design patterns*, because they originally pertained to designing code). A pattern is a general solution to a class of problems occurring in practice. Think of it as a template that covers the class but must be filled in to fit any individual situation. Consequently, the pattern helps you fit your specific needs into solutions that have proved successful in similar situations.[9] In short, it is a means of capturing tacit process knowledge.

Mary Lynn Manns and Linda Rising (and others) have moved the patterns approach from design into organizational change. As Manns and Rising explain, "It is not top-down or bottom-up, but participative at all levels—aligned through a common understanding of a system."[10] Unlike the more institutional approach of Kotter, Manns and Rising work by infecting others with the new concept so that they will *want* to become involved in it. However, in line with Bridges and Kotter, they note that, based on research, people tend to base their decisions on emotions, then justify them with facts. The first hundred pages of the Manns and Rising book explain the change-management process using patterns, introducing appropriate patterns as they go, then the last 60 percent of their book describes forty-eight patterns using a standardized format. Although each pattern receives a few pages of discussion devoted to it in their book, they choose the pattern names carefully so that the name alone suggests much of what you must know about it. (Their patterns appear in italics when I first mention them in the upcoming paragraphs.)

Organizational change using patterns usually starts with an *Evangelist*, someone with a passion for a new concept who introduces it to the organization. Most of the other patterns support the Evangelist in gaining widespread adoption of the concept. The Evangelist may not be the expert on the topic, and, in fact, should be quite willing to share the role with others, who become Evangelists too. The main objective of each Evangelist is to gain exposure and credibility for the new concept. The Evangelist's core set of patterns includes *Test the Waters* (try some patterns and evaluate the result), *Time for Reflection* (take time regularly to assess what is working and what needs adjusting), *Small Successes* (celebrate small successes), and *Step by Step* (proceed iteratively, exploiting what you learn).

At first, the Evangelist must spread the word about and expand interest in the new concept, so Manns and Rising offer several patterns for getting people's attention and building interest: *Piggyback* (find ways to attach the new concept to an existing concept or forum), *Brown Bag* (hold an information meeting at noon and encourage people to bring their lunches), *Do Food* (provide food to draw more people and build interest, as illustrated in Figure 10.3), *The Right Time* (when scheduling events, avoid crunch periods), *Plant the Seeds* (place materials about the new concept in opportune places), *External Validation* (provide sources of outside information about the concept), *Next Steps* (at the end of an event, identify or announce the next one), *Stay in Touch* (maintain contact with your key supporters), *e-Forum* (build an interactive electronic forum), and *Group Identity* (put a catchy name on the initiative).

Later on, when you have some supporters, you should expand to gain a critical mass. Other patterns can help here: *Trial Run* (convince the organization to try the concept for a limited period, which reduces resistance to it), *Guru Review* (have a *Guru on Your Side* evaluate the concept), *Big Jolt* (invite an impressive outsider to demonstrate and discuss the concept), *Royal Audience* (arrange for management to meet the Big Jolt visitor), *Hometown Story*

Figure 10.3   First, Get Their Attention (Use Food–*Brown Bag* or *Do Food*–Which Naturally Increases Levels of Trust)

Illustrator: Lyn Doiron.

(encourage those who have had a positive experience with the concept to share it), and *Just Enough* (avoid overload; provide only what people can absorb).

Manns and Rising, in keeping with the more ad hoc style of agile development, provide patterns for many involved parties, such as Guru on Your Side. This is in contrast with Kotter, who prefers a formal chartered team responsible for running the program.

You will meet resistance. Prepare for it and defuse it with these patterns: *Fear Less* (swing resistance to your side by asking resisters to help you), *Bridge-Builder* (pair someone who is resisting with an advocate), *Champion Skeptic* (ask a respected resister to be your "official skeptic"), *Corridor Politics* (informally work with key decision makers before a vote by addressing their concerns), *Whisper in the General's Ear* (meet privately with key executives to address their concerns), and in general, *Personal Touch* (show people how the concept can help them personally).

I have mentioned about half of Manns and Rising's patterns, which should provide a vivid picture of how you might use these tools. These authors also list additional organizational change patterns from other sources. Notice that two important themes pervade these patterns: communicate to all and involve everybody. Privacy and possessiveness are death to organizational change programs.

Summary

Here are the points to keep in mind as you move into implementation:

- However interesting the concepts in this book may be, they have no business value until you implement them: do something!
- Do not implement more than you can sustain; you can always add more later, but restarting the program is an uphill battle.
- There are paradoxes in implementation approaches; consider these carefully and customize your implementation to your objectives and culture.
- Some tools that meet heavy resistance might be exactly the ones you need most.
- See-feel-change is far more likely to precipitate change than is analysis-think-change.
- Consider combining Kotter's framework with Manns and Rising's tool kit, keeping in mind that it is Bridges' transitions that harbor the difficulty.
- Involve everybody and communicate continuously and openly.

Closing

Congratulations! You have stayed the course and finished this book. You have now learned the first half of flexible product development: use these tools to *defend yourself* against changes that will occur during development, that is, to roll with them and minimize the damage they can do. The second half, Flexibility 102, if you will, is to use the same tools *on the offensive* to create change, bewildering your competitors. Fortunately, the same tools presented here also apply on the offensive, but you must be more expert at using them. So start with this material, Flexibility 101, and plan to move on to the Flexibility 102 as you master it.

Consider what Quadrus Development, a Calgary-based software company, achieved recently in developing an online drugstore application for a Canadian pharmacy.[11] This is a contentious business domain, fraught with many regulatory and legal challenges that create extremely high rates of change for the project. In addition, the client was playing catch-up with other online pharmacies and trying to capture market share. To accommodate the rapid changes, Quadrus used very short (two-day) development cycles (iterations) and weekly deployments of the next release to overcome the challenges and lead the change. By having short cycles and an open attitude toward change, Quadrus responded to competitor offers and regulatory changes faster than competing online pharmacies, thus delivering competitive advantage.

With these tools and techniques, you can get inside your competitors' business cycles too! Best wishes for your journey.

Notes

Introduction

1. *Iteration* comes from the software development world (see Chapter One). In the lean manufacturing and lean product development fields, the related term is *small batch size*, for which see Reinertsen's *Managing the Design Factory*.

Chapter One

1. See the Boston Consulting Group's *Innovation 2006*.
2. Membership in the Project Management Institute stands at 237,000 (as of March 2007) and has grown at 22 percent per year over the past three years. See the Project Management Institute's Member Fact Sheet.
3. This is a short discussion of change in modern business. For a longer and more strategic treatment, See Brown and Eisenhardt's *Competing on the Edge*.
4. Arthur Fry and Spencer Silver invented the sticky note in 1970, based on Silver's 1968 invention of the "low-tack" adhesive involved. It was 1979 before 3M found a means for marketing it successfully. See en.wikipedia.org/wiki/Spencer_Silver and inventors.about.com/library/inventors/blpostit.htm (both accessed April 23, 2007).
5. See Smith and Reinertsen's *Developing Products in Half the Time*.
6. For a contemporary treatment, see Cooper, Edgett, and Kleinschmidt's *Portfolio Management for New Products*. For good

coverage of the balance between new and mature products, see Roussel, Saad, and Erickson's *Third Generation R&D*.

7. See Boehm's *Software Engineering Economics*, p. 40.

8. See Boehm and Turner's *Balancing Agility and Discipline*, pp. 218–219.

9. See Terwiesch, Loch, and De Meyer's "Exchanging Preliminary Information in Concurrent Engineering." They provide detailed cost-of-change information for three automotive components, and their results support the 10X/phase rule. However, this is an example of the worst part of the Pareto principle. They only investigate the two most expensive transitions in the development process (toolmaking), which together yield a 100X cost increase.

10. See Larman's *Agile and Iterative Development*.

11. See agilemanifesto.org/principles.html, accessed April 23, 2007.

12. This discussion draws from Beck's *Extreme Programming Explained*. Although this book comes in two editions (dated 2000 and 2005), it is actually more like parts 1 and 2. The first edition lays out the basics, and the second edition, requiring some existing knowledge of XP, describes it more broadly, provides case studies, and covers more advanced topics, such as the roles of project planning and software testing and the scalability of XP to large teams, dispersed teams, and life-critical applications. Consequently, this discussion follows the first edition more than the second one. Also see en.wikipedia.org/wiki/Extreme_Programming (accessed April 23, 2007).

13. Although commonly used, the term *pair programming* is misleading even for software development, because these pairs not only program but design, test, integrate, and document. Compare to the shift from *concurrent engineering* to *concurrent development*. Thus I use simply *pairing* from here on.

14. See Boehm and Turner's *Balancing Agility and Discipline*, pp. 230–232.

15. See Beck's *Extreme Programming Explained* (First Edition), pp. 64–70, for more such relationships.

16. en.wikipedia.org/wiki/Extreme_Programming (Origins section) or www.informit.com/articles/article.asp?p=20972&rl=1 (both accessed April 23, 2007).

17. See Beck's *Extreme Programming Explained* (First Edition), pp. 29–34. The second edition adds respect and suggests that others, such as safety, predictability, and quality of life, may be important in certain situations.

18. See Boehm and Turner's *Balancing Agility and Discipline*, p. 231.

19. See Eckstein's *Agile Software Development in the Large*.

Chapter Two

1. I use *specification* and *requirement* interchangeably to mean the written description of the product going into development, but I know that some people make a clear distinction here. Some say that requirements are the wish list at the beginning of the project, while specifications appear in the catalog after commercialization. Others believe that requirements are for your product, and specifications relate to purchased components or materials. Please picture the term you prefer for the up-front description of what the product should be.

2. Basic data are from Thomke and Reinertsen's "Agile Product Development," updated via personal communication with Donald Reinertsen, December 11, 2006.

3. See MacCormack's "Developing Products on 'Internet Time': The Anatomy of a Flexible Development Process," "How Internet Companies Build Software," and "Creating a Fast and Flexible Process: Empirical Research Suggests Keys to Success."

4. See Boehm's "Prototyping Versus Specifying: A Multiproject Experiment" for details.

5. Source: The Standish Group, www.standishgroup.com, as reported at the 3rd International Conference on Extreme Programming and Agile Processes in Software Engineering (XP 2002), Alghero, Sardinia, Italy, May 2002.

6. Lynn and Reilly's *Blockbusters* lists a clear and stable product vision as one of five factors that distinguished what they call "blockbuster" products from others in a ten-year study of seven hundred development projects. For more examples of vision statements and how to create them, see their book.

7. From Jeffrey K. Liker, *The Toyota Way*, McGraw-Hill, 2004 (Figure 5-4). Reproduced with permission of The McGraw-Hill Companies.

8. See Morgan and Liker's *Toyota Product Development System*, p. 123.

9. See Morgan and Liker's *Toyota Product Development System*, p. 260. Also, private communication with the authors, November 6, 2006.

10. See Sobek's "Principles That Shape Product Development Systems," p. 226.

11. Cooper's *The Inmates Are Running the Asylum* describes this technique.

12. For more on this topic, see Cockburn's *Writing Effective Use Cases*.

13. For more on this topic, see Cohn's *User Stories Applied*.

14. You can often drive user stories to a higher, more change-resistant level by writing "epics," as Cohn describes.

15. See Hohmann's *Innovation Games*.

16. *Customers* (those who pay for your products) are not necessarily *users* (those who use them). For consumer products, the two are often the same, but for industrial products, they are usually different: a buyer or a manager may purchase the computer on your desk at work, but you have to use it and cope with it every day. I use the terms interchangeably, but please apply the pertinent one.

17. Sometimes Marketing and Sales personnel are nervous about letting engineers talk to customers, fearing that they might say something inappropriate. If so, train those involved using Hohmann's guidance described in *Beyond Software Architecture*, p. 60.

18. See Scoble and Israel's *Naked Conversations* for much more on business blogging.
19. In Hohmann's *Innovation Games*.
20. Both Toyota examples are from Morgan and Liker's *Toyota Product Development System*, p. 30.
21. For example, see Mariampolski's *Ethnography for Marketers*, and Perry and her colleagues' "Creating the Customer Connection."
22. For more on lead users, see von Hippel's *Sources of Innovation*, and for other examples and the 3M infection study, see his "Creating Breakthroughs at 3M."
23. See Christensen's *The Innovator's Dilemma*.
24. See Highsmith's *Agile Project Management*, p. 13.

Chapter Three

1. From Stevens, Myers, and Constantine, "Structured Design," p. 117. Quotation attributed to Constantine, who is considered the originator of the structured design technique used in software development and was the teacher of Stevens and Myers.
2. Adapted from The PDMA Glossary for New Product Development. See pdma.org/library/glossary.html (accessed April 23, 2007).
3. For more on platforms and platform architecture, see Meyer and Lehnerd's *Power of Product Platforms* or Feitzinger and Lee's "Mass Customization at Hewlett-Packard: The Power of Postponement."
4. This shift between integral and modular architectures may appear to contradict Christensen and Raynor's observations in *The Innovator's Solution* (pp. 127–137). These authors work at the level of industries and describe how, in the early stages of an innovation (when I suggest that the need for flexibility and thus modularity is greatest), its performance falls below customer desires, so designers squeeze performance from the design

(integral architecture). Later, as the technology improves, performance exceeds needs and customers are unwilling to pay extra for performance, so the industry shifts to a modular architecture that allows more flexibility in tuning the product to individual needs at minimal cost. Observe that this strategic modularity aims more at changes during manufacture and distribution, that is, it is more of a platform architecture approach. In the early stages of an innovation, there is still a great need for designers to isolate areas of uncertainty and provide for reserve performance where needs are likely to grow, so wise designers apply modularity selectively at the design level, especially in the early stages of an innovation. This illustrates why flexibility techniques must be applied selectively so that performance will not suffer excessively just when Christensen and Raynor advise that it is most important.

5. Quotation from ferrariusa.com/design_f430text.php, accessed April 23, 2007.

6. These techniques are old. David Parnas provided an elegant (but technical) description of them for software nearly three decades ago. See Parnas' "Designing Software for Ease of Extension and Contraction."

7. Here I follow Ulrich and Eppinger's *Product Design and Development*.

8. For more on considering interfaces as design rules, see Baldwin and Clark's *Design Rules*.

9. See Thomke's "Role of Flexibility in the Development of New Products" for further discussion.

Chapter Four

1. Sources, respectively: Thomke's *Experimentation Matters*, p. 6; nmlites.org/standards/science/glossary_2.htm; and www.math.tamu.edu/FiniteMath/FinalBuild/Fall2001/Module9/Introduction0.html (both accessed April 23, 2007).

2. Source: Archibald Lemon Cochrane. See his *Effectiveness and Efficiency*, p. 43.

3. See Thomke's *Experimentation Matters*, pp. 211–214.

4. For an extensive discussion of exploration and hypothesis-based experimentation, see Garvin's *Learning in Action*, chapter 5 (specifically what he calls the probe-and-learn process).

5. See Iansiti and MacCormack's "Developing Products on Internet Time."

6. The Orion case study was published by Z Corporation in 2001 but is no longer available.

7. See Thomke's "Capturing the Real Value of Innovation Tools."

8. See Smith and Reinertsen's *Developing Products in Half the Time*, chapter 2.

9. See, for example, Montgomery's *Design and Analysis of Experiments*.

10. The lock analogy was inspired by Thomke's *Experimentation Matters*, p. 110. For more on parallel versus sequential strategies, see Thomke and Bell's "Sequential Testing in Product Development."

11. *Testing* in its broadest sense includes testing an idea, a prototype, or even a hunch. Here I consider the narrower interpretation of testing a design, a product, or a part of a product.

12. See Peters and Austin's *Passion for Excellence*, p. 130. My first engineering job was for a manufacturer of aircraft engines twenty-plus years before their book appeared. At that time the test used a two-pound seagull, but the procedure was the same. This was regarded as the final test of an engine.

Chapter Five

1. Yogi Berra was a famous American baseball player from several decades ago, but today he is known better for his illogical but direct manner of speaking.

2. Engineering changes do *not* constitute flexibility. Engineering changes originate internal to engineering and in most cases arise from poor engineering judgment. Flexibility stems from

changes external to engineering. Thus flexibility is beneficial when external change is likely, but engineering changes are usually an indication of mistakes.

3. See Ward, Liker, Cristiano, and Sobek's "Second Toyota Paradox." This article is also the source of the concept for Figure 5.4.
4. See Pugh's *Total Design*, section 4.8.
5. For additional details, see Morgan and Liker's *Toyota Product Development System*, pp. 269–274. For examples of A3 reports, guidance on writing them, and templates for writing the basic types, see www.whittierconsulting.com/lpdresourcecenter.php (accessed April 23, 2007). For examples directly from Toyota Central R&D Labs, see www.tytlabs.co.jp/eindex.html (these are actually A4 reports—half the size of an A3 report). For example, for one on a fuel tank cap, see www.tytlabs.co.jp/english/tech/e_saf_fuelcap.pdf (both accessed April 23, 2007).
6. See Sobek, Ward, and Liker's "Toyota's Principles of Set-Based Concurrent Engineering."
7. The examples in this and the following few paragraphs come from Durward Sobek's Ph.D. dissertation.
8. Suggested by Katherine Radeka of Whittier Consulting Group.
9. See Ward, Liker, Cristiano, and Sobek's "Second Toyota Paradox."

Chapter Six

1. From Turner and Boehm's "People Factors in Software Management."
2. The book is Boehm and Turner's *Balancing Agility and Discipline*.
3. See Boehm's *Software Engineering Economics*.
4. See Quinn's *Building the Bridge As You Walk On It*. However, only the title of this book is pertinent here, as the book deals with personal change rather than project change.
5. See MacCormack's "How Internet Companies Build Software" for more on experience.

6. See Loch, DeMeyer, and Pich's *Managing the Unknown*, p. 41.

7. See Cockburn's *Agile Software Development*, pp. 14–18, and Boehm and Turner's *Balancing Agility and Discipline*, p. 48.

8. This has no connection with Douglas McGregor's Theory X, which postulates managers who regard workers as lazy and unwilling to work without strong structure and control.

9. This figure results from a multiyear study in a major electronics company that categorized engineers' activities as either value-adding or not adding value to their development projects.

10. In a 2006 article of the same name, Scott Ambler uses the term *generalizing specialists* and discusses both their benefits to the team and the techniques for cultivating them.

11. See agilemanifesto.org/principles.html, accessed April 23, 2007.

12. See Figure 8-7 (p. 156) of Smith and Reinertsen's *Developing Products in Half the Time*.

13. Many people call this a "virtual team," but I dislike this term. Teams exist to enhance performance, and it clouds the performance issue to use a term that means "being such in essence or effect though not formally recognized or admitted" (webster.com, accessed April 23, 2007). Are the members virtual, are the activities virtual, or what is it that exists only in essence or effect?

14. See Allen's *Managing the Flow of Technology*. His more contemporary *Organization and Architecture of Innovation* (pp. 58–61) reinforces his earlier work and concludes that electronic communication media, such as e-mail, lack the fidelity to substitute for face-to-face communication as distance increases.

15. As suggested at the beginning of this section, because effectiveness drops off gradually, various distances are used to define co-location. Reinertsen is somewhat more liberal in his definition than I am. Stephanie Teasley and her colleagues (quoted a few paragraphs later) are still more liberal.

16. The Olsons' article appeared in *Human-Computer Interaction* in 2000.

17. This work was published by Teasley, Covi, Krishnan, and Olson as "How Does Radical Collocation Help a Team Succeed?" Both of the quotations that follow this paragraph are reprinted with permission from that article, copyright ACM.

18. See Cockburn's *Agile Software Development*, pp. 84–88.

19. See Williams and Kessler's *Pair Programming Illuminated*.

20. From Duarte and Snyder's *Mastering Virtual Teams*. Used with permission.

21. See Duarte and Snyder's *Mastering Virtual Teams*, p. 42.

Chapter Seven

1. Quoted in Maier and Rechtin's *Art of Systems Architecting*, p. 272. Robert Spinrad is a retired vice president of technology strategy and director of the legendary PARC laboratories at Xerox. He is also a member of the prestigious National Academy of Engineering in the United States.

2. For example, see Deck's "Decision Making: The Overlooked Competency in Product Development."

3. "The last responsible moment" was coined in about 2000 by the Lean Construction Institute in work they were doing with the British Airports Authority to create the construction process for Terminal 5 at London's Heathrow Airport. They needed flexibility because the airlines' strategic plans were likely to change numerous times during the eight years needed to build the terminal. In *Lean Software Development*, Poppendieck and Poppendieck brought the term into agile software development, and I elaborate further.

4. In developing this section, I consulted some experts on building consensus. Each had a somewhat different way of using the consensus gradient. Consequently, what you see here is truly a consensus version of the topic, keeping the elements separate so that you can assemble them to suit your needs.

5. For this section, I am indebted to chapter 6 of Savage's excellent book, *Decision Making with Insight*. This chapter introduces

decision trees and provides XLTree, an Excel add-in, for creating them. All decision trees in this chapter were created using XLTree. (The "student" version of XLTree bundled with Savage's book is full-featured but limited to trees of the size in this chapter. For larger trees, get the "commercial" version from analycorp.com.) For more powerful but much more expensive alternatives, see treeage.com or www.palisade.com.au (all accessed April 23, 2007).

6. For an introduction to utility theory and utility measures, see Savage's *Decision Making with Insight,* pp. 194–195.

7. For an example of real options applied to the product development process, see Huchzermeier and Loch's "Project Management Under Risk."

8. For a starter on real options applied to new product development, see Faulkner's "Applying 'Options Thinking' to R&D Valuation," Angelis' "Capturing the Option Value of R&D," and van Putten's "Making Real Options Really Work." Several other helpful articles are available in *Research-Technology Management* and the *Harvard Business Review.*

9. Traditionally, such valuations are made using discounted cash flow (DCF) methods, which assume the project will be completed according to the original plan. Even when used with a phased development process, where the purpose of the phases is that one can kill the project rather than continuing to invest, the project is still evaluated on the assumption of completing the plan. In contrast, the real options approach allows a project to be evaluated more flexibly by making future investments contingent on interim results.

10. For a discussion of how real options are equivalent to decision trees, see Faulkner's "Applying 'Options Thinking' to R&D Valuation."

Chapter Eight

1. The referenced guide is the Project Management Institute's *Guide to the Project Management Body of Knowledge.*

2. Several other books on agile project management have appeared in the last few years. I list DeCarlo's and Highsmith's because they generalize beyond software development better than most of the others, I believe.

3. Chapter Nine shows how to combine structured and flexible development processes in the same project, depending on the project's specific demands. You can use the same approach to adjust project management to the specific characteristics of a project.

4. See the Project Management Institute's *Guide to the Project Management Body of Knowledge*, p. 356.

5. See Portny's *Project Management for Dummies* (Second Edition), p. 14.

6. See the Project Management Institute's *Guide to the Project Management Body of Knowledge*, p. 369.

7. Chapter Nine covers anticipation relative to adaptation, which is investing in the capability to react quickly when anticipation is not possible or cost-effective.

8. See Figure 9.4 for an illustration of the way a project naturally shifts from anticipation to planning as it progresses.

9. For additional information on this method, see Githens's "Using a Rolling Wave for Fast and Flexible Development."

10. For more detail on agile loose-tight planning, see Cohn's *Agile Estimating and Planning*.

11. See Thomke's *Experimentation Matters*, pp. 168–169.

12. See Highsmith's *Agile Project Management*, p. 42.

13. Smith and Merritt's *Proactive Risk Management* is a good example of this literature.

14. Although most agilists have replaced waterfall (phased) processes with iterative ones, Jim Highsmith has created a means of combining a phased governance process (for managing project investments) with iterative development (for flexibility). See his "Agile for the Enterprise: From Agile Teams to Agile Organizations."

15. See Loch, DeMeyer, and Pich's *Managing the Unknown*. Although valuable, this book is unfortunately also very

expensive. However, you can read a lengthy review of it gratis at www.newproductdynamics.com/book_reviews06. htm#ManagingUnknown (accessed April 23, 2007).

16. See Weick and Sutcliffe's *Managing the Unexpected*.

17. Summarized with permission from Weick and Sutcliffe's *Managing the Unexpected*, pp. 10–17.

18. This metric was inspired by Iansiti's "Shooting the Rapids," Figure 1.

19. I intentionally use *feel* here, but I recognize that some people are quite uneasy in expressing their feelings or hearing about others' feelings. In this case, please see Derby and Larsen's *Agile Retrospectives* (p. 10) for ways of obtaining this information without using that *f* word directly.

20. See Morgan and Liker's *Toyota Product Development System*, p. 211.

Chapter Nine

1. See Boehm and Turner's *Balancing Agility and Discipline*, pp. 36–37 and p. 152.

2. See note 14 in Chapter Eight.

3. See Cockburn's "Learning from Agile Software Development."

4. For a description of how IT might be used to capture and manage product development knowledge, see McGrath's *Next Generation Product Development*.

5. For more on how Toyota manages tacit knowledge, see Morgan and Liker's *Toyota Product Development System*, pp. 204–205, 229, and 279–280. I describe A3 reports and engineering checklists in Chapter Five.

6. As discussed in the Introduction, using *structured* as the opposite of *flexible* has difficulties in that flexible development is very structured in certain subtle ways. Agilists speak of high- and low-ceremony processes. Nevertheless, *traditional* (used in the rest of the book) seems to miss the mark when discussing

process, so I will proceed with *structured* here, knowing that it is not a perfect antonym.

7. See Boehm and Turner's *Balancing Agility and Discipline*, chapter 5. For non-software projects, their approach must be modified in two ways. One is to shift it to a physical product, and the other is to narrow it to a focus on flexibility (Boehm and Turner consider other differences between agile and traditional approaches, such as scalability). Also, I do not follow their complete five-step process. For an alternative means of adjusting the process used to the needs of a specific project, also see the Project Analyzer discussed at the end of Chapter One.

8. The infrared measurement technologies and algorithms described here are fictitious.

9. Goldratt and Cox's *The Goal* (a business novel) is the classic on this topic, but more descriptive material can be found on the Web, for instance, en.wikipedia.org/wiki/Theory_of_Constraints (accessed April 23, 2007).

10. For bulk arrivals, there is no formula for the answer, so I used the Extend discrete-event simulation package from Imagine That, Inc. and covered in Savage's *Decision Making with Insight*. I assumed that arrivals appear in uniformly distributed clumps of one to five items (mean of three), as well as being exponentially distributed in time. Extend generated Figure 9.7 too.

11. From "What Testers Can Do About Technical Debt" by Johanna Rothman, www.stickyminds.com, accessed April 23, 2007.

Chapter Ten

1. Brooks managed development of the OS/360 software system for what was perhaps IBM's most successful product line. The quote comes from his *Mythical Man-Month*, p. 242. "System" to him means the software or hardware.

2. From Kotter and Cohen's *Heart of Change*, p. 40.

3. For more on pilot projects, see Smith and Reinertsen's *Developing Products in Half the Time*, chapter 15.
4. From Bridges' *Managing Transitions*, p. 37.
5. From Kotter and Cohen's *Heart of Change*, p. 2.
6. From Patterson's *Leading Product Innovation*, pp. 262–264.
7. See Schaffer's *Breakthrough Strategy* for more on this momentum-building process.
8. From Morgan and Liker's *Toyota Product Development System*, p. 227.
9. For more on patterns, see en.wikipedia.org/wiki/Software_pattern, accessed April 23, 2007.
10. From Manns and Rising's *Fearless Change*, p. 5.
11. Readers residing outside North America may need some explanation here. Canada has a national health care system, and the United States does not, so drug prices are regulated at considerably lower levels (for the same drugs) in Canada than in the United States. Consequently, Canadian pharmacies have a huge potential market serving U.S. customers online. But drug manufacturers and the regulatory authority (the Food and Drug Administration) in the United States oppose this, as it undercuts their power and authority. This creates volatile conditions as the various opposing parties act constantly to enhance their positions.

Bibliography

Allen, Thomas J. *Managing the Flow of Technology*. Cambridge, MA: MIT Press, 1977.

Allen, Thomas J., and Gunter W. Herr. *The Organization and Architecture of Innovation: Managing the Flow of Technology*. Amsterdam: Butterworth-Heinemann, 2007.

Ambler, Scott W. "Generalizing Specialists: Improving Your IT Career Skills," 2006. Available online: agilemodeling.com/essays/generalizingSpecialists.htm. Accessed April 23, 2007.

Angelis, Diana I. "Capturing the Option Value of R&D." *Research-Technology Management* 43(4): 31–34 (July–August 2000).

Avery, Christopher M. *Teamwork Is an Individual Skill: Getting Your Work Done When Sharing Responsibility*. San Francisco: Berrett-Koehler, 2001.

Baldwin, Carliss Y., and Kim B. Clark. *Design Rules: The Power of Modularity*. Cambridge, MA: MIT Press, 2000.

Beck, Kent. *Extreme Programming Explained: Embrace Change*. Boston: Addison-Wesley, 2000.

Beck, Kent, and Cynthia Andres. *Extreme Programming Explained: Embrace Change* (Second Edition). Boston: Addison-Wesley, 2005.

Boehm, Barry W. *Software Engineering Economics*. Upper Saddle River, NJ: Prentice Hall, 1981.

Boehm, Barry W., Terance E. Gray, and Thomas Seewaldt. "Prototyping Versus Specifying: A Multiproject Experiment." *IEEE Transactions on Software Engineering* SE-10(3): 290–302 (May 1984).

Boehm, Barry W., Ellis Horowitz, Ray Madachy, Donald Reifer, Bradford K. Clark, Bert Steece, A. Winsor Brown, Sunita Chulani, and Chris Abts. *Software Cost Estimation with COCOMO II*. Upper Saddle River, NJ: Prentice Hall, 2000.

Boehm, Barry, and Richard Turner. *Balancing Agility and Discipline: A Guide for the Perplexed*. Boston: Addison-Wesley, 2004.

Boston Consulting Group. *Innovation 2006*. Boston: Boston Consulting Group, Inc., 2006.

Bridges, William. *Managing Transitions: Making the Most of Change* (Second Edition). Cambridge, MA: Da Capo Press, 2003.

Brooks, Frederick P., Jr. *The Mythical Man-Month: Essays on Software Engineering, 20th Anniversary Edition*. Reading, MA: Addison-Wesley, 1995.

Brown, Shona L., and Kathleen M. Eisenhardt. *Competing on the Edge: Strategy as Structured Chaos*. Boston: Harvard Business School Press, 1998.

Christensen, Clayton M. *The Innovator's Dilemma: When New Technologies Cause Great Firms to Fail*. Boston: Harvard Business School Press, 1997.

Christensen, Clayton M., and Michael E. Raynor. *The Innovator's Solution: Creating and Sustaining Successful Growth*. Boston: Harvard Business School Press, 2003.

Cochrane, Archibald Lemon. *Effectiveness and Efficiency: Random Reflections on Health Services*. London: Nuffield Provincial Hospitals Trust, 1972.

Cockburn, Alistair. *Writing Effective Use Cases*. Boston: Addison-Wesley, 2000.

Cockburn, Alistair. *Agile Software Development*. Boston: Addison-Wesley, 2002.

Cockburn, Alistair. "Learning from Agile Software Development—Part One." *Crosstalk: The Journal of Defense Software Engineering* 15(10): 10–14 (October 2002).

Cohn, Mike. *User Stories Applied: For Agile Software Development*. Boston: Addison-Wesley, 2004.

Cohn, Mike. *Agile Estimating and Planning*. Upper Saddle River, NJ: Prentice Hall, 2006.

Cooper, Alan. *The Inmates Are Running the Asylum: Why High-Tech Products Drive Us Crazy and How to Restore the Sanity*. Indianapolis: SAMS, 1999.

Cooper, Robert G. "Your NPD Portfolio May Be Harmful to Your Business's Health," *Visions* 29(2): 22–26 (April 2005).

Cooper, Robert G., Scott J. Edgett, and Elko J. Kleinschmidt. *Portfolio Management for New Products* (Second Edition). Cambridge, MA: Perseus Books, 2001.

DeCarlo, Doug. *eXtreme Project Management: Using Leadership, Principles, and Tools to Deliver Value in the Face of Reality*. San Francisco: Jossey-Bass, 2004.

Deck, Mark J. "Decision Making: The Overlooked Competency in Product Development." In *The PDMA ToolBook 1 for New Product Development*, Paul Belliveau, Abbie Griffin, and Stephen Somermeyer, eds. New York: Wiley, 2002, pp. 165–185.

Derby, Esther, and Diana Larsen. *Agile Retrospectives: Making Good Teams Great*. Raleigh, NC: Pragmatic Bookshelf, 2006.

Duarte, Deborah L., and Nancy Tennant Snyder. *Mastering Virtual Teams: Strategies, Tools, and Techniques That Succeed* (Third Edition). San Francisco: Jossey-Bass, 2006.

Eckstein, Jutta. *Agile Software Development in the Large: Diving into the Deep*. New York: Dorset House, 2004.

Faulkner, Terrence W. "Applying 'Options Thinking' to R&D Valuation." *Research-Technology Management* 39(3): 50–56 (May–June 1996).

Feitzinger, Edward, and Hau L. Lee. "Mass Customization at Hewlett-Packard: The Power of Postponement." *Harvard Business Review* 75(1): 116–121 (January-February 1997).

Garvin, David A. *Learning in Action: A Guide to Putting the Learning Organization to Work*. Boston: Harvard Business School Press, 2000.

Githens, Gregory D. "Using a Rolling Wave for Fast and Flexible Development." In *The PDMA ToolBook 3 for New Product Development*, Abbie Griffin and Stephen Somermeyer, eds. Hoboken, NJ: Wiley, 2007.

Goldratt, Eliyahu M., and Jeff Cox, *The Goal* (Third Edition). Great Barrington, MA: North River Press, 2004.

Highsmith, Jim. *Agile Project Management: Creating Innovative Products*. Boston: Addison-Wesley, 2004.

Highsmith, Jim. "Agile for the Enterprise: From Agile Teams to Agile Organizations." *Cutter Consortium Agile Project Management Advisory Service Executive Report* 6(1) (2005).

Hohmann, Luke. *Beyond Software Architecture: Creating and Sustaining Winning Solutions*. Boston: Addison-Wesley, 2003.

Hohmann, Luke. *Innovation Games: Creating Breakthrough Products Through Collaborative Play*. Upper Saddle River, NJ: Addison-Wesley, 2007.

Huchzermeier, Arnd, and Christoph H. Loch. "Project Management Under Risk: Using the Real Options Approach to Evaluate Flexibility in R&D." *Management Science* 47(1): 85–101 (January 2001).

Iansiti, Marco. "Shooting the Rapids: Managing Product Development in Turbulent Environments." *California Management Review* 38(1): 37–58 (Fall 1995).

Iansiti, Marco, and Alan MacCormack. "Developing Products on Internet Time." *Harvard Business Review* 75(5): 108–117 (September-October 1997).

Kerth, Norman L. *Project Retrospectives: A Handbook for Team Reviews*. New York: Dorset House, 2001.

Kotter, John P., and Dan S. Cohen. *The Heart of Change: Real-Life Stories of How People Change Their Organizations*. Boston: Harvard Business School Press, 2002.

Larman, Craig. *Agile and Iterative Development: A Manager's Guide*. Boston: Addison-Wesley, 2004.

Loch, Christoph, Arnoud DeMeyer, and Michael T. Pich. *Managing the Unknown: A New Approach to Managing High Uncertainty and Risk in Projects*. Hoboken, NJ: Wiley, 2006.

Lynn, Gary S., and Richard R. Reilly. *Blockbusters: The Five Keys to Developing Great New Products*. New York: HarperBusiness, 2002.

MacCormack, Alan. "How Internet Companies Build Software." *Sloan Management Review* 42(2): 75–84 (Winter 2001).

MacCormack, Alan. "Creating a Fast and Flexible Process: Empirical Research Suggests Keys to Success." *Product Development Best Practices Report* 10(8): 1–4 (August 2003).

MacCormack, Alan, Roberto Verganti, and Marco Iansiti. "Developing Products on 'Internet Time': The Anatomy of a Flexible Development Process." *Management Science* 47(1): 133–150 (January 2001).

Maier, Mark W., and Eberhardt Rechtin. *The Art of Systems Architecting* (Second Edition). Boca Raton, FL: CRC Press, 2002.

Manns, Mary Lynn, and Linda Rising. *Fearless Change: Patterns for Introducing New Ideas*. Boston: Addison-Wesley, 2005.

Mariampolski, Hy. *Ethnography for Marketers: A Guide to Consumer Immersion*. Thousand Oaks, CA: Sage, 2006.

McGrath, Michael E. *Next Generation Product Development: How to Increase Productivity, Cut Costs, and Reduce Cycle Times*. New York: McGraw-Hill, 2004.

Meyer, Marc H., and Alvin P. Lehnerd. *The Power of Product Platforms: Building Value and Cost Leadership*. New York: Free Press, 1997.

Montgomery, Douglas C. *Design and Analysis of Experiments*. Hoboken, NJ: Wiley, 2005.

Morgan, James M., and Jeffrey K. Liker. *The Toyota Product Development System: Integrating People, Process, and Technology*. New York: Productivity Press, 2006.

Olson, Gary M., and Judith S. Olson. "Distance Matters." *Human-Computer Interaction* 15(2–3): 139–178 (2000).

Parnas, David L. "Designing Software for Ease of Extension and Contraction." *IEEE Transactions on Software Engineering* SE-5(2): 128–138 (March 1979).

Patterson, Marvin L. *Leading Product Innovation: Accelerating Growth in a Product-Based Business*. New York: Wiley, 1999.

Perry, Barbara, Cara L. Woodland, and Christopher W. Miller. "Creating the Customer Connection: Anthropological/Ethnographic Needs Discovery." In *The PDMA ToolBook 2 for New Product Development*, Paul Belliveau, Abbie Griffin, and Stephen M. Somermeyer, eds. 201–234. Hoboken, NJ: Wiley, 2004.

Peters, Tom, and Nancy Austin. *A Passion for Excellence*. New York: Random House, 1985.

Poppendieck, Mary, and Tom Poppendieck. *Lean Software Development: An Agile Toolkit*. Boston: Addison-Wesley, 2003.

Portny, Stanley E. *Project Management for Dummies* (Second Edition). Indianapolis, IN: Wiley, 2007.

Project Management Institute. *A Guide to the Project Management Body of Knowledge* (Third Edition). Newtown Square, PA: Project Management Institute, 2004.

Project Management Institute. Member Fact Sheet. Available online: pmi.org (search on "Fact Sheet"). Accessed April 23, 2007.

Pugh, Stuart. *Total Design*. Wokingham, UK: Addison-Wesley, 1991.

Quinn, Robert E. *Building the Bridge As You Walk On It: A Guide for Leading Change*. San Francisco: Jossey-Bass, 2004.

Reinertsen, Donald G. *Managing the Design Factory: A Product Developer's Toolkit*. New York: Free Press, 1997.

Roussel, Philip A., Kamal N. Saad, and Tamara J. Erickson. *Third Generation R&D: Managing the Link to Corporate Strategy*. Boston: Harvard Business School Press, 1991.

Savage, Sam L. *Decision Making with Insight*. Belmont, CA: Brooks/Cole, 2003.

Schaffer, Robert H. *The Breakthrough Strategy: Using Short-Term Success to Build the High-Performance Organization*. Cambridge, MA: Ballinger, 1988.

Scoble, Robert, and Shel Israel. *Naked Conversations: How Blogs Are Changing the Way Businesses Talk with Customers*. Hoboken, NJ: Wiley, 2006.

Smith, Preston G., and Guy M. Merritt. *Proactive Risk Management: Controlling Uncertainty in Product Development*. New York: Productivity Press, 2002.

Smith, Preston G., and Donald G. Reinertsen. *Developing Products in Half the Time* (Second Edition). New York: Wiley, 1998.

Sobek, II, Durward Kenneth. "Principles That Shape Product Development Systems: A Toyota-Chrysler Comparison." Ph.D. dissertation, University of Michigan, 1997.

Sobek, II, Durward K., Allen C. Ward, and Jeffrey K. Liker. "Toyota's Principles of Set-Based Concurrent Engineering." *Sloan Management Review* 40(2): 67–83 (Winter 1999).

Stevens, Wayne G., Glen J. Myers, and Larry L. Constantine, "Structured Design," *IBM Systems Journal* 13(2): 115–139 (May 1974).

Teasley, Stephanie, Lisa Covi, M. S. Krishnan, and Judith S. Olson. "How Does Radical Collocation Help a Team Succeed?" Proceedings of the 2000 ACM Conference on Computer Supported Cooperative Work, Philadelphia, pp. 339–346, 2000.

Terwiesch, Christian, Christoph H. Loch, and Arnoud De Meyer. "Exchanging Preliminary Information in Concurrent Engineering: Alternative Coordination Strategies." *Organization Science* 13(4): 402–419 (July/August 2002).

Thomke, Stefan H. "The Role of Flexibility in the Development of New Products: An Empirical Study." *Research Policy* 26(1): 105–119 (March 1997).

Thomke, Stefan H. *Experimentation Matters: Unlocking the Potential of New Technologies for Innovation*. Boston: Harvard Business School Press, 2003.

Thomke, Stefan H. "Capturing the Real Value of Innovation Tools." *Sloan Management Review* 47(2): 24–32 (Winter 2006).

Thomke, Stefan, and David E. Bell. "Sequential Testing in Product Development." *Management Science* 47(2): 308–323 (February 2001).

Thomke, Stefan, and Donald Reinertsen. "Agile Product Development: Managing Development Flexibility in Uncertain Environments." *California Management Review* 41(1): 8–30 (Fall 1998).

Turner, Richard, and Barry Boehm. "People Factors in Software Management: Lessons from Comparing Agile and Plan-Driven Methods." *Crosstalk: The Journal of Defense Software Engineering* 16(12): 4–8 (December 2003).

Ulrich, Karl T., and Steven D. Eppinger. *Product Design and Development* (Third Edition). New York: McGraw-Hill, 2003.

van Putten, Alexander B., and Ian C. Macmillan. "Making Real Options Really Work." *Harvard Business Review* 82(12): 134–141 (December 2004).

von Hippel, Eric. *The Sources of Innovation*. New York: Oxford University Press, 1988.

von Hippel, Eric, Stefan Thomke, and Mary Sonnack. "Creating Breakthroughs at 3M." *Harvard Business Review* 77(5): 47–57 (September–October 1999).

Ward, Allen, Jeffrey K. Liker, John J. Cristiano, and Durward K. Sobek II. "The Second Toyota Paradox: How Delaying Decisions Can Make Better Cars Faster." *Sloan Management Review* 36(3): 43–61 (Spring 1995).

Weick, Karl E., and Kathleen M. Sutcliffe. *Managing the Unexpected*. San Francisco: Jossey-Bass, 2001.

Wheelwright, Steven C., and Kim B. Clark. *Revolutionizing Product Development: Quantum Leaps in Speed, Efficiency, and Quality*. New York: Free Press, 1992.

Williams, Laurie, and Robert Kessler. *Pair Programming Illuminated*. Boston: Addison-Wesley, 2003.

Customer Council

Many people have contributed generously to this book, for which I am most grateful. Without them, the book would not have been possible. However, I would like to acknowledge in particular a "customer council" of lead users of flexibility techniques, the people who have played a key role in reviewing chapters, suggesting improvements, offering examples, and providing sources of associated material. I am especially grateful to these individuals on the customer council, each of whom has made an important contribution to the book:

Name	Affiliation	Country
Bob Becker	Product Development Advantage Group	United States
Chuck Blevins	LifeScan, Inc. (Johnson & Johnson)	United States
Jim Callahan, PMP	C-Cor, Incorporated	United States
Alan Chachich	Breakthrough NPD	United States
Frankie Chan	T&K Industrial Company Limited	Hong Kong (China)
Mike Clem	Cordis Accelerated Medical Ventures (Johnson & Johnson)	United States
Mike Cohn	Mountain Goat Software	United States
Mike Dowson	Draeger Safety	United Kingdom
Ricco Estanislao	Johnson & Johnson Worldwide Emerging Markets Innovation Center	China

John Farnbach	Silver Streak Partners LLC	United States
Gregory D. Githens, PMP, NPDP	Catalyst Management Consulting, LLC	United States
Mike Griffiths	Independent Consultant	Canada
David Gunderson	Micro Power Electronics, Inc.	United States
Greg Krisher	GE Water & Process Technologies, Analytical Instruments	United States
Jeff Oltmann, PMP	Synergy Professional Services, LLC	United States
Barry Papoff	Harris Corporation	Canada
David Petrie	California State University, Fullerton	United States
Roman Pichler	Pichler Consulting Ltd	United Kingdom
Katherine Radeka	Whittier Consulting Group, Inc.	United States
Radhika Ramnath	Cadence Design Systems	India
John Shambroom	Shambroom Associates, LLC	United States
Kulbhushan Sharma	Quark Media House India Pvt. Ltd.	India
Thomas Sigemyr	IVF	Sweden
Reardon Smith NPDP, CMC	Business Vectors Inc.	United States
James Joseph Snyder	Medtronic, Inc.	United States
Gary J. Summers, Ph.D.	Skillful NPD	United States
John Tepper	Alpha Med-Surge, Inc.	United States

The Author

Preston G. Smith received a Ph.D. in engineering from Stanford University and served for the next twenty years in engineering and management positions in the aerospace, automotive, highway safety, defense, and diversified industries. In 1984 he initiated a corporate program to accelerate product development, and for the past twenty years, he has been an independent management consultant specializing in advanced product development techniques. Consulting and training engagements for products as diverse as supercomputers and footwear have taken him to hundreds of venues in twenty-five countries.

Smith's interest in development flexibility has been brewing for years. His first book, *Developing Products in Half the Time* (with Donald Reinertsen; originally published in 1991), covered the core of flexibility—iterative and incremental development—in its fourth chapter.

Another part of flexibility, responsive experimentation (Chapter Four of this book) includes rapid prototyping, which Smith started following in 1988. More important, super-rapid prototyping machines, often called 3-D printers, appeared in 1996. Although some people denigrated 3-D printers as a "poor man's rapid prototyping system," he saw the very low costs and rapid responsiveness of such systems as opportunities to change the way organizations develop new products radically by harnessing this quick, inexpensive feedback. He followed these developments closely, having keynoted at a rapid prototyping conference in Australia in 1995 and participated in six others in

Australia, the United Kingdom, South Africa, and the United States since then.

Over the past decade or two, Smith has helped product architecture (Chapter Three of this book and the sixth chapter of *Developing Products in Half the Time*) to move from a solely technical matter to a business strategy topic, although its role in enhancing flexibility during development is still not widely appreciated.

The tipping point for him was in 2004, when the Agile Development Conference (ADC) invited him to keynote. Agile development aims precisely at flexibility, except that it only pertains to software development. Having started his career in the 1960s immersed in programming, he had been observing software development for years. It impressed him that software development projects have experienced more than their share of spectacular failures, but this community has studied these failures, done impressive research on methodologies, and improved—to a greater extent than product development in other fields, he believes. Notwithstanding that software developers have a lead in understanding their methodologies, the 2004 ADC invited Smith to speak—characteristically—to see what they could learn from an allied field. They rather confused who was the teacher and who was the student. As a result, he attended other agile conferences since then, joined the Agile Alliance, and was a founding member of the Agile Project Leadership Network (apln.org)—and he took many notes. As a result, what the agilists have achieved in software development inspired him to write this book, which provides comparable means for developing other types of products flexibly.

Index